The Pandaw Story

Also by Paul Strachan

Pagan: Art and Architecture of Old Burma

Mandalay: Travels from the Golden City

A Burma River Journey

THE PANDAW STORY

On the Rivers of Burma and Beyond

Paul Strachan

IRRAWADDY FLOTILLA COMPANY

For Antoni Strachan

First Published in 2015 for the Irrawaddy Flotilla Company
by Kiscadale Publications, Scotland
1st Printing in the United Kingdom

2nd Printing in (November), 2015, Yangon, Myanmar
Published in Myanmar by
Daw Thin Thin Mon (Thinn Publishing House) 00372
No. 19, Kaw Tha Ka Street, Mingalar Taung Nyunt Township, Yangon

Printed by
Daw Shwe (Thukha Press) 00719
No. 128, 46th Street, Botahtaung Township, Yangon

No of books: 1,000

Price: $12.00

ISBN 978-1-870838-43-6

British Library Cataloguing-in-Publication Data
A catalogue record for this book is available from the British Library

Cover Design: David Lumsden
Front Cover Photo: Barry Broman

Contents

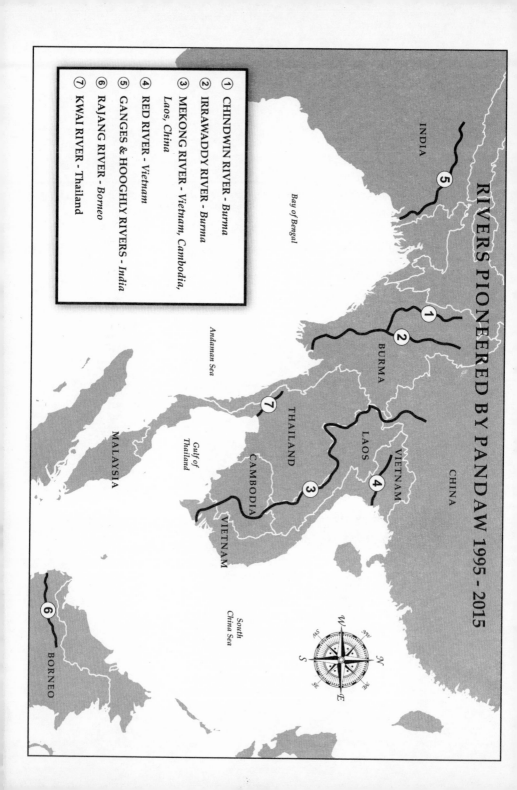

Foreword

For Burmese place names I have tended to use the old names such as Rangoon instead of Yangon and of course have used Burma instead of Myanmar to designate the country itself.

In doing so I have followed the current usage of the UK's Foreign and Commonwealth Office and indeed that of Daw Aung San Suu Kyi who, among many more significant acts of resistance, declined to go along with the name changes peremptorily forced upon the country by the military government in 1997.

While political and historic personages such as General Ne Win or General Khin Nyunt appear as themselves, the names of many of the other characters who appear in these pages have been changed.

Writing this memoir has reinforced my gratitude for the support of my wife Roser and my son Antoni, to whom this book is dedicated. His adoption of us as parents is described within. They have followed these adventures, ups and downs, with a general air of bemused tolerance. As will become clear, they have had much to put up with.

I am very much obliged to my old friend Colin Donald, a passenger on the maiden voyage of the Irrawaddy Princess in 1995, who has helped get my manuscript into shape for publication.

Finally I thank all the Pandaw team, from captains and their crews, to managers in their offices, for their parts in realising this great adventure.

Introduction

This is the story of how our company Pandaw built a river cruise business in one of the world's most repressive dictatorships. Not that it seemed so bad at the time.

Burma of the mid 1990s was an optimistic place, full of ideas and full of hope. Money grew on trees, ripe for harvesting by any enterprising person, Burman or foreigner. Many, including ourselves, were driven not just by the profit motive, but by the prospect of helping to take an ancient nation into the modern world.

As these pages will relate, it did not exactly turn out that way. The mid-90s glimmers of hope were brutally snuffed out, and we found ourselves at the mercy of a coarse kleptocracy whose exploitation of — and contempt for — its subjects was a throwback to Burma's blood-soaked pre-modern history.

In the background to the Pandaw story is a morally treacherous political landscape, where well-intentioned people caused bad things to happen, and malevolent forces inadvertently did good. Our story will show that our own good intentions did not always work out, but I hope it will justify the pride we feel in having tried to make things happen in Burma, against all odds.

What follows is a tale of ups and down, good moments and bad, both personal and commercial. Living and working in Burma is a perpetual game of snakes and ladders. One moment you are winning, and then...

I hope I have conveyed the intensity of this roller-coaster well enough for the reader to excuse the occasional self-pity and paranoia that seep through the hard-luck stories contained in this narrative, possibly forming a bit of a pattern. These may go beyond even what is standard for an entrepreneur's memoir.

While I have not resisted the opportunity to settle the occasional score, I am painfully aware that the price of doing so is to reveal my shortcomings as a businessman. 'I Did It My Way', but I often did it wrong.

From publishing books on Burmese art to running cruises and then building ships; the story does at times seem ridiculously far-fetched. My wife Roser and I feel privileged to have lived in Burma at a time when such things were possible.

Building something great out of nothing has been the crowning experience of my life. Despite many disasters and the occasional tragedy we feel it was worth doing. Readers will come to their own conclusions as to whether we are right to do so.

This is not a book about Burma's struggle to escape military oppression and achieve democracy. Burma's best known political figure Daw Aung San Suu Kyi, whose first western publisher I am proud to have been, does not feature in the story directly. Much as I admire her, I do question the effects of some of the policies promoted by "The Lady", and the way they were interpreted by western governments — my own included — in the long years she suffered in isolation under house arrest.

In the early 1990s I used to visit "Suu", then under house arrest at her University Avenue house, a predicament she bore with exemplary courage and patience. I would take her parcels of books as she had nothing to read, and I think she quite enjoyed sparring with me on current affairs. Perhaps not surprisingly given her circumstances, her view was very black and white and she had little patience with my belief that it was in the grey areas that any hope might lie.

As this account will make clear, my experiences of Burma made me think that Daw Suu's universally-admired iron resolution came regrettably close to being a refusal to see perspectives other than her own. Ultimately I feared that her position was doing the country more harm than good, a conclusion also reached by some who were far closer to her than I ever was.

However well-intentioned, the sanctions regime she promoted — which included even basic aid — took a terrible toll on Burma's poor, without much impacting the generals and their cronies, who just got richer and more powerful.

This is certainly not a "how-to" guide to doing business in Burma, or indeed anywhere, although I like to think that my experience of leading an organisation in complex circumstances might impart some "do's" and even more "don'ts".

In fact some parts could be read as an account of how not to run a company. Pandaw's business model, or lack of a model, could only have emerged in a country as eccentric as Burma.

Yet it did work, and at the time of writing it still works well. Applying to new operations in new areas is proof that management school does not always supply the answers.

Success is built on failure and when people see a Pandaw ship, serenely gliding the Irrawaddy or Mekong they do not know of the disasters, the sleepless nights, and the agonies behind it.

At times we grew over-ambitious and moved too fast once again, resulting in the loss of a much loved ship in India, a nagging hurt I will always carry. We grew too fast and important detail was overlooked.

Glory turned to disaster in 2003 when an innocent person lost her liberty as a result of my misreading of prevailing politics. Thankfully she survived the experience, and lessons were learnt, though I will never forgive myself for that failing.

In our relief operation in the aftermath of Cyclone Nargis in 2008, all the pieces fell into place. The years of perfecting, the honing of skills, the discipline and camaraderie came together to save lives and do something worthwhile. It was definitely Pandaw's finest hour and something we can be proud of to our dying days.

Also a matter of pride are the three hundred-plus people we employ, and the fact that the people we started with in 1995 are now sending their sons and daughters to work on the ships, just as I hope my own son will in a few years time. When we are all together on the rivers, we are one big and very content family and it all seems worthwhile.

Ultimately I think that the Pandaw Charity, currently running seven outpatient clinics in Middle Burma, and with twelve schools to its name is our greatest success and testimony to the generosity and involvement of our passengers.

Pandaw has a policy of never borrowing. It is entirely debt-free and a portion of profits is ploughed into community projects through the Pandaw Charity. Up until very recently, we have never spent money on advertising, PR or marketing – our ships fill by word of mouth and by returning passengers. I hope that speaks for itself.

Ultimately, there can be no more striking example of team-work than a well-run ship. Unlike a car, a train or even an aeroplane a ship cannot be moved by one man on his own. You need the master on the bridge, the crew pulling ropes, engineers cranking up motors, and all working together in finely-tuned harmony. So it is with Pandaw, everyone depending on each other and everyone as important as each other in the great scheme of things.

Bohmu and the Return to Burma

Descending the steps from the aircraft onto the apron at Rangoon's Mingaladon Airport we found ourselves singled out from the other passengers. Excited men in Ray-Ban aviator glasses bustled us into a minivan with blackened windows parked at the foot of the plane's steps. They gathered our bags straight off the plane.

A short yet broad man sitting in the front of the car introduced himself as "Bohmu", a military rank equivalent to colonel. We were asked to pass over our passports, which he pocketed.

Loaded up, the car sped off across the airfield to a gate that was hastily swung open by surprised guards snapping too. We were back in Burma. But at the same time we were not. Our visit was to be unrecorded. There would be no immigration, no customs.

The car sped from the airport but at the Prome Road junction swung right. The police on duty at the traffic lights instantly switched the lights to green as they saw Bohmu's unmarked car approaching. This was the case wherever he went – the lights just turned instantly green – every policeman in Rangoon knew that car and was ready to flick the switch. Worryingly we were heading away from the city centre. I was too nervous to ask where we were going. I knew the Rangoon area well from several previous long stays and we were headed in the direction of the north-western suburb of Insein, best known for its notorious prison.

The car turned off the Insein Road and sped down back streets and lanes where much new building was evident. Five years ago none of this was here. Now there were brand new suburban villas built or being built everywhere. Insein Jail loomed large to our right, in British colonial times a model panopticon prison, now a byword of human rights abuse, with thousands of political prisoners left to rot for their part in the failed 1988 "people power" rising. Were we being taken there? Had we been hoodwinked into coming back so that the State

7

Law and Order Council (SLORC) could exact revenge for past misdeeds? The thought was a real one.

We passed the jail and drew up at a new-built house in a quiet lane. The gates swung open and the watchman saluted.

Bohmu was more relaxed now, smiling and being generally genial. We felt more welcome. His English was marginally worse than my Burmese and we communicated in a combination of the two tongues. This was one of his houses. We were to stay here a few days until he could arrange for us to meet his boss.

His boss was General Khin Nyunt, then the head of military intelligence.

Only if the general liked us and approved of our projects could we then officially enter the country. Meanwhile we were to rest here until the general, a busy man, had time to see us.

It transpired later that the general had not been told we were here, in fact no one had. Bohmu would need the right moment to get the general alone and explain our case and beg an interview. We were not in Insein Jail but we were effectively under house arrest. The servants were our jailors, briefed to watch and report on every move.

Though new, the house was not comfortable, with heavy teak carved and varnished armchairs that dug into your back. Being of modern construction with low ceilings it got very hot and stuffy. Being an army house there was at least a good power supply, a rare thing in Rangoon, and we had air conditioning. The food prepared by an old Indian retainer of Bohmu was not intolerable, though we were fed an inordinate number of eggs.

Altogether we were somewhat dismayed at this turn of events. We had expected to be staying at a hotel with a pool and basking in the attention of the many old Burmese friends we had looked forward to seeing again. This was Roser's first visit to the country and not a great start.

Since I first went there at the age of eighteen, my story has been interwoven with events in Burma. Our return in 1993 was part of a rehabilitation following a four year banishment. Explaining these circumstances requires a brief recap of personal history.

B urma was a country that I had loved since the first of my long stays in 1981. I had managed to get a 'gap year' job working for John Brown Engineering. My father worked most of his life for the company which in earlier times built great ocean liners. This was an extraordinary six months spent mainly in the pleasant riverine town of Prome. The country was then deeply immersed in its great post-War political experiment known as 'The Burmese Road to Socialism'.

We may giggle now at this bizarre synthesis of Theravada Buddhism, Fabian socialism and the superstitious whims of its dictatorial author General Ne Win. One forgets that up till the mid 1980s this extraordinary philosophy was taken seriously not just by hundreds of thousands of party members throughout the country but also by western academics and philosophers. The influential British economist EF Schumacher in his 1973 book *Small is Beautiful* devoted an entire chapter to a solemn consideration of the Burmese dream.

I was eighteen and living on the fringe of a socialist work camp cleared from the jungle outside Prome. We were building a gas turbine power station. There were nimble little women engineers clambering up scaffolding in boiler suits alongside the great hulking Scotsmen sent out to advise them. The Burmese we worked with were developing their country. The power generated would serve nearby textile mills being built by an Irish company.

These projects were all funded by British government aid. In these Cold War years Burma was non-aligned, steering a middle path between the Russians, the Chinese and the Americans and happily taking development aid from all of them. The country ran on aid – not food parcels but new industries and infrastructure. Ne Win enjoyed cordial relations with the British royal family culminating in the visit of the Princess Royal, then Princess Anne, in 1986.

The terrible wars Ne Win fought against communist insurgency in the north of Burma remained uncensored by the west, for he was only doing the work that the British had taken on in Malaya and the Americans in Vietnam and Cambodia, without the west having to foot the bill. These were the days before the Berlin Wall came down and a concern for political appearances replaced rampant Cold War adventurism in US and British foreign policies.

In those days the Burmese countryside seemed prosperous to my youthful eyes. People dressed gaily and were forever taking days off for various jolly festivals. Under Ne Win not much was happening: there were no private businesses, no imports, no exports, few luxury goods. People had time on their hands and plenty to eat. Intellectual and artistic life was rich. Café or rather tea house society was populated by gentleman scholars discussing Dostoevsky or Tolstoy, usually read in Burmese translation. The BBC Burmese Service was then the most listened to BBC foreign station in the world. As a result people were surprisingly well informed about world events. Lending libraries abounded, and with one of the highest literacy rates in the developing world, people were reading everywhere: on buses, in cafes or just sitting in their porches. As in some visions of Utopia, education was an activity in itself. Young people collected degrees and diplomas without any thought to applying this education to anything practical.

All in all, life in the People's Union of Burma in the early 1980s was far from unpleasant so long as you behaved yourself. The greatest possible crime would be publicly to criticise General Ne Win. Yet privately thousands of jokes abounded about the general, his wives, his wealth and his many eccentricities. There was plenty of mirth. The Burmese are a self deprecating people, they love to laugh at themselves. The Ne Win circus at the heart of their country, with all its lunacy, reflected something primordially Burmese, and was the biggest joke of all.

With no non-essential imports or exports under the Burmese Road to Socialism everything had to be made. "People's Industries" produced everything. Pharmaceuticals, dinky little motor cars, toothpaste and soap, beer and rum, they printed their own money and made their own automatic weapons — all the essentials of life. The country had abundant oil and gas. Exporting a surplus of rice, rubies and jade they could earn the necessary foreign exchange to buy the arms needed to fight several wars on several fronts.

Burma between the 1960s and the 1980s was a closed country. Not just closed for trade but for the transit of people and for any contact with the world. A large slice of the Indian and Chinese communities packed up and left following the 1962 Revolution when Ne Win started seizing their houses and businesses. Rich Indian ladies were forced to take off their jewellery at the airport before leaving. It was Burma's gold.

By then nearly all the western businesses had already left during the anarchic 1950s. Conditions were very different from how they had been under British imperial rule. Very soon after Independence in 1947 corruption and state interference started making business inoperable.

From 1962 when Ne Win and his "Revolutionary Council" took power following a coup, foreign visitors were few. Foreign diplomats were corralled up in Rangoon, only allowed to visit each other's embassies in an endless circuit of cocktail parties and dinners. Only in 1979 was a seven-day tourist visa issued. By the late '70s as development started to flow, the first expats came in.

Arriving aged 18 in 1981 having done no background reading and being totally unfamiliar with culture or history, I rapidly found myself immersed in a captivating new world. My duties at John Brown's were hardly onerous and, after acquiring a bicycle, I took to exploring Prome and its environs, rich in archaeological treasures and contemporary Buddhist life.

Soon I was wearing a *longyi*, the universal Burmese wrapped cloth skirt, and communicating in broken Burmese. My expat colleagues, mainly rough and ready Scots from Clydebank, outside Glasgow, found this hilarious.

Returning to Britain I read history at Bristol University and took as many courses as possible in Asian history and spent much spare time mugging up about Burma in the library. I would travel to London regularly for lectures at the Britain Burma Society and to explore the School of Oriental and African Studies (SOAS) library with its rich collection of Burma materials. I had but one plan during my three years as an undergraduate and that was to go back to Burma and live there for an extended period after graduating.

With the seven days visa rule you could not just go and live in Burma. I had by now forged contacts with the Burmese department at SOAS which had a staff of two and, in a good year, a student body of one. I planned to enroll for a master's degree in Burmese art history (I was interested in pagodas), which would allow me to apply for a research visa. Burma was just beginning to open up a little and student exchanges were taking place. During a first year at SOAS in 1984-85 I took a course in Burmese, which included reading and writing. I was not very proficient, having no great aptitude for languages, but it gave me a solid grounding that I was able to build on when I was there.

Then after several months of letter writing to our embassy in Rangoon I got my visa and was off in early 1986. I have written about that year in Burma elsewhere. It was a formative period for me, and the foundation upon which, without prior design, life has unfolded.

I became quite ill with dysentery and dengue fever and had to return home, shrunk from fifteen stone to ten. Having fattened up I went back again for another six months in 1987. The result was my book on Pagan.

Then came the great pro-democracy uprising, known by its auspicious date of 8/8/88 which I followed from a London bedsit. At one moment I was euphoric that the monster Ne Win had finally been toppled and then horrified by the coup and brutal repression that followed. I longed to be back with Burmese friends, to be with them in that moment of glory that reached its apogee on 8/8/88 when the entire nation rose, civil servants, police, navy, air force and much of the army, and said 'enough!'

Burma was the first left wing tyranny, to revolt against totalitarianism since the Prague Spring of 1968. It pre-empted the Tiananmen Square uprising by eight months and the collapse of the Berlin Wall by a year, although it received only a fraction of the attention due to Burma's relative obscurity and the near-complete absence of foreign TV cameras.

The SLORC counter-coup of 15 September 1988 was swift and brutal and the crackdown horrific, resulting in up to 10,000 deaths.

I was back briefly in 1989 as a guest of the British Council to promote my book on Pagan and the situation was the opposite of the carefree happy-go-luck Burma I had known a couple of years earlier. There were Army checkpoints on every road, nests of barbed wire and machine guns on street corners, a curfew at dusk and a rule forbidding public gatherings of more than six people, resulting on one grim occasion in the gunning down of an entire bus queue.

Even back in 1989 under SLORC things were changing fast. The country's name was changed to Myanmar as were long-Anglicised city names – Rangoon became Yangon, Pagan – Bagan and Moulmein – Molamyein. Indeed, Rangoon woke up one morning to find that, with extraordinary efficiency, all the street signs had been changed overnight. York Road became Yaw-min-gyi Lan, Boundary Road became Dhamazedi Lan, etc. Rangoon was redesigned mainly to prevent future gatherings of people (all parks were fenced in with railings) and dual carriageways replaced the once-winding country lanes of suburban Rangoon. Everywhere smart young officers in Ray-Bans were shouting orders. Most of these captains were MI or Military Intelligence.

I flew into Sandoway (now Thandwe) on the Arakan coast for a few days at the beach and had an introduction to such a captain, who met me at the airport in his jeep, Ray-Bans and all. Everything happened for this guy, things moved, doors opened. I had never seen this before in Burma, young men in a hurry getting things done. It was extraordinary.

The vast Burma Socialist Programme Party, that had employed as many people as the bloated civil service, was disbanded. Government was honed down and the civil service cut. The new regime seemed anxious to modernise and make up for lost time. All around roads were being built and rivers bridged. By the early 1990s Rangoon doubled in area as satellite towns grew up and inner city populations relocated, often more for strategic reasons than because of the normal dynamics of human settlement.

I left in 1989 with a bad feeling. That very Burmese mirth, that had infused all aspects of life and activity, had gone. This was a country deeply traumatised by the events of '88 and its aftermath. Still to this day there is no clear body count, there are no memorials or days of remembrance. Every time I drive over the White Bridge on Prome Road, scene of one of the most vicious student massacres I shudder, but not a bunch of flowers marks the spot.

Sometimes I think that the Burmese suffer from a voluntary amnesia. Like the tens of thousands of women enslaved by the Japanese in the war to work as 'comfort girls' a sense of shame drives them to bury their memories and move on.

Even as Burma currently edges slowly towards democracy, discussion about war crimes or retribution for human rights violations are still clearly off the agenda. Perhaps not dwelling on the past is a good thing, it lets people move on. Those who have not experienced such horrors are in no position to judge.

By about 1990 reports were coming in of increasing military brutality, but I was busy having started a publishing business in Edinburgh. Letters from Burma were few and far between. I was out of touch.

What made the difference for me was the forced re-location of Pagan village in 1990. I had spent six months here in 1987 working on my book on the monuments at Pagan. This had been one of the happiest times of my life when I had been adopted by a Burmese family, and lived amongst them as if Burma born and bred.

I learned that one night the entire village was moved at gunpoint to a new location about seven miles to the south, now called New Pagan, without warning. The new site was devoid of power, water or sanitation. I was beside myself with shock, pain and anguish for my friends and the community I had once lived in.

There was no email then and all phones had been disconnected. News came to me from my old friend the archaeologist Pierre Pichard whom I had worked with at Pagan. Pierre worked for a Unesco restoration programme and had witnessed the relocation at first hand. As a Unesco official he could not openly write about it but would I?

Photos of demolished houses and the wasteland of 'old Pagan' were forwarded and I wrote a very emotional and, I thought, poignant piece that was published by the dissident Burmese press and was then picked up by the international media.

Still to this day no one is very clear just what was behind the forced relocation. I am not sure even SLORC clearly thought it through. They just felt they had to shift the village to open the place for tourism, when ironically the village, with its many traditional teak houses and ancient caretaker community, was a tourist attraction in itself.

The result was that I was immediately put on the PNG (Persona Non Grata) list, the blacklist for visas. Kiscadale Publications, my little publishing house, meanwhile moved away from books on art and history to more topical works on Burmese politics and human rights.

We were Aung San Suu Kyi's first European publisher (for her 1991 biography of her father *Aung San of Burma)* and we went on to publish a rather difficult Swedish journalist called Bertil Lintner. His book on the 1988 rising (*Outrage*) and his trek across insurgent occupied northern Burma (*Land of Jade*), both lost money but Pagan was doing well and helped to subvene them.

There followed an interesting period of visiting Burmese refuge camps along the Burma-Thai border researching for future book projects. I managed a short stay at Mannerplaw, the Karen insurgent capital where I met the famous Karen leader General Bo Mya. Later Mannarplaw was bombed out of existence.

By the mid-1990s, now married to Roser, and living in rural Stirlingshire, I found myself missing Burma more and more. Things were changing, Saw Maung the general behind the late 1980s atrocities had been locked up in a palace coup and General Khin Nyunt had apparently taken charge. He was said to be more moderate and westwards leaning. There was a relaxation, an encouragement of investment and tourism. There was talk of modernisation and opening up.

Khin Nyunt, then in his 50s, was interested in art and culture and had apparently been impressed by our publication of Pierre Pichard's magisterial *Inventory of Monuments at Pagan* (seven volumes co-published with Unesco and the Ecole Francais d'Extreme Orient).

I was approached by a little man at Burma's London embassy and asked if I would like to return to Burma, unofficially. All our right-thinking friends said don't go. In the wake of the human rights violations Burma was taboo. If we went we would face social ostracism at home. I would be branded a turncoat, a hypocrite, and a fool.

Yet I knew better than they did that the military regime was there to stay, so the only hope of change would be through a combination of investment and development, hand in hand with education and cultural exchange. A bunch of activists chanting piously outside the Myanmar Embassy was not going to change anything.

Neither the power of the internet nor the freedom of mobile communications had as yet been unleashed. The world of two decades ago was very much different from today. A number of projects in Burma beckoned. Already colonial Rangoon appeared doomed as developers razed Palladian mansions and neo-classical villas in favour of tacky tower blocks of cheap flats. I had to get out and photograph what remained (nearly all the houses I photographed for my book *Old Rangoon* are now gone).

Also, I missed Burma. After five years out in the cold I was "homesick" and desperate to get back. And thus it was we returned in 1993 under the somewhat bizarre circumstances described above.

As mentioned we were not actually invited by General Khin Nyunt, but there on the initiative of Bohmu and his faction within the MI. We were there on approval to see if the General liked us or not. I am not sure what Bohmu thought was in it for him. Brownie points with the general if it worked out? A lucrative book distribution deal? Books were talked about but Kiscadale was hardly Random House.

The days went by and we negotiated permission to go out each day and visit various old friends, heavily chaperoned by Bohmu's minders. Anyway, we were in a car that every policeman in Rangoon knew to be Bohmu's so we were not going to get far.

Tubby and short, Bohmu proved to be an affable character; he dressed down and did not for a moment resemble the remorseless instrument of a brutal regime. On one occasion we needed to make a phone call and went into a downtown shop where we could see a phone on the counter. Bohmu asked very politely if we could use the phone. Now in Burma such a request would never have been refused but in this case the shopkeeper, an Indian, said no.

Bohmu was visibly shaken. Then all he said was 'MI' and suddenly the shopkeeper, quivering with fear offered the use of the phone.

With much time on our hands Bohmu liked to drive me around himself and with a contented beam on his face would point out various businesses he claimed to own, or at least have a share in.

There was the golf shop on York Road; a huge Chinese dim sum restaurant; supermarkets and coffee shops, even a bakery. In these early days of 'opening up' any Chinese entrepreneur considering a start up would contact Bohmu and offer him a share in the business and in return Bohmu would see through the licences and make sure they were left alone. This classic protection racket filled Bohmu with pride and joy, he would lunch in one of his restaurants, shop in one of his stores, try out the latest golf clubs from his golf pro shop and never seemed to pay for anything.

This was the system by which Burma ran from the 1990s until the 2010s. A connected military man fronted a business and the investment and management came from Chinese business people in the background. Even today a number of Burma's largest conglomerates follow this formula.

Just what Bohmu did, other than swan around his various business interests was never very clear, there was mention that he took care of the General's security in certain sectors of the city. It seemed there was literally a whole army of people out there caring for the General's security, no one unit could be trusted exclusively and thus units rotated geographically and periodically.

Clearly Bohmu, at certain moments at least, had the General's ear and could drop hints or make suggestions, which made him immensely powerful. Bohmu like so many senior officers came from a provincial background, in his case the northern town of Katha, and had risen up through the ranks, serving for many years on the frontline.

His entourage was hugely loyal and protective of him, for his power and wealth descended to raise the prestige of the lowest of his servants.

This was the Burmese feudal system, essentially one of barons and knights and squires owing fealty to each other, dependent on the whims of great magnates themselves jockeying to greater proximity to the throne.

Indeed, pre-internet Burma often felt very much as if one had been transported into the Middle Ages. There was deep piety fenced around by wickedness, rich spirituality blending into superstition, compassion countered by cruelty, ancient wisdoms overcast by ignorance.

Overall there was domination, a blind obedience sprung from the Buddhist cult of "respect": due to the patriarch in the home, the monk in his monastery, the master in his atelier, the general in his camp. From the Burmese perspective, if democracy is unthinkable in the home, the monastery, or the workplace, how could it be applied to a state?

Eventually the big day arrived and Bohmu arrived at the safe house in a state of great excitement. I was told to get ready and Bohmu supervised my wardrobe insisting on a jacket and tie despite the seasonal heat. We were whisked through Rangoon to another safe house apparently to await the next order.

Was this where they held Rangoon's "disappeared", in a suburban archipelago of torture chambers and mortuaries? Feigning a search for the bathroom I opened a number of closed doors but found little of interest.

Bohmu appeared very anxious, sweating a lot and giving me lots of 'you'll be fine' smiles. The phone rang and Bohmu's team sprang into action. We set off with a vehicle in front.

This time the traffic light police were really on the ball and every light across town switched to green to let us through, Bohmu's men had radioed ahead. We reached the War Office compound on Signal Pagoda Road with its sentries and barbed wire and tank-stoppers. The gates were open and we did not even slow down but speeded up a drive of sentries all in dress uniforms with their machine pistols braced in a salute.

Gosh all this for me? I felt very important, but that was the trick that SLORC played with so many foreign visitors, many of whom, like myself, were rather dubious. Treat someone like a head of state and you have a friend for life.

Ushered into the Dagon Yeiktha, a sort of pavilion erected to receive foreign guests, the entrance hall was filled with a levee of what can only be described as courtiers, people who danced attendance on the general.

Aides, decorated officers in fancy uniforms, ministers and countless officials formed groups in this Ruritanian court setting. I was met by a colonel who described himself as head of protocol and ushered into a side room and asked me to sit on a sofa positioned to the side of a very throne-like armchair.

Minutes later there was the sound of cars drawing up, the babble of chatter in the hall stopped, and in a second General Khin Nyunt himself danced beaming into the room.

He had been well-briefed and knew my Burmese name 'Ko Hpone Myint' and insisted that we talk Burmese. He was all charm, even putting an arm round me for the photographers and TV cameras. I presented him with my book on Pagan with which he professed himself delighted. We talked art and culture. He promised me any help I needed with our publishing projects in Burma.

Then he was gone, ushered into the next audience in a room adjacent. It transpired the Singaporian foreign minister was due any minute and all the dress uniforms, sentries and all the pomp were for him, not me.

Never mind, it had made me feel for the first and last time in my life incredibly important. I was whisked away by a jubilant Bohmu who had decided that everything had gone to plan and that the meeting had been a success. Back at the safe house Roser and I were told we were free. Just like that. We could go and stay in a hotel and do whatever we liked. And sure enough after that one encounter there were no constraints at all and for the remainder of the trip were able to travel freely around the country without let or hindrance.

Little did we know that one year on we would be running river ships on the Irrawaddy. And so the story begins.

The Irrawaddy Princess

In September 1995 we found ourselves steaming up the Irrawaddy in a river boat that resembled a giant crate astride a pair of canoes. The mood was celebratory: surrounded at all stops by flags and bunting, accompanied by thirty mainly British travellers and all feeling rather pleased with ourselves.

This was a first. The first river voyage in Burma for foreigners since before the Second World War and one of the first groups of tourists to visit since the country reopened in the early 1990s.

It was also the maiden voyage of a brand new Burma-built ship. Neither Roser nor I could quite work out how we had ended up in this bizarre situation, so remote from our past aims and occupations.

We were headed from Pagan to Bhamo, at least we thought we were — we never actually arrived. We had little idea what we were in for, originally planning to sit back and enjoy the ride, we soon found ourselves doing the jobs of a dozen crew members.

It all came about from a visit to Rangoon earlier that year. I was in town taking photographs for a book on the city's rapidly disappearing colonial architecture. A friend had lent me a scooter and I was enjoying myself buzzing around the town setting up tripod and camera in people's front gardens. There was little traffic back then, but the writing was already on the wall for so many of the city's splendid old Raj-era buildings. Already the bulldozers were at work as great old houses in their one-acre compounds were divvied up for demolition and replacement with cramped apartment blocks.

My little-known publishing firm, Kiscadale Publications, specialised in such cultural conservation projects. These were rarely remunerative but in retrospect pleasingly altruistic – for any book that turned a profit there would be half a dozen losers. Somehow we had muddled along for several years, ever in the red at the bank but just about managing to pay the bills. Whilst researching and taking

23

photographs for *Old Rangoon – City of the Shwedagon* a friend invited me to the launch of what was to be Burma's first ever river cruise ship, the Irrawaddy Princess.

Possibly one of the ugliest ships ever to be seen on the Irrawaddy, this vessel had been built by the retiring director general of the Myanma Oil and Gas Corporation (MOG). In socialist, and more so post-socialist Burma, this post had been considered one of the cushiest of billets for any government official, with many a plump contract being signed with lavishly generous foreign oil companies. U Win Pe, a Burmese of Chinese extraction, had amassed a considerable fortune and boasted that he owned every house in his street. Enormously fat, he dressed in an immaculate silk *paso* (the male Burmese *longyi* or skirt); his index finger was all but obscured by a giant ruby almost the size of ping pong ball. On retirement from MOG he had decided to treat himself to a little retirement present and had ordered the construction of this ship in the department's shipyard. An intimidating character he was surrounded by an army of assistants and servants, all clearly terrified of him.

At the launch, the boat was filled by such people, the dependents and sycophants with whom any senior Burmese official or army officer is accompanied. Like a feudal magnate, he is surrounded by vassals, and he in turn owes fealty to his own overlord, in this case the minister of energy.

Also at the launch were a motley bunch of travel agents, mainly Swiss ladies who all seemed to hate each other – looking daggers whenever any one opened their mouth. U Win Pe presided over a gross feast of very rich and oily curries in the ship's dining room, positioned in the stern over the engine room and thus very noisy and hot.

There were a great many cabins ranged over three decks constructed off plywood partitions with western-style bathrooms. I asked the great man what his intentions were. He told me that tourists would soon be arriving in their thousands, and that cruising the river was the most logical way to see the country. The Irrawaddy was to

Burma, he said, as the Nile was to Egypt, the great artery through which all things passed, that linked cities ancient and modern.

Yes, very well, but what of marketing? How would he find these tourists? Long pause, during which the idea came to me. I would do it.

Kiscadale had a good list of names and addresses of people who bought books about Burma – we would make a 'reader offer'. Terms of hire were agreed with U Win Pe.

Returning to Scotland a week later we set about making a leaflet, Roser, who is a keen artist did a sketch of the boat and I wrote a blurb. In those pre-email days we spent about fifty pounds on stamps and photocopying and sent it out to a couple of hundred people we knew to be Burma buffs. A couple of days later the phone never stopped ringing. We never looked back. It is thus true to say that we really did start Pandaw on under a hundred dollars.

Cheques bearing deposits came pouring in. What was intended as a lark, a one-off charter of the ship to take a bunch of like-minded Burma enthusiasts up the river for the first time since the war, overnight became a serious enterprise. In those days people phoned. The day was spent talking with war veterans and old colonials, keen to revisit Burma after decades of isolation. Then there were the writers and journalist. A man from the BBC wanted to make a radio documentary about the Irrawaddy Flotilla Company. Various film makers got in touch. One old boy was incredulous, telling me I was a fraud and what we proposed to do was impossible. Another, likewise told me that we could not "pull the wool over his eyes", he had been up and down the Irrawaddy (about 50 years before) and therefore knew what we were up against.

My old friend and mentor on river matters Alister McCrae, former general manager of the IFC after the war, rang to say "You're not running boats on the river now?" He then proceeded to give me detailed instructions on best mooring positions and where rocks were to be avoided.

We would take thirty passengers, and soon the cabins were filled. We announced two further consecutive trips and additional charters were secured with U Win Pe. Then a further three trips for first part of 1996 were offered and those soon sold out as well.

At this point the doubts set in. We knew nothing of ship, hotel or tour management. A couple of hundred people had booked and an awful lot could go wrong, particularly in a place like Burma. Ships could break down and the Princess's build quality was questionable with safety appliances non existent. River navigation was uncertain with few aids and no charts. Food hygiene in Burma was probably the worst in Asia if not the world — you would feel ill just browsing the menu.

Also, the country was ruled by what was widely described as a brutal military dictatorship, whose past record of xenophobia had left a legacy of a mass of restrictions on travel for foreigners.

Worried, we booked a Nile cruise to see what happened on river cruises; having never been on a cruise in our lives.

It was ghastly, or rather the cruise was. We had no complaints about the Nile. We sat down and made a list of all the 'do nots' and have stuck to this list ever since.

A further visit was made to Yangon that summer to check on the ship and discuss arrangements with U Win Pe. The Russian-built Inya Lake Hotel, a vast concrete pile built in the 1960s as a carbon copy of a Soviet resort on the Black Sea Riviera, was undergoing a restoration under a friendly Scottish manager. Rooms, then at exorbitant rates due to a lack of hotel beds in Rangoon, were secured. I found U Tin Tun, a former Burmese ambassador to Britain, whom I had known well during student days in London. He had been 'retired' for his involvement in the democracy movement in 1988 and had started a travel company who would undertake the ground arrangements: transfers, coach hire, sightseeing and excursions.

In the early '90s Rangoon was an exciting place to be. Things seemed to be 'opening up', a much vaunted expression then. Many middle class Burmese saw tourism as a golden goose. Life savings were invested in turning family homes into guest-houses or 'inns' as they liked to call them. Restaurants and bars started opening everywhere. People were importing second hand buses to start transport businesses or used cars to drive as taxis.

Once devoid of traffic, Rangoon streets suddenly became quite busy. Car transport ships, huge floating car parks, would moor alongside Strand Road and a thousand cars would be driven off and auctioned on the spot. Old gas-guzzling Toyotas and Hondas from Japan or Singapore, countries which were becoming more strict on carbon emissions were being shipped off to Burma where the ownership of a car, once a remote dream, became a reality for so many middle class Burmese. Pollution, previously unheard off, joined the host of other inconveniences of Rangoon life, along with the seven-month monsoon, power cuts, blocked drains, garden snakes and ubiquitous mosquitoes. New cars were on sale too, Land Rover opened a dealership and car show rooms were popping up everywhere. Everything seemed possible.

The SLORC years, were routinely depicted by journalists then, and by historians since, as dark and sinister times. General Khin Nyunt, emerging as the regime's strongman, was portrayed as a dark, and dangerous figure. The head of Burma's feared MI, he had engineered a palace coup in 1991 to displace General Saw Maung, founder and chairman of the repressive SLORC regime in the aftermath of the repression of the 1988 Uprising.

General Saw Maung was said by military rivals to have gone mad and to have come to think of himself the reincarnation of an ancient Burmese king, who like most ancient Burmese kings, had conquered Thailand (the Thai capital Ayutthaya was sacked seven times by the Burmese in the 18th Century). Saw Maung was said to be planning a further invasion of Thailand.

Thinking themselves reincarnated kings was, and remains, an occupational hazard for post-War Burmese dictators. General Ne Win had similar fantasies and enjoyed a mini court life, surrounded by Brahmanic astrologers just as past kings had. However Ne Win was an undemonstrative, low-key character, which was a big part of his success. Later General Than Shwe took regal fantasies to new heights, relocating his palace-city, just as Burmese kings of old would, surrounding himself with courtiers who addressed him with royal titles. Given the sycophantic tendencies of Burmese officers before a superior it is hardly surprising that, with lack of education or experience beyond the confines of the military cantonment, vain delusions can shade into clinical territory.

Khin Nyunt was not like this. He was one of the few senior officers who had an education. He had a university degree and came from a middle class Sino-Burmese family of merchants in Kyauktan, south of Rangoon. Furthermore, he had travelled abroad as a flunky in the Ne Win entourage. What the Burmese call an 'umbrella holder', holding the sun shade over the dignitary, an ancient court office that is now the preserve of an aspiring army officer. Back in the 1960s, '70s and even '80s Ne Win was much feted on his annual trips abroad. Everyone wanted to be his friend and win concessions into Burma. A German arms manufacturer would send a chartered Lufthansa jet to collect the General and his party. Ne Win would load the plane with strong boxes of gold and jewels to be deposited in the vaults of a Swiss bank. Hotels in Austria or Switzerland would be taken over. Embassies were requisitioned, one former diplomat told me that Ne Win went everywhere with his favourite cook, an Indian called Raju.

Raju was to become one of the most important men in Burma as he had direct access to the throne and people would pay dearly to get a word or a hint dropped before the great man. On such overseas visits Raju would call up the embassy commissariats and order bottles of Scotch whisky which he would then sell off to mates on the outside.

It was in this rarefied world of schloss and spa, Swiss bank vaults and black market whisky that Khin Nyunt had at least caught a glimpse of the outside world. In more recent times he had visited Singapore and nurtured dreams of transforming Rangoon — a decayed colonial city partly reclaimed by the jungle, with creepers entwining buildings and the great stuccoed facades gone green with moss and mould — into a 'garden city' of tree-lined boulevards and manicured little parks. The secret behind his masterstroke of silencing Saw Maung, placing him under house arrest in his Inya Road mansion for the remainder of his life, was to ensure in advance that the 'real army' rather than the dictator's intelligence service would support the coup.

Back then the 'real army' seemed distant and opaque. No one really knew who the supreme chief was. General Ne Win may have 'retired' but he was said to enjoy a weekly scrabble game with Khin Nyunt, reputedly when the latter would receive his instructions.

In 1995 few foreigners had heard of General Than Shwe, Khin Nyunt's patron and eventual nemesis. He appeared to be a remote geriatric figurehead, wheeled out for parades on National Day. In fact, the real army were remote from both domestic and foreign affairs, they were concerned with their own affairs – in the 1990s the military more than trebled in size and re-equipped itself with new weaponry, MIG fighter jets and a new fleet for the navy supplied by Russia and China. Khin Nyunt was effectively a sort of Grand Vizier, delegated to run the country and ensure the military received its procurement budget, and that there would be no more domestic uprisings.

In 1995 it was still possible to sit in the cocktail bar at the Inya Lake Hotel and get into conversations with sundry carpet-baggers who would offer you a million dollars to help set up a project for them. Everyone was on the lookout for opportunity. Burma was a country of low hanging fruit. Old colonial epithets abounded once again: 'the rice basket of Asia', 'Rangoon the pearl of the orient', even the 'Petrol pump of Asia'. The Inya Lake Hotel was being transformed into a Western-standard five star hotel, as was the Strand and other old state-owned hotels. New hotels were springing up around town. The enormous Traders Hotel (now the Shangri-la) occupied the site of the old Armenian cemetery and some fine old cinema halls. The wrecker's ball and bulldozer were transforming a once-charming colonial downtown, and not for the better. Giant sign boards proclaiming joint ventures, import and export emporia or travels and tours agencies seemed to subsume whole buildings. Down at the docks a hotel ship arrived, called the Central Floating Hotel, so great was the need for hotel rooms for all the businessmen pouring in. There was an ebullience in the air.

Khin Nyunt, who styled himself as 'Secretary One', and was known by all as S1, set about an ambitious programme of reform. After the malaise of quarter of century of somnolent "socialism" the Burmese became enthralled by his energy. TV news each night narrated his seemingly inexhaustible activities with his personal aircraft whizzing off to land at remote airstrips across the country, inspecting budding hydro dams, new roads and railways, irrigation schemes, power stations, schools and of course making offerings at diverse Buddhist monasteries. As one friend told me, 'Khin Nyunt understands the Burmese mentality, everyone says yes and then does nothing'.

To get his many projects completed he had to keep visiting them to keep officials on their toes. To win hearts and minds he had to be a devout Buddhist, visiting every monastery great and small paying respect and making generous offerings.

In 1988 the Buddhist *sangha* hierarchy had supported the people against the military. Khin Nyunt set about wooing, some would say corrupting, the *sangha* with his generosity. Ne Win had rarely interfered in *sangha* affairs his interests lying more in the subculture of nat or spirit worship and astrology. By contrast, Khin Nyunt became preoccupied with official religious matters and was determined to bring "church and state" closer together. I witnessed the effects of this on several occasions. In little known village monasteries the monk would point to a new pump for a well, or a fine new shrine and say "S1 donated this … a good man". Distinguished monastic scholars and nationally revered abbots were 'invited' to Rangoon and enthroned in splendid state-sponsored temple monasteries, literally showered with gold, sacred objects of veneration under the government's watchful eye, to all intents and purposes under house arrest. New pagodas and *dhamma-yon* or preaching halls, much elaborated with gilded stucco in a slightly kitschy style associated with the Khin Nyunt years, sprang up all over Rangoon. The national TV stations reeled off hours of military-religious propaganda, endless films of generals pagoda-building or feeding monks, the principal general always being S1.

For these reasons the mid-'90s mood in Burma was dynamic, even electric. After a thirty-year slumber the Burmese had awoken. Like Khin Nyunt everyone was full of beans, and full of projects and ideas. Buying their first cars, opening their first businesses, going shopping in Bangkok or Singapore for the first time. Or for those who could not afford the bribe to get a passport then fancy shopping malls were opening offering western fashions and the latest electrical goods. The Burmese were determined to catch up and to move ahead.

By the late 1990s however such plans had been put into abeyance; Khin Nyunt's power ebbed away and the hardliners won the day. Aung San Suu Kyi, her moral authority reinforced by the Nobel Peace Prize she won in 1991, had long called for a boycott of tourism and for economic sanctions. But with catastrophic consequences, she demanded a withdrawal and denial of any aid or assistance to the country

Isolated and stigmatised by the west, the generals retreated into their bunkers, seeking succour from less fastidious governments: China, North Korea and Russia. This story will be told in a later chapter.

Whilst still in the ascendant, the Khin Nyunt regime prided itself on its international relations. He himself was keen to show off to the west the many changes and improvements he was making, particularly

31

new hotels, tree-lined boulevards with roads leading everywhere and lots of bridges.

Cynics might speculate that these infrastructure improvements were designed to facilitate the movement of troops in civil emergencies, and while this may be true but an inescapable side-effect was that the economy was stimulated and new businesses abounded.

Meanwhile back in the UK New Labour came to power and a new foreign secretary Robin Cook proclaimed an 'ethical foreign policy', while the Clinton administration in the United States took a similar moralistic tone. The western powers were not talking to Khin Nyunt. They had been advised by Aung San Suu Kyi to keep their distance.

In their place, various suitors appeared in Rangoon. Indeed Khin Nyunt seemed to work his way through a gamut of potential Asian 'partners'. First the South Koreans, then the Malaysians, followed by a flirtation with Thailand and a longer affair with Singapore. State visits were exchanged. Joint ventures signed, visionary projects of mutual co-operation shared. None of these friendships seemed to last – the Koreans built factories, the Malaysians hotels, the Singaporeans ports. All these projects seemed doomed to failure as a result of a mixture of inertia on the Burmese government's part and a collapse in trade caused by the sanctions. But the relationship that did endure was the one with the People's Republic of China.

By the end of the first decade of the 21st century, China had effectively 'occupied' Burma, turning the country into a virtual colony on various levels. Firstly, through migration – no fewer than a million ethnic Chinese came to live in Burma during this period, occupying first Mandalay and later Rangoon. This turned them into Chinese cities, in which they bought out the Burmese, through land, property and business deals.

This influence was mirrored at a governmental level through credits, loans and barter agreements that have resulted in the division of key economic resources between Chinese corporations, with the result of making the Burmese government financially beholden to the Chinese.

Finally the takeover was completed strategically through military co-operation that started with rearmament, and which developed via 'training' and 'joint exercises', particularly naval, in the Bay of Bengal. The end result is permanent Chinese military bases within the country's borders.

Beijing's effective colonisation of Burma only became fully apparent to western observers by about 2010 but the process had been started years earlier by a desperate Khin Nyunt, anxious to find friends and aid in the face of western rejection.

The irony was marked. There was Khin Nyunt, educated and savvy, and temperamentally pro-western, desperately needing aid and investment to keep the hardliners at bay, forced to turn to the Chinese in the face of this rejection. For all her moral stature on the world stage, the unpalatable truth is that had Suu Kyi not urged western investors and donors to 'stay away from Burma' things might have been very different.

What is inarguable is that running a river expedition up the Irrawaddy prior to the Khin Nyunt 'liberalisation' of the 1990s would have been unthinkable. By around 1995 everything seemed possible: people were talking about ski resorts in the Burmese Himalayas; a canal that would cut across the Kra Isthmus, from the Burmese Andaman Sea to the Gulf of Siam, and cut out Singapore. There was a crazy Frenchman with a project for a massive container port in Mergui. The South Koreans were going to build a futuristic new city across the river at Dalla. And we were going to take travellers up the Irrawaddy to Bhamo. It is hardly surprising that people put our river cruise business into a similar category of laughable fantasy.

Our first voyage was planned for the 15th September. Embarking at Pagan we would aim for the Upper Irrawaddy and Bhamo. I knew sections of the river system and a number of historical sites from my wanderings with a monk in the mid-1980s, which are described in my travel book *Mandalay*. Roser and I flew out a couple of weeks in advance, to prepare the Princess.

The ship was very basic, the cabins partitioned by thin plywood and rather rickety. When the engines were switched on everything rattled.

Somehow U Win Pe had thought that a twin hull, essentially a catamaran, would draw less and be more suited to the shallow conditions of the Irrawaddy. Nothing could have been further from the truth and the vessel's poor design became even more apparent in its lack of trim, the stern sunk deep and the bows projecting at a rakish angle, a bit like a crouching water skier.

Roser did a great job with flowers and pictures and various local objects bought to decorate the ship and jolly it up a bit. The passengers arrived, and thus began probably the most exciting and exhausting ten days of our life.

Imagine simultaneously hosting a cocktail party, delivering a series of lectures, running a house party requiring three meals a day, while at the same time pioneering an unchartered river in a poorly designed vessel with a totally inexperienced crew.

Despite these hurdles there prevailed that euphoric feeling of doing something totally new, something radical, and of being onto something. Orient Express, the upmarket train and hotel operator were soon after to launch their own vessel on the river, a totally unsuited 1960s Rhine cruiser that was to run into all sorts of difficulties on account of its disproportionate size. We were very pleased to be the first to take travellers up the river, at least since the 1930s when a river voyage with the old Irrawaddy Flotilla had been an essential component to any imperial tour.

The sense of adventure we experienced was aided by the cast of passengers who had elected to join this bizarre expedition. These were not the sort of people you would find on a normal package holiday.

Indeed our bunch were probably amongst the most interesting and eccentric — in the best sense of that word — group of characters conceivable in the current era. Agatha Christie, herself a keen river cruiser, would have reveled in the possibilities.

There were three fabulously wealthy American ladies, all married to English noblemen who came dressed in bee-keeping outfits, muslin and gauze reaching from head to toe. A pair of gentleman travellers called Dr Hook and Colonel Cook, the latter a veteran of the wartime Burma campaign. There was a retired vicar who took rather too pronounced an interest in the cabin boys. There was a refined lady from Edinburgh's Morningside who had been born in Burma and was travelling with her tiresomely right-on daughter. There was an awkward Italian-American called Frank who wore football shirts, long before this became a fashion who (deliberately) annoyed the British by always being late. There was other rather mysterious retired American colonel, who had been a defence attaché at the US Embassy and seemed to be on a mission of his own, prompting excited whispering of the initials "CIA". There was an architectural historian who was an expert on colonial architecture and a man from the BBC making a radio documentary. Nearly everyone had either been born in Burma, or had a parent born in Burma, had fought in Burma, had served in Burma or was a Burma fanatic of some sort or the other.

This was to be expected. The country tends to get a hold of you and stay with you all your life. A rich and diverse culture like Burma's offers much to preoccupy.

Finally there was an extravagantly dull suburban couple from Surrey who had clearly booked the wrong trip, and easily upset by the contingencies of tropical terra incognita

Twenty years later I seem to be able to recall exactly every moment of those ten days. Ups and downs, highs and lows, conversations and events all come back in detail. All the other expeditions and voyages seem to merge into a great blur of riverine experience but not this one.

Embarking at Pagan there were the usual tours of the monuments and museums. Pagan then was entering its darkest hour. The 1990s SLORC-sponsored 'restorations' of temple fabric, motivated in one part by piety and on the other part as a cash-generating racket for the army, were causing greater destruction and loss of heritage than the 1976 earthquake.

Already the brickies were at work, dismantling and rebuilding entire monuments with modern brick and cement, replacing ancient tile bricks that were virtually mortarless. Unexcavated mounds were transformed into fantastic and unhistorical mini *stupas*. Complex and venerable ruins were transformed into themed stereotypes. All of this treatment was applied according to the clouded aesthetics and scant archaeological understanding of the military restorers.

Having known Pagan as a boy and having lived there as a young man in the mid 80s what I witnessed hurt deeply. Even twenty years later when I 'transfer' from the airport to the river bank I try to keep my gaze firmly on the car's dashboard.

Today's tourists do not see these things, not having known it before. They still think Pagan is wonderful. Back in 1995 the worst damage was yet to happen.

The Irrawaddy Princess pushed off and all seemed well. We were headed for Pakokku, a city rich in great collegiate monasteries, markets and a host of architectural gems from the 18th and 19th centuries. Trishaws were engaged for a city tour and thus began the great round-Pakokku trishaw race, a Pandaw tradition that continues to this day. In fact on this expedition a pattern for shore excursions and sightseeing was set that remains almost unchanged two decades later.

As with any Burmese enterprise the Princess was ridiculously overmanned. There was a captain, several deck officers and an incalculable number of crew. At the end of the trip when it came to dishing out tips at least fifty people lined up and all sorts of people emerged out of the woodwork that I had never seen before including three lady accountants, previously confined to a sort of bookkeeper's purdah in some lower deck cubby hole.

A young man, a distant nephew of U Win Pe had been appointed manager. Clearly Ko Zaw, as he was called, lacked the training, experience and ability to handle such a charge. Much of his time was spent in his 'office' pouring over great ledgers. His remit seemed to be to ensure that not a cent was spent over budget. The budget was a mean one, not at all what we had bargained for in our negotiations with U Win Pe. Meals were sparse, the greatest expenditure being an array of tomato ketchup and HP Sauce bottles arranged on the tables that rather set the tone.

I would spend hours on the phone to Rangoon trying to persuade U Win Pe to provide more fruit or vegetables (which are both abundant and ridiculously cheap in tropical Burma) only to be fobbed off with insincere promises. Such parsimony knew no limits. When we went ashore on our explorations the manager would switch off the ship's generators to save diesel. We would come back, hot and bothered, to rooms like furnaces. Hot water was erratic and early on in the voyage the loos started backing up and overflowing, effluent running out under the cabin doors and down the decks. Rat infestation, normal in any ship out east, grew to horror film proportions. One night I was woken by a rodent crawling across my face and screamed so loudly that I woke every passenger on the ship. In ten days this new ship aged ten years.

Indeed the U Win Pe management style seemed to encapsulate the entire Burmese system responsible for the many woes that have befallen this otherwise wonderful country. Ko Zaw, a poor and minor relation, addressed U Win Pe as 'Daddy'. You would hear him on the phone saying 'yes Daddy, no Daddy, of course Daddy, right away Daddy', in an entirely subservient manner. Between voyages Pe Kyi would fly up to Pagan and sit himself down at a desk he had arranged in the middle of the deck and berate Ko Zaw, abusing him loudly with curses and threats in front of all the crew. Ko Zaw, and indeed most of the crew, were paid almost nothing but were totally beholden to 'Daddy' for their jobs. Nearly every member of the crew had some form of family connection with him. If not a family member then a parent would have worked in U Win Pe's department or have been some form of dependent, a servant or client of some sort.

As mentioned the crew had swollen to over fifty and there was a complex pattern of demarcation between jobs. An engine oiler would not touch a generator. The generator man would not touch the anchor winch and so on.

Needless to say our philosophy of team-work and task-sharing was a world apart from the Burmese norm, but amongst the younger Burmese on board it struck a chord and as we controlled the tips, which were like lottery prizes, we soon formed a core team who we could work with and who could work with us. Most of these colleagues are still with us nearly twenty years later and many have risen to responsible positions in the company. Though we had no experience of running hotels or restaurants we did know the difference between a fork and a spoon and how to set a table, which the local lads had yet to learn.

We were perhaps just one step ahead then. Today they are all serious professionals whilst we remain hopeless amateurs.

Meanwhile the parsimonious fare on offer was beginning to demoralise even the most stalwart amongst us. Daily calls to Win Pe were to no avail. Ko Zaw, his nephew-manager lacked the funds to buy additional fruit and Win Pe's plan was clearly to try to get us to start supplementing the victualing from our own pockets. This caused considerable tension between us and Ko Zaw. On one occasion as I remonstrated for more bananas – which cost about 2p for a big bunch. He could take no more and grabbed a machete that came to hand and went for me. I skirted round the room and got out the door just in time and ran down the passage to my cabin and bolted myself in. He came after me and started hacking at the door.

Disarmed by the crew he calmed down and later apologised. 'Daddy' had put him under incredible stress, with the daily calls accusing him of stealing, cheating, wasting food and fuel, etc. This is perhaps a metaphor in this anecdote for the Burmese system – patience is deep, but it has its limitations, and in the end something has to give. Every fifteen years or so the whole population will crack, witness the 1974 U Thant Funeral Uprising, the 1988 Uprising, and the 2009 Saffron Revolution.

E venings onboard the Princess were convivial. Usually I would give a talk on some aspect of Burmese art or culture, illustrated by a slide show on a rickety projector in which slides would be invariably back to front (which was not much picked up on) or upside down (which was). Lubricated by lashings of local rum punch, these talks tended to go down quite well and would lead to a lively discussion forum. As mentioned, nearly all our passengers had a Burma connection, or at least a strong interest, and the sessions could produce debate as lively and informed as any found in a university seminar.

Roser sprang into action on the kitchen front. The galley consisted of a sort of garden hut hung loosely off the back of the ship. This smoke-blackened hell-hole, perched above the swirl of the propellers — conversation rendered inaudible by the growls and groans of the over-strained diesel engines beneath — was the domain of our chef U Maung Maung. An Indian, he had achieved some level of fame as cook to General Ne Win at the state guest house at Pagan (Ne Win always kept Indian cooks, like the aforementioned Raju).

U Win Pe presented U Maung Maung's recruitment as something of a personal coup. It turned out that U Maung Maung had served as a cook in the 1950s on the Paddy Henderson & Co, the Glasgow-headquartered sister company of the old Irrawaddy Flotilla Company, where long before one of my great-grandfathers had served as a captain. In fact, U Maung Maung was the survivor of a famous sinking in the Bay of Bengal. He carried in his head a wonderful menu of British maritime favourites – the sort of food one would have eaten when travelling out to India to take up a colonial posting, or en route to Malaya for military service: fish and chips, bangers and mash, Lancashire hotpot, shepherd's pie, and other school dinners were featured along with spotted dick and bread and butter pudding. This accounts for the HP sauce and tomato ketchup. We wanted stir-fry and curry.

Roser quickly devised a series of simple dishes based on local produce that were easy to prepare and more in keeping with a tropical environment. Abundant avocados made excellent guacamole, excellent local beef could be ground to make a passable chili con carne. Fish and prawn were favoured over the proffered fatty pork and scrawny chicken.

Yet the functioning of our galley was shrouded in strange mysteries. Why was the deep freeze continually being switched off and on? No one could tell us. Who was this ghost threatening us all with salmonella poisoning?

Finally we realised that U Maung Maung was chucking items into the freezer without bagging them. As they tended to stick together the only way to get something out was to switch the freezer off and wait for it to semi defrost. Plastic bags were introduced.

One day I visited the galley to find U Maung Maung shaving in the kitchen sink over stack of fish fillets – our lunch.

U Maung Maung's assistant Po Koh remains with us today and is an excellent cook. In Burma master-disciple lineage counts for much, this being a country where monks can trace their lineage back a thousand years. It is pleasing to know that in the culinary department we have a line going back to the days of Paddy Henderson.

Alas the ramshackle arrangement of a kitchen hut hanging off the back of the ship was not to last. One hot afternoon for no apparent reason it fell off and disappeared downstream. Fortunately no one was lost as all the crew were then enjoying their siestas. A new galley was soon created elsewhere on the lower deck. The Burmese can set up a camp kitchen in a moment almost no where and produce amazing meals. Service was resumed without interruption.

The loss of the galley may have been inconsequential, and barely noticed by passengers. However the near-loss of the ship was a more pressing concern. Once above Mandalay we hit some strong monsoon storms. Though at the tail end of the monsoon September can be very wet and sees some of the strongest tempests. The Princess chugged on up through such a storm and then the alarm was raised. Waves blowing down stream were breaking over the low bulwarks of the bow and flowing down the lower deck. The alarm raised, we rushed down to find the deck under a foot of water and the ship going down. Amazingly, the up till then rather complacent captain, who had not inspired great confidence, did exactly the right thing. He revved up the engines and with full power rammed the ship up a nearby river bank thereby preventing sinking and enabling any water taken on to drain back and out of the ship.

The Lower Deck cabins were flooded. Passengers entered to find their luggage bobbing up and down in the muddy, oily waters. Lighter furniture like rattan stools were floating off in little eddies together with buoyant footwear and toiletries. The high society American ladies found it hilarious "so much more fun than the QE2". The lady from Surrey, already showing signs of nervous tension, broke down in tears blaming her husband for taking her on the trip wailing "We should have gone to Bali".

That night, whilst their cabins dried out, the lower deck passengers were accommodated in the bar and saloon.

Near-sinking apart, it soon became clear that U Win Pe's schedule of one week to reach Bhamo from Pagan and then three days back to Mandalay was optimistic. Bhamo clearly was too far and at our current speed, against a very strong downstream current, bolstered by rains we were clearly not going to manage it. This announcement at my daily

41

briefing was received with equanimity by most except the "retired" American colonel who declared "we must go to Bhamo" with vehemence that renewed speculation about his real agenda. I felt partly vindicated on the day we saw a bullock cart overtake us on the river bank. Clearly the Princess's engines were not up to speed.

We did manage to reach Katha, perhaps the most delightful and perfectly Burmese town in Burma. Our arrival was spectacular. All the way up the river entire populations of villages and even towns turned out to greet us. We were cheered by hundreds of people along the river banks. Never had such a strange ship bearing such a strange cargo of foreigners been seen before. North of Mandalay few Burmese had ever seen a foreigner in the flesh. There was a real sense of excitement. Our arrival seemed to herald a new dawn – the opening of the country, the ebbing of decades of repressive isolation in favour of new possibilities and opportunities.

At Katha several thousand people turned out to line the river banks half a mile either side of the jetty. Cheering, waving, singing, the excitement continued for several hours. Some people even camped out all night on the river bank, staring at the ship in a state of rapture. Our passengers played to the crowds with gusto. Taking photos, waving, and acting out comic roles from the decks. Clearly we were the objects of interest, the curiosities. We were the entertainment and they the spectators, it was we that were the human zoo.

Katha lies on the edge of vast teak and hardwood forests. I had been here in the mid 1980s when I had been arrested and later lavishly entertained by the local military commander. Then Katha was a front line town in Burma's chronic civil wars and just up river at Shwegu, where I was permitted to travel to under heavy military escort, at night I could hear mortars popping and by day men hobbled into town with freshly bandaged wounds.

By the mid-1990s Khin Nyunt had made peace with the Kachin Independence Army (KIA) and indeed nearly all the insurgent groups with the exception of certain Karen groups. This was perhaps Khin Nyunt's greatest achievement. Anyone else, in any other country, would have merited a Nobel Peace Prize. Burma had been ravaged by ethnic conflicts for half a century and Khin Nyunt managed to wind them up in a couple of years through mediation and good will.

I had a friend in Katha, a retired *saya* (school teacher) and antiquarian U Hla Myint whose little house was filled with artifacts he had excavated from the surrounding area. Such antiquarians are not uncommon in these remote towns, corresponding with great professors in Rangoon and Mandalay. Such *saya* were passionate about the history and faded importance of their home towns, which once princely capitals or royal citadels. Saya U Hla Myint had connections with the forestry department and was able to arrange a visit to an elephant camp. An old truck was hired, buses being unavailable, and our valiant group of thirty climbed aboard, clinging to its wooden sides or railings as we hurtled down jungle tracks, fording streams, towards the hills. Elephant camps can be elusive. These are working camps not tourist attractions and they tend to move around. However, we found the camp and the *oozi*, as elephant riders or *mahouts* are called in Burma, were somewhat reluctant to arrange a demonstration.

Unfazed by the arrival of truck-load of foreigners they explained that this was the elephant's rest time and they would be very angry if disturbed. A 500 kyat note (then about $6) did the trick, with the *oozi* not the elephant. It was quickly persuaded out of a bamboo grove with a commensurate bribe of a branch of bananas.

Whilst the elephant was being put through his paces Dr Cook brought it to my attention that Colonel Hook was missing. Search parties were sent out into the surrounding forest and the colonel was soon found wandering in the verdant growth, misty eyed, reliving a poignant wartime memory from half a century before.

It was tough playing so many roles – tour manager, guide, lecturer, genial mine host, with Roser doing the catering and battling with house keeping. At the end of each voyage we would collapse and sleep for a couple of days. About five days into each trip I would loose my voice and communicate in a hoarse whisper. The hardest part of the job was keeping up the banter, and answering endless questions. Sometimes so spaced out with exhaustion one would come out with the wrong response. 'What's that tree over there?' 'The Lord Buddha ascending to the heavens'. 'What are they fishing for?' 'The Irrawaddy elephant'.

On the later trips we took on a manager, a retired naval officer who was going to take charge of the expedition arrangements. They say the services train you to be ready for anything. This chap seemed ready for nothing, spending most of his time in the bar, glass in hand telling long boring naval anecdotes. The only time he was galvanised into action was when he attempted to calculate the speed of the vessel by throwing a knotted line off the stern. It did not look too professional, even to our landlubber guests, but after a few days on the Irrawaddy they had ceased to be surprised by anything.

We learned from these early trips that people respond well if things are explained clearly and openly, intelligence is not insulted, and you never, ever, tell a lie.

Thus we involved the group in every situation and decision. Yes, the engines are so bad that there is not a chance of getting there but never mind we are going to do lots of other interesting things instead. Yes, the food is rubbish but we are working on it. No, the bus has not shown up but we have hired thirty trishaws instead. Yes, the plane has been mysteriously cancelled and we will have to bus you to another airport. Yes, the bus broke down. Yes, the a bridge was swept away in a flash flood. But eventually people got there, saw everything, and were astonishingly grateful. Nothing could be planned, itineraries and schedules proved worthless bits of paper. People realised that early on. Everyone was on our side as they could see what we were up against.

These were people who had served in the War or at least lived through it. Theirs was a 'soldier on' attitude where anyone who complains is a rotter. On many an occasion I witnessed a whinger being taken to task by fellow passengers. They policed themselves. Take the difficult French couple on a later voyage who were always late back to the ship and always holding us up. A retired brigadier shouted "next time you go ashore take your passports as we are not hanging around waiting for you again".

Sadly a new generation has come along now and if we are late or miss an appointed excursion, all the retired lawyers are reaching for their Blackberries, sending back compensation claims before the holiday is even over.

The Princess made it through to the end of that first season. We had made six river voyages and no two were the same. Twenty years later and we can make the same boast: no two voyages are ever the same. In that first season the ship had aged six years in six months and would clearly not last another season. Already an array of temporary generators had appeared on the main deck as the originals had given up the ghost. Plywood partitions between cabins were beginning to peel off. Passengers were incredulous that this ship was not even a year old.

Despite this, the experience had been instructive – we now knew an awful lot about the river and the sort of ship that would work on it. We had learnt about how to take care of people and their arrangements, how to firefight and crisis manage. An understanding of Burma, the Burmese and their language was perhaps my winning ticket and nipped in the bud many a misunderstanding. The fact that I could stand up and talk without notes about 13th century Burmese mural painting or 19th century Konbaung dynasty wood carved monasteries helped too, so one was not just a flustered courier, or not all the time anyway.

The Irrawaddy Princess was literally falling to pieces only six
months after her launch. One passenger threatened to sue on the
grounds that the brochure said it was a new ship, and he suspected it
was twenty years old.

The old pirate, U Win Pe, refused to reinvest in the vessel and
would not fork out on basic maintenance. He failed to appreciate that
ships have to be maintained and the need for reinvestment is constant.
He worked on the time-honoured Burmese principle of build
something, then sit back and do nothing and let the money role in.

Ships do not work that way. We could no longer trust Win Pe in
any form of business relationship. The poisonous atmosphere he
injected into anything he came into contact with resulted in a terrified
hopelessness amongst his staff and crew. We were buying in additional
food to stop the passengers from going hungry and to support his fifty,
virtually unpaid, crew members.

The Win Pe business model was another microcosm of the
Burmese state: fear-induced inertia against a background of neglect
and decay. Then to cap it all Pe Kyi wrote to our key tour operator
clients and offered to charter his ship direct to them cutting out 'Mr
Strachan'.

Yet we still wanted to carry on. Here was a chance to pursue
everything we loved – exploring further into Burma, mucking around
in boats, working with the Burmese and getting a chance to show
intellectually curious people the real Burma.

After eight years in publishing, with long days spent editing the
unremunerative books of ungrateful authors, this seemed a far more
exciting way to spend one's time. Tourism in Burma looked like it
would boom. Every week new hotels seemed to open, new travel
companies came in and set up offices. The government seemed keen

on inward investment and encouraged foreigners to come in with expertise and finance to get things going.

So began the search for a new ship. We thought about refitting an old colonial vessel but we lacked the experience — or rather the courage. Someone mentioned that the Burmese Navy had the former 'state yacht' used by General Ne Win. This was a state-of-the-art vessel built in Burma but, unlike the Irrawaddy Princess, no expense had been spared, with top-quality German engines, vastly overpowered for its requirement. The only way we could get our hands on it would be through General Khin Nyunt.

At this time all government departments and branches of the military had been instructed to form joint ventures with foreign investors in order to self-finance themselves, in the absence of revenue from taxes.

In other words departments and divisions had to be self-financing by whatever means possible to pay wages. Military companies abounded, whether vast conglomerates controlled by the generals themselves or tea shops and restaurants run by top soldiers' wives. Khin Nyunt agreed to meet me. It had been a couple of years since our last meeting. This time it was a low profile affair, without the guards of honour, the TV cameras and associated glitz.

The General appeared tired to the point of being drained, which was hardly surprising as each day we could follow his punishing schedule on the TV as he toured the country in his official plane visiting his infrastructure projects, worshipping in pagodas, making offerings to the monks and giving 'necessary instructions', as the papers put it, to serried ranks of officials.

Khin Nyunt was friendly enough but not really interested in my project. Of course as an "old friend" he would help me, and would arrange a meeting with the Quartermaster General. He ended by saying anything I wanted he would help with, a promise I was later to take him up on in personal matter, of which more later.

This occassion was the only time official help was ever asked for the business, and no great help was forthcoming. Looking back now, there was an air of melancholy about the general, as if he knew that already his days were numbered, and his great hopes narrowing in the face of reactionary forces within the military. He was to carry on for another seven years until 2003 but his power to effect real change gradually whittled away.

A meeting with the Quartermaster General was arranged and in the meantime I was allowed to visit the state yacht. Built more like a battle cruiser than a river boat she was everything that she was cracked up to be, and more.

A dozen or so smartly dressed naval officers showed me around with obvious pride. The problem was that the vessel had been designed for the comfort of one man only – General Ne Win. He had a vast suite of rooms that included dining, conferencing, study, living and bed rooms. There was a private galley in his state rooms, as the general feared poisoning and travelled everywhere with Chef Raju. The presidential stateroom was shielded by rooms for bodyguards through which you had to pass to gain entry.

Eccentrically, the naval architecture was subservient to the principle of preventing a palace coup. The rest of the ship was designed for his suite – further body guards, aides, secretaries, accompanying officials, soothsayers and other members of the Ne Win court who followed him on his peregrinations. They all got poky little cabins on the decks below with communal toilet and wash areas. In short it would take a prohibitively massive investment to convert all this to tourist class accommodation.

Colonel Hla Min was sent along to hold my hand, for it soon transpired that the Quartermaster General, General Tin Hla, was not at all pleased to meet me and acted with extreme formality that was as intimidating as it was intended to be. He was like a seething little sergeant-major, on the verge of volcanic explosion. Exchanges followed a strict protocol. After a short speech in which he said he would assist General Khin Nyunt in his request to help me, he said that Navy would be interested to rent us the ship for a charter rate of $10,000 a day. I gasped. When officials start as high as that it effectively means no. There is no point in negotiating. In fact Burmese generals do not negotiate, as to negotiate is to climb down and lose face.

Even Hla Min was embarrassed by this direct snub, and we respectively bowed out as fast as we politely could. The refusal was intended as one in the eye for Khin Nyunt, in retrospect a sign of how little power this falling star had over the "real military", even as early as 1996.

So it was time to start looking again. Inland Water Transport were approached by a friend who had a cousin who was the general manager there. An informal meeting was arranged at the IWT headquarters in wide and tree-lined Pansodan Road, formally Phayre Street, named after the first Commissioner of British Burma.

This was an interesting location, for the IWT had superseded the Irrawaddy Flotilla Company in 1947 on its nationalization. These offices were once home to the IFC. It is an impressive building built in a monumental 1920s style and not unlike the great steel-framed office buildings of central Glasgow where the company's head office was located.

Ushered through a grand-colonnaded portico and up a sweeping marble central stair I found myself in the General Manager's teak-paneled room, with vast desks and elegant cabinets, surely unchanged from the days of the IFC. Here my old friend Alister McCrae would have sat – the last in a long succession of Scots managers sent out to run the greatest privately owned fleet of ships the world had ever seen.

The meeting was cordial and GM was very co-operative. Yes they had been told to bring in foreign exchange and to work with foreign companies. Indeed, they had a ship, the Myat-thanda just delivered from China as part of a Chinese lend-lease programme to rebuild the country. It was a VIP ship, too good to be mucked up on daily public services and currently being used by the minister for inspection tours.

A visit was arranged to see the ship moored in the Rangoon River and amazingly with a bit of imagination we saw how it would work. The ship itself was ugly as sin, a modern-style vessel that is typically found on the Yangtze. Yet she was high powered and, with a flat bottom, very shallow draft. There were ten cabins with their own bathrooms, between a dining room to the aft and an observation lounge with a bar forward.

The rest of the ship consisted of open decks for passengers and their baggage and cargo holds in the hull. We could make something of this. A bit of decoration with antiques and pictures would soften the edges. Letters were exchanged and a reasonable hire agreement reached to the satisfaction of both parties. All seemed well.

Then I received a summons to the minister of transport's office. This was located in a decrepit building down by the docks, the stairs stained with expectorated betel nut juice, an all-embracing aroma of faeces filling the building. I was ushered into an enormous room past two sentries in full combat rig, clasping machine guns across their chest. Around the limits were ping pong-sized tables with models of airports sporting numerous terminals and runways. These were the projected models for new airports in upcountry places like Pegu, dreamed of as a new air hub for Southeast Asia, larger and more modern than Bangkok or Singapore. As the road to Pegu was at best of times barely passable there seemed little the chance of the minister realising his vision.

Portraits of obscure generals, chests festooned with tiers of medals and scowling faces adorned the walls. I expect Than Shwe was among them but back then I, like most people, did not even know what he looked like. Sofas, seemingly a bulk order from MFI back in the sixties, and now much in need of reupholstering were set at right angles to a plinth upon which a great teak carved throne stood, its cushions

51

embroidered in rich Chinese fabric, still covered with the maker's plastic. Neon lights flickered. An ancient air conditioner intermittently clattered and roared, without discernible impact on the humid and airless room.

Suddenly the sentries went from slouch to stiff, as in stormed a melee of uniforms. I stood up nervously and as the majority of officers backed off to an outer ring of seats I was left facing this midget-like character in what seemed to be the dress uniform of an Air Chief Marshal festooned in medals like a dwarf Christmas tree.

"Who the fuck are you?" He yelled at me in English, his face centimetres from my own. I bowed, offering a business card that was brushed away. "How dare you?" Blushing, I studied his toe caps.

"Do you know who I am?" The Minister of Transport? I suggested "A fucking fighter pilot and you don't try and screw a fighter pilot" I gasped.

The general sat and I was waved to the sofa. In addition to all the uniformed officers who followed the proceedings with nonchalant expressions at least a dozen officials in formal Burmese costume made copious notes in enormous ledgers.

"You want my boat you talk to me, not these fools." The general waved at a group of IWT officials including my friend the GM who had gone the colour of betel nut spit, and was visibly shaking.

"You don't do deals with brokers and middle men, you talk to me." I attempted to explain that the IWT general manager and managing director did at least have the appearance of being decision makers. No they had no right to interfere in the matter. They would be punished. Did I want the ship? Yes. Again a monstrous figure was quoted, it was clearly a no-negotiation situation. The Myat-thanda only had ten cabins, and it would be hard to make a return on this even with a sensible charter rate. To attempt to press further would be dangerous as one enters that Burmese minefield of 'face'. Having picked a figure out of the air it would be impossible to bring him down as then he might lose face. Thus it is that in Burma few deals get done.

We returned to Scotland despondent. On the surface I had given up, but deep down I could not let go. There had to be a way to find a ship.

Some months later I fired a fax off to IWT agreeing to the minister's terms but inserting a clause stating that we would pay the charter rate on operating days only rather than the 365 days a year he had insisted on. Amazingly I got a fax back agreeing. I was on the plane back to Yangon.

This is compromise Burmese-style. Someone big says something and everyone jumps and says yes. Then everyone waits till someone big has forgotten what he said and can then 'reinterpret'.

My offer was in the spirit of the General's original decree, only we had changed the charter period. Everyone was happy apart from the poor GM who had been rusticated and banned ever from talking to me again. Whenever I ascended the white marble staircase at IWT's Pansodan Street headquarters he would be seen scuttling out of a side entrance.

I now had to deal with the managing director himself. He was a retired naval officer, a gentleman of the old school trained by the Royal Navy at Dartmouth, with perfect English. Back in the 1990s these figures were the last of a generation educated in the democratic 1950s, well-travelled and erudite. Despite thirty years of Ne Win rule, when nothing much happened in Burma, they had retained a last veneer of metropolitan courtesy and civilisation before the lost generations took control.

By the turn of the millennium a new cadre of officials had assumed power. They were stepped-up soldiers from Burma's badlands – the frontiers and war zones. Barely educated, their only experience of foreigners were Yunnanese drug barons and tribal insurgents. Kleptocracy came to replace bureaucracy.

Money was paid, the ship handed over and contractors called in to build the dozen or so officers' cabins on the main deck, and to make various other adjustments. Though it was brand new and just delivered from China nothing really worked. Additional air conditioning had to be installed in the dining room which had ill-advisably been put over the engine room so it got incredibly hot.

Hot water only worked when the main engines were running which is useless on a riverboat which stays tied up for 75% of its time. Shower scuppers did not drain and instead shower water tended to flow into the cabin.

Roser scoured the antique markets and found lots of colonial knick knacks – old gramophones, parafin-powered brass fans, old ship's navigation lights and lots of fun things to give it a bit of atmosphere. A Chinese furniture maker was commissioned to make tables and chairs and other furnishings. Textiles were hung in otherwise soulless cabins. At the end of it a very dull, modern Chinese river boat was transformed into something bright, colourful and characterful.

Experiences with the Princess had proved that managing these ships was no easy task. Too much can go wrong: mechanically (engines breaking down), navigationally (getting stuck on sandbanks), governmentally (nasty officials trying to stop us), medically (sick passengers), and socially (passengers not getting on with each other).

That is before consideration is given to the hospitality side of things like providing palatable meals and teaching people who live in bamboo huts with earthen floors the principals of the vacuum cleaner, or explaining to people who at home eat with their hands the difference between steak knives and fish knives.

We needed a manager. Rather than hire an old salt from the Royal Navy as we did the previous year we decided to try and find a professional hotel manager. An advert was placed in the UK magazine *Innkeeper* and a few days later my desk was piled with over 300 applications. Clearly a lot of British innkeepers were stirred by fantasies of tropical climes and the romance of going up rivers.

In 1996 Burma had yet to join the ranks of pariah regimes, and to many older Brits the country still conjured up dreams of a colonial idyll. Once the applications were sifted through, eventually what seemed the perfect man was found, a Mr Crammond, who had been an army cook, then a chef in the merchant navy followed by several years as hotelier.

Outward going, full of ideas and enthusiasm Mr Crammond was the man. He would take a crew of Burmese lads who had never seen a knife and fork before and give us silver service. Professional management at last.

Mr Crammond came out and joined us after insisting that, for the sake of ensuring the respect of the crew, he would be uniformed in full merchant marine officer's kit. It seemed a good idea, though I was a bit shocked when the bills came in from naval outfitters for orders of several tropical uniforms including full mess dress. It was though important that the man felt happy in his working attire.

Crew were recruited including several old hands from the Irrawaddy Princess who were very keen to come and work for us and escape from Uncle Win Pe. IWT would supply the marine crew and we would provide the hotel crew. An opening party was announced and the British Ambassador made an appearance. Tourism was not yet sanctioned and we were happy to receive the warm support and encouragement of our embassy.

The IWT managing director or 'Emdee' as he is called in Burma also deigned to come. His office in Phayre Street is situated one hundred meters from the Phayre Street Jetty. I was to accompany him. He emerged down the great white marble stairs in best silk *longyi* and white taipon jacket leading a crocodile of similarly-dressed officials. Outside the police had sealed off the street. A cavalcade of motors awaited, Emdee getting into the first one – a box-like land cruiser made in Burma under Korean patent, the other officials filling the fleet of other vehicles. Slowly we progressed the hundred meters crossing Strand Road and entering the jetty area, which had likewise been cleared of the usual scrum of vendors, hawkers, beggars and touts galore.

Here was our ship, moored in all its splendour. Emdee and his suite debussed and were ceremoniously piped aboard. Dozens of splendidly uniformed officers and other ranks from the IWT fleet appeared on the quayside in a sort of guard of honour. And this was just for a head of a government department. Imagine it was a general or Khin Nyunt himself.

The Myat-thanda had many shortcomings. These were not just technical glitches, but included the fact that its massive engines and fast operating speed resulted in the sort of fuel consumption you would expect of an ocean liner. Further, IWT paid their huge crews next to nothing we also had to pay their wages as traditionally crews were funded by selling off fuel, smuggling and other activities.

This was hardly going to be a profitable exercise, but amazingly we got through two years of hire, just about breaking even. With only ten cabins we were not going to make the sort of money we made on the Princess but that did not matter. The main thing was to keep the show on the road until we could develop a project for a ship of our own.

I studied river vessels and operations in Burma and on other rivers, learnt something of ship design and naval architecture, read books and talked to lots of people. I built up the contacts and connections in shipyards and amongst people who might help finance such a project. The two Myat-thanda years were a big part of the learning curve.

Part of the process was dealing with IWT and the government in general. On the Princess we had been innocently oblivious to the red tape nightmares of doing business in Burma.

We had deliberately not requested permission to sail north of Mandalay as in Burma if you ask for anything you immediately create the possibility of a 'no'. It is much better to go and do what you want to do and when officials see that it works then you legitimise it.

On the Myat-thanda the dramas began with the officers and crew. Having hired the ship at an exorbitant daily rate we were informed that the ten deluxe cabins (with the leaky showers and tingly pink chandeliers) were assigned to the ship's ten officers. Foreign tourists were to be deck cargo and would have to sleep outdoors on deck.

The Myat-thanda officers were all university graduates, middle class boys granted this sinecure on account of some connection with Emdee. Few had ever actually been on a ship. The chief engineer had a BSc in engineering but had never lifted a spanner in his life. The real work was done by a bunch of hardened ratings, old river rats who knew their business and got on with it whilst the officers argued about who got which cabin.

When I suggested that we give the ten deluxe cabins to the tourists the idea sparked outrage. I was a racist, an imperialist, putting down the poor Burmese. Eventually it was agreed that on the open main deck, where cargo would normally be stacked, we would frame up at our expense ten plywood cabins.

Face was saved and we plied the great waterways with two tourist decks — our paying passengers on the upper deck and our paid passengers on the main deck. Essentially we paid the ship's officers to do nothing. This is the art of the bribe in Burma. In other countries you pay an official to do something – to get something done. In Burma you pay an official not to do anything — not to meddle or interfere or cause trouble.

The captain was another thing altogether. Whilst the officers were quite happy to be paid to do nothing whilst being fed continuously with gargantuan meals from our galley, Captain U Maung Maung Lay had other things in mind. This was to be his last posting and the chance to set himself up nicely for his retirement. A Karen, he spoke very fluent English having been to a mission school in the 1950s prior to their nationalisation in the 1960s and the forbidding of teaching English.

IWT high command had been guarded about his appointment. He was their only captain with any English so they felt they had to appoint him, at the same time they warned me he was very tricky and not to be trusted. Of course a Burmese Buddhist would say this about a Burmese Christian but I could see that even Emdee regarded the appointment with some trepidation.

Our captain was a charmer and spent most of his day chatting merrily to the passengers. Indeed he was something of a star. Yet the extortion soon began. We would awake and the ship despite a long planned schedule, gone over with the captain the night before, would remain moored, going nowhere. Captain why are we not moving? My children (the crew) are tired and hungry. But we gave you money for food only yesterday. All gone. Progress up or down the river was a carrot and stick business. More carrot than stick. Little of the money for food, clothing, welfare etc actually got to the 'children' rather these funds seemed earmarked for other uses.

As we prosecuted our first voyage upstream, at the first stop of Thayetmyo we were met at the landing stage by a handsome Burmese lady with two young children all turned out in their Sunday best. "My wife and children" the captain happily proclaimed. Funds were distributed. The next day we pulled into Magwe and were met with a similar sight, this time a very pretty young girl with a baby. My other wife! Funds were distributed. A few days later at Pakokku the process was repeated again with an older lady with a gaggle of kids. My ex-wife! Funds were distributed.

We counted at least three such arrangements but the captain was not content with this. Single ladies travelling on the vessel were prey to his many charms. One early morning he was seen returning from a village with a German divorcee riding pillion on his scooter.

Mr Crammond proved the perfect foil for Captain Maung Maung Lay. Theirs was a double act from the first day. There was an Ealing comedy feel to it, it was 'Carry on Up the Irrawaddy'. This was exacerbated by Mr Crammond's high camp Ruritanian uniforms – he was often present on the bridge splendidly epauletted and capped with gold braid, more admiral than cook.

Mr Crammond was a rather large and flabby man, prone to heavy perspirations, whilst the captain by contrast small and wiry. When other ships passed Mr Crammond would leap onto the wings standing to attention for the some minutes it would take for the ships to pass and salute majestically whilst the captain, grinning merrily, tooted the horn. At other moments Mr Crammond would call out "Full steam ahead captain" and the captain would chant back "Aye, aye Mr Crammond, full steam it is" and other such nautical pleasantries gleamed more from boy's own papers than any experience at sea. It was later discovered that Mr Crammond had served as corporal in the catering corps.

If Mr Crammond's role-playing verged on fantasy, that did him no harm in the crazed atmosphere of a military dictatorship. On one occasion, when flying from Pagan to Rangoon, he arrived at the airport attired in one of his most splendid uniforms, was wafted through formalities, escorted by senior airport officials, the guards all snapping to attention, and given the best seat on the plane. Asked about this, he explained "…Oo, they all think I'm a naval attaché".

Alas Mr Crammond's management skills were not all that they were cracked up to be. Before the sailing season's start, whilst preparing the vessel at Prome, Roser and I returned to Rangoon to pick up some supplies leaving Mr Crammond in charge with our newly recruited hotel staff. That evening we received a panicked phone call from Prome "It's a mutiny, they've deserted, I'm all on me own". Rushing back the next day we discovered that Mr Crammond had become over-excited and shouted at the hotel staff. The foreigner in Burma never raises his voice. Burmese can shout at Burmese but the moment a foreigner looses it everything just stops. Face is lost, the post-colonial chip, that tragic motivator of much that has held back post-war Burma, clicks in.

A number of key people including the chef, all recruited from top Rangoon hotels had simply walked off in the face of this trauma. The first group of passengers were arriving the next day. That night, over a particularly good fried rice in the San Francisco Chinese Restaurant, I called the cook over – a Karen lad of about sixteen years old, and asked him if he wanted a job. This was Ko Saw Thar Gay, still with us today and a brilliant chef.

Meanwhile Mr Crammond pulled too and did a marvellous job acting as cook, waiter and barman all in one, while we recruited new kids as we progressed up stream.

The atmosphere on the Myat-thanda was convivial. The ten cabins ranged off a corridor connecting the dining room with a front saloon. As said, we had made a good job of decoration and refurnished it elegantly. The dining room had been furnished with fine long teak tables and chairs made by a Chinese carpenter in Rangoon. On the first night, as dinner progressed one passenger after another, mainly the heavier males, keeled over onto the deck as the chairs beneath them collapsed. Everyone took this in good part, the days of Health and Safety and compensation culture still far off.

At that time drinkable wine was incredibly cheap in Rangoon, the government having not yet worked out how to impose duties, so we offered free wine with meals. I gave my talks before dinner and took care of the guiding. Mr Crammond flapped around making endless lists of essential supplies and overspending the budget massively. When he eventually left we improved the meals no end and on a budget of less than half of what he was spending. Clearly the captain was not the only one on the take. Thus we experienced for the first time the biggest problem any hotelier faces – cost control in the face of rapacious managers.

The Myat-thanda was on a fairly easy routing. Having failed to get to Bhamo in the previous year on the Princess, despite three tries, we had decided to cut out the Upper Irrawaddy. Instead we offered a ten night trip from Prome to Mandalay called the 'Golden Land'.

The schedule and itinerary remain virtually unchanged to this day. Passing through Middle Burma, which is arid and in parts a desert, with the Yoma mountains always running on the east bank we explored the cultural heartland of the real Burma. Thareyakittiya, home to the first great Burmese civilisation between the 5th – 8th centuries, with its proto Pagan monuments and first-rate museum was just outside Prome.

At the colonial British frontier post of Thayetmyo we discovered the oldest golf course in Burma with a sign declaring they were twined with the Royal and Ancient St Andrews – a claim later denied by the R&A's Secretary.

We visited the Italian-designed 19th century royal forts at Gwechaung and Minhla. Buddhist treasures included and great gold pagoda of Magwe, the wood carved monastery at Sale and of course the three thousand monuments at Pagan, then being vandalised by the so called restorations sponsored by the military.

As an art historian I had explored many of these places in the 1980s and was able to guide the official guides, who previously had never experienced such places. These were places that you would not find in any guide book and I like to think our river expeditions offered an exceptional insight into the art, culture and real daily life of Burma.

Sometimes I was over-ambitious in our plans, forgetting the hazards of travel in such places and the limitations of elderly travellers. I wanted to cram as much as possible into any trip and as the Myat-thanda with her high speed engines (and massive fuel consumption) tended to get to our designated stops far too early (so the captain could visit a wife or mistress and the crew ajourn to the nearest tea house) so we had time on our hands.

On one voyage it was decided to take the group to Shwesetdaw, a pilgimage site located deep in the west bank hills near Minbu. An ancient bus was hired from a local contractor. The coachwork timber-framed, the seats raised high off the bus's floor to enable sacks, bales and boxes to be crammed beneath the seating area. The roads were poor and rivers were forded as we traversed wild inhospitable scrub jungle of the sort that had worn down the Fourteenth Army in 1945.

The shrines inspected, the sacred mount climbed and the colourful encampments of the pilgrims toured, we set out on our return through the heat and dust. The bus moved at an astonishingly slow speed, I expect a land cruiser would have taken thirty minutes to our three hours. Eventually the bus just ground to a slow halt. As with all Burmese buses in addition to the driver an entire crew came with it, including a couple of mechanics. They sprang into action and proceeded to start stripping down the ancient Hino engine.

Clearly we would be in for a long wait. Was there a village near by? Yes just up the road. I suggested that we hike to it and find shelter from the sun and refreshment whilst alternative transportation might be arranged. We set out. It was far further than indicated and in that heat and humidity was hard going for the best of us. Yet not a moan or complaint was to be heard from this ragbag army of fairly elderly travellers as they marched into the village like heroes of one of General Slim's campaigns. We were received in the monastery and fed fruit and green tea.

The abbot summonsed a village elder who owned a lorry, a vehicle even more ancient than our bus but apparently operable. In we piled, seated on benches or hanging onto the sides as we chugged back to the waiting Myat-thanda and Mr Crammond's tender ministrations. Never has so ugly a vessel been such a welcome sight.

We ran the Myat-thanda for two seasons 1996/7 and 1997/8. By running the ship back-to-back on a ten night itinerary between Prome and Mandalay we were able to run enough sailings and carry enough people to break even. Just.

By now we were working with a number of UK tour operators who specialised in adventure travel. We were getting a great reports in the travel press. When Roddy Forsyth, the well known Scottish football writer, came out, fascinated with the IFC story, his full page feature in the Daily Telegraph alone filled the ship for the whole of the next season.

In the second year we found a nice young English hotel manager called Jake who proved personable with the guests and sympathetic with the Burmese. We were able to divide our time more between the ship and Rangoon where we had set up a small administrative office taking care of passenger's inbound arrangements and liaising with IWT, a time-consuming daily haggle over things like fuel supply and over-manning. I was spending more time in the shipyards and getting to know naval architects and engineers who could help us with our dream – a ship of our own.

Our Burmese friends in Rangoon were enchanted by our dream of reviving the old Flotilla. Leo Nichols, one of these friends, was an institution of a man. The Nichols family were of Greek origin and had controlled the stevedore business in the ports of colonial Rangoon becoming fantastically wealthy in the process.

"Uncle Leo" was outspoken and demonstrative man and when you went into his house you were confronted by a full length photo of Daw Suu, surrounded by flowers and candles like a shrine to a Madonna. I think Uncle Leo was the only person in Burma who would dare to display such a photograph. He always referred to Suu as 'thami' or daughter and was forever doing favours for her and her party the National League for Democracy (NLD), lending them cars and drivers, sending round hampers of food, and the such like.

Roser and I went to see Uncle Leo to see if he could help find us a ship. "Come on!" he ordered, and we piled into his car and headed down to the docks. He stood, monumentally, a great hulk of a man with his bald head, and pointed at the nearest ferry boat. This was a typical double decker from colonial days. You just get one of these, do her up, knock up some rooms and you are off. And he was right. By this point a huge crowd had gathered around us, the attraction being Uncle Leo not us.

He exuded charisma, people loved him. He started questioning the people, You are a sailor? You a captain? How much for the ship? Too much. How much? And suddenly we were in the midst of a dock side auction with everyone having lots of fun and not taking this very seriously.

Uncle Leo then announced that the sun was going down and it was time for his gin and tonic. Give the people money, Paul. Hand out a thousand kyat, they have earned it. And so I did and learnt one big thing from Uncle Leo, in Burma generosity is everything.

Tragically not long after Uncle Leo was arrested and died in jail. He was always getting arrested and normally he was in and out after making the customary payments. On this occasion the Danish ambassador to Thailand (Leo had been the Danish honorary consul) flew in to protest. Then, in a typically Burmese way, fearing international scrutiny the authorities felt they had to do things by the book and kept him locked up. As a result Leo was denied his medication and died.

This was just one of many examples of the catastrophic consequences of western diplomats failing to understand the Burmese way of doing things. Leo had spent most of his life giving away his wealth and sponsored dozens of often obscure organisations – nuns who took care of lepers, a Muslim hospital, orphanages and the like. All that stopped when Leo went. I still feel I owe it all to Leo for pointing me in the right direction, both in the matter of ships and of what to do with any surplus cash.

The Pandaw

The Irrawaddy is timeless and exquisite in its beauty. Look in any direction and you see a perfect picture, for 1,300 miles from source to delta. Everywhere human life is intimately intertwined with the river's flow. Growing things, catching things, making things, moving things. A nation's prosperity is tied up with that great mass of water moving from north to south, from the mountains across great plains to the ocean.

It mattered to our own prosperity too of course. After three years, a small, almost cultish, network of passengers had been established. Passengers recommended the trip to friends and others came back each year for more. We grew by word of mouth rather than advertising. Travel agents and tour operators were finding us without any PR on our part. Travel writers and journalists wrote enthusiastically about this unique experience.

We had bought time with the Myat-Thanda. Only in its second year of operation, after Mr Crammond had returned to his native Lincolnshire, were we able to make savings and turn a small profit. I yearned for a ship of our own and during these two years had explored a variety of possibilities – importing an old ship, building a new ship or renovating an old one in Burma. We lacked the finance for the first two options but there were any number of old vessels still plying the Irrawaddy. Conversations were had with various ship owners.

We came close to securing a 200ft barge, that had been formed out of the mid section of a great steamer that had broken its back when it hit the bottom. With the flowering of enterprise in the mid 1990s salvage operations up and down the river abounded and amazingly a considerable number of the 500 plus vessels scuppered by the retreating British in the Second World War, were salvaged – some to float again, wholly or partly, and others broken up for their high quality steel.

The barge was owned by two Chinese brothers who lived in Rangoon. I tracked them down to a ramshackle shop house in the back-streets of Chinatown. They wore tattered shorts and singlets, the shop house a muddle of children, grandchildren, stacked merchandise and cooking smells. I asked them how many ships they owned: over twenty! We were close to a deal but annoyingly the tour guide, who had interposed himself as a go-between, scared them off.

Inland Water Transport or IWT from whom we had hired the Myat-thanda operated a number of steamers that had been built in Scotland just after the War. The M class ships, 200 foot long, had been classic Irrawaddy side-paddlers designed for the Rangoon – Mandalay run. In 1947 six of these had been ordered from Denny's of Dumbarton by the Irrawaddy Flotilla Company, then still in existence and anxious to rebuild its lost fleet and get business going again. The company was nationalised in 1948, one of the first acts of the newly independent Burma. The IFC became the IWT. A number of Scots stayed on to assist with the management, though few lasted with the seeping corruption and no doubt the frustration they felt as masters-turned-servants. IWT then ordered a further six P class ships, stern wheelers of 150 foot length with a shallower draft for the upper rivers. These were built at Yarrows on the Upper Clyde and amazingly were sailed out to Burma under their own steam. I have a photo of one of them cruising down the Firth of Clyde with snow on the hills.

On an evening walk with an interested friend, along the riverbank at Mandalay, talking about the old flotilla, various vessels were moored, some trading and some laid up. To illustrate a point about 1940s ship design we boarded one such vessel and walked over the decks. Rusted, the steel work buckled, the hull hogged (curving upwards), there were pigs, chickens and naked babies running about then main deck and on the upper deck a sort of squatter camp of makeshift sleeping nets. The ship had clearly not sailed anywhere for a long time. An old sailor told me that the ship had been built in Scotland. He remembered it new in the 1950s, brass shining everywhere. Even brass grips on the steps. Now all that brass had been stripped away and melted down to make Buddhas. He remembered the ship officered by Indians before the 'kalay-pyan' as he called it, the 1960s expulsion of the Indians who had run Burma for the British. With no spare parts the vessel had been laid up for a year, the crew with no income (crew can do well on the rich pickings of a working vessel) were reduced to foraging for gazun-ywe, or rabbit weed, that grows alongside roadside ditches.

It was then that the lightning struck. We would renovate her, restore her to her former Clydebuilt glory. We could fit her out just as she would have been, only with proper cabins constructed across the open decks once reserved for cargo and deck passengers. Pacing the deck, quick on the spot calculations were made – keeping the original first class saloon on the upper deck the old first class cabins would be extended aft to fill the entire upper deck. There was just enough space for a dining room and more cabins on the main deck. The upper deck was solid teak and still inches thick. The muck and grime of half a century would scrape and sand off. An observation or sundeck could be extended aft of the flying bridge above.

An approach was made to the owners, IWT. They laughed. It is hard to convey just how ridiculous my regular meetings with the IWT 'board' actually were. I would be ushered into a teak-panelled meeting room, once the preserve of the Scots IFC executives or 'assistants' as they were called. At least a dozen departmental heads would be ranged round a U-shaped table arrangement. The MD would arrive and all chatter would cease in a respectful hush as he took his place at the head. Usually I went alone. The greater the MD's suite of retainers, the more confident I felt on my own. This is quite contrary to Burmese business practice where everyone goes around with several assistants and the more important you want to make yourself out to be the more people you brought along in your wake. My singularity spoke more eloquently than a dozen assistants. It helped focus minds, reduce distractions and red herrings and helped give a useful impression of general impecuniousness, thereby reducing the risk of an official demanding some large sum that then for reasons of face he would later be unable to discount.

Yet face did come into play at every level. The $2000 per day plus fuel that we paid them for the Myat-thanda earned them more dollars than the rest of the fleet combined. IWT ran a fleet of over five hundred vessels but at any one moment only about fifty were actually working because they lacked the cash for fuel and spares. Our one little ten-cabin charter ship was funding the entire fleet. Vital services to remote areas, the passage of goods and commodities essential to local economies, medical supplies, student travel to colleges and universities, were all being paid for by twenty politically incorrect foreign passengers.

In the top echelons of IWT this rankled. Then there was also the fact that we had their flagship. This vessel, designed for 200 deck passengers and 1000 tons of cargo, paid for with a not-so-soft loan from China at a price several times higher than its actual value, had been kept in pristine condition in case the minister deigned to make an inspection tour of up country stations. I had witnessed such tours, the minister never disembarking other than to visit particularly auspicious pagodas, travelling in state in a sort of medieval progress to receive the obeisance of local officials: the manager of each port, the superintendent and engineers of the Mandalay shipyard and various other vassals.

Now I had asked for the Pandaw. The room erupted into laughter. It was a wreck, a hulk, long abandoned. Yes but I would pay dollars for it. Dollars! More laughter. I would pay $500 a day and would pay the restoration costs but they would have to fix the engines. They could not believe this. Lots of jokes about whether Mr Paul was feeling well. This was madness.

Yet I had made my calculations and the extra rooms we could built, the fact that we would buy fuel on a consumption basis rather than per exorbitant running hour charged on the Myat-thanda all made sense. In a way it fitted with their idea that tourists were extremely stupid people who paid good money for nothing. Agreement from His Excellency The Minister of Transport was sought and received and a deposit paid.

With astonishing rapidity the old Pandaw was recommissioned for the journey south and dispatched to Rangoon for renovation. With some difficulty I found a contractor who understood what I was attempting to do. U Soe Naing was a civil engineer with his own construction company who had been twenty years in government service so he understood bureaucratic mentalities. He had also been abroad, working a number of years as a seaman, as so many Burmese of this period did to bring home some foreign earnings and set up his family.

He ran a family company and provided an excellent example of management Burmese-style, so different from the U Win Pe model of intimidation. It worked remarkably harmoniously based on the *saya-debe* relationship or master-disciple. U Soe Naing was *saya*, surrounded by a group of young engineers who were *debe*. It is this 'atelier' model that has created Burma's many art treasures over the past 1,000 years. It is paternalistic and wholly benign. U Soe Naing would often apologise for overcharging me, explaining that he had so many people to look after. Humanity came before efficiency. In Burma, people, workers, are motivated less by financial gain than by respect and loyalty. But they have to have someone worthy of respect and loyalty and this loyalty is reciprocated with a fatherly care for the workers and their families. Taking care of someone is quite different from paying a good wage. Each atelier is a family, a community. This works well for a small business but goes seriously awry when it comes to assembly line production on a larger scale. Then the Burmese system tends to fall apart.

The Pandaw manoeuvered itself into Rangoon's Sinmalike dockyard where a wharf had been hired. Work began. Whole tree trunks would arrive on the dockside to be sawed up by a sort of mobile sawmill. Generators were installed along the wharf with snake-like cables powering welding units and arc lighting enabling twenty four hour shifts. I had very clear ideas of design, particularly the cabin with its fixed berths and brass fittings.

There was a pool of talent out there – draughtsmen who realised often convoluted ideas on paper. Brass foundries would take classic marine items, like bulkhead caged lamps, carried from specialist shops in London, and copy them perfectly. A water treatment plant, designed by a Rangoon University professor, worked amazingly well. Many of the carpenters were also talented wood carvers and could turn their hand to anything. Mouldings were carved by hand as there was a scarcity of machinery. U Soe Naing adopted the attitude of why use a machine if there was a man who could do it by hand? It was cheaper too. There was even a strange American expatriate who ran a factory that produced opulent teak and brass loo seats.

The idea for the distinctive teak tongue-and-groove panelling came from a visit to the Royal Yacht Britannia, now on its last mooring as a museum and corporate entertainment venue in Leith, near Edinburgh. The berths were typical yacht berths with stowage cupboards and drawers beneath. I designed a natty way to hide the aircon units over a wardrobe. Amazingly twenty years later we are still building ships with the exact same cabin concept and design. Very little has changed though some American cruise operators who long term charter our ships are insisting on hotel style beds which I am forced reluctantly to go along with.

Work progressed through the monsoon of 1998 with our first cruise planned for September that year. Working with U Soe Naing and his team the atmosphere was terrific – there was a buzz in the air as we collaborated on design and technical issues. Our core team, many dating back to Irrawaddy Princess days, came with us and as soon as the cabins were ready we began the task of cleaning them up and fitting them out.

The ship moved off the wharf to a mooring buoy in the middle of the Rangoon River where we took over the finishing work from U Soe Naing's men. We already possessed a store full of goods, crammed into a rented property at Prome, with furniture, kitchen equipment and antiques ready to go onto the new ship. On one occasion, I met a diver, in an ancient suit complete with massive brass helmet coming up from alongside. I asked what was going on. There was one of those awkward silences. It transpired that Khin Maung San, one of the waiters had dropped an antique lamp over the side when passing it aboard and had gone off and hired the diver to try and retrieve it, which needless to say he failed to do. After such a display of initiative the matter was quickly forgotten about.

As mentioned, IWT was responsible for the engineering side. The Pandaw was propelled by twin diesel engines powering an outboard propulsion arrangement of two Hydromaster rudder propellers. This system had replaced the steam-driven quarter wheel, or stern paddle, supplied by Denny of Dumbarton. The changeover to diesel-powered rudder propellers in the 1970s had been part of British government aid and all but one of the Scottish-built ships had been converted. The advantage of the outboard propulsion system was draft reduction, manoeuverability and ease of maintenance as the propellers could be swung out of the water on hydraulic pistons. The disadvantage was noise, high fuel consumption and unreliability resulting in an insatiable appetite for scarce parts. The Pandaw engine room consisted of great heaps of disassembled machinery, stripped down and never put together again. Pistons and shafts, cracked propellers long inoperable and oil drums lay everywhere. A long-abandoned generator sat in the lower deck, having apparently once powered the bilge pumps. What machinery did function was held together with string and bits of wire. Above all stood a shrine to the Engine Room Nat, the spirit god of the place who in benevolent moments ensured swift passage but when displeased inflicted no end of technical disasters.

The Director of Engineering (DE) was a short fat man of dark complexion, said by his enemies to be of Indian origin. He was notoriously corrupt and at the outset of the project had told me that he would only visit the ship if we gave him 'one green'. By this we assumed he meant a $100 bill. This was very unusual at that time as I had found all my dealings with IWT and the Burmese Government in general untainted by such requests. (Ten years later Burma had become one of the most corrupt countries in the world). Invitations to the DE to visit the ship were accordingly few. As a result nothing was done. The promised overhauls and reconditioning of the engines never took place. A month before sailing, we invited MD to visit the ship for drinks and a sunset cruise on the Rangoon River. It looked immaculate, almost brand new and I think they were all genuinely surprised and happy at the outcome. I then explained that we could not go for the promised cruise as the engines did not work. MD was embarrassed, he realised what would happen if the tourists arrived and the ship could not sail. There was a panic and the next thing we heard was that DE had been 'retired' and a new team arrived to start work on the engines.

For the maiden voyage we had invited Sir Eric and Lady Yarrow out from Scotland. Eric, then in his mid seventies, and Joan were old family friends and at one time my grandfather had worked at Yarrows, possibly on the Pandaw. Eric had served with the Royal Engineers in Burma during the war and loved to tell how before the encroaching Japanese arrived he would sink Yarrow-built ships. It may have been an 'act of denial' but Eric was gleeful, knowing that they would get the reorders after the war.

Our guest of honour, Eric gave a marvellous opening speech at the formal re-launch of the ship exactly fifty years after the original launch on the Clyde. All the IWT board were there, on their best behaviour and at their most charming. Her Britannic Majesty's Ambassador to Burma sent his regrets, the UK was now following the late Robin Cook's "ethical foreign policy", which in Burma was led by Aung San Suu Kyi.

Following the party, our guests disembarked and we set off on our first voyage from Rangoon to Prome down the Twante Canal and across the Delta. Along with the Yarrows we had a bunch of travel agents on board, a number of them the ubiquitous spiky Swiss ladies, who for some reason seemed to dominate the Burma travel scene, and were forever at each others' throats. Fortunately, given the highly convivial atmosphere an unspoken truce between seemed to quell hostilities. There was dancing by night on the sundeck and excursions into the Delta towns by day. At Henzada we nearly lost Sir Eric, who disappeared on a trishaw, intent on finding the railway station which apparently he had also blown up in 1942.

Despite the fun and festivities I grew increasingly anxious. The ship was only making about three or four miles per hour upstream. There was no way we would keep to promised future schedules. Worse we were not going to get to Prome in time and a number of our guests including Sir Eric and Lady Yarrow had onward connections. The *set-saya* or chief engineer, U Hla Shwe, laboured day and night to keep the engines turning. A diminutive tubby man he remains one of my great river heroes. Each night he would strip an engine and rebuild it ready for the next day. He would disappear into jungle villages to find a workshop where a part could be welded or re-cut. U Hla Shwe was much stressed, and like so many ship's engineers before him had too close a relationship with the bottle. Working in such conditions it was hardly surprising. Never have I met a man with such a work ethic combining integrity and honesty. Somehow U Hla Shwe got us to Prome.

Meanwhile Sir Eric and Lady Yarrow were in danger of missing their flights and a car was waiting for them at Prome. We had no radio or telephone communications at all. (Only recently have cellphones appeared along the river. For a decade and more we ran these ships quite efficiently without communications of any sort other than messengers and runners and irregular calls to the office when in a larger town.)

The decision was taken to land about twenty miles south of Prome on the west bank where a road ran parallel to the river. We would flag the first vehicle down. I went with the Yarrows, and we scrambled up the river bank and after a short walk in the scrub jungle found the road. Crew set down the matching set of Samsonite cases on the roadside and we settled down to wait. It was hot and steamy, nothing was moving on the road. The ship had moved off and we began to despair a little when a Willy jeep of Second World War vintage, chugged up the road driven by a soldier. We explained our situation and the soldier readily agreed to help. In we jumped and I calculated that we would just make it. Suddenly the vehicle careened off the main road and headed into the jungle down a muddy track. Eric declared that it was just like being back in the war. On enquiry we learnt that they were off to load up with *aw-za-thi* or custard apples, a speciality of the Prome west bank. This done, the Samsonites buried beneath great baskets of custard apples we made our rendezvous with the car that would take the Yarrows to their flight to Bangkok.

The Pandaw captain was one U Nyunt Wei. A rather shifty character, he was less flamboyant than Captain Maung Maung Lay but equally devious. Captains and crews had long been unpaid and were left to forage their own livelihoods on the rivers. A working ship on a return voyage to Bhamo could amass a considerable profit, the crew with their own cargo allowances, the officers renting out their cabins whether to passengers for the duration of the journey or shorter times for the "river girls" to ply their trade in when in port. The engineers made their money from selling off the fuel. The cook, from operating a canteen, and so on. Though laid up for at least a year and in a state of near malnutrition when we had found them the captain immediately launched a campaign to recoup past losses.

Gone apparently were the rich pickings of their usual river trade; his children were hungry, with families to support; and they had no clothes to wear. All this despite the fact that seemingly vast quantities of leftovers joined a very generous food allowance and new uniforms had been provided, which they would never wear, keeping them in good nick to sell on later. Anyway, the arrangement with IWT had been that we would provide the hotel team and they the marine crew.

The result was a disaster as the government-employed crew of fifteen were unused to regular work. They were unimpressed with the idea that they had to do anything at all other than eat and sleep, occasionally tying up the ship or putting out a gangplank so they could slope off to the nearest tea house. On the bridge half a dozen crew would be involved in the navigation of the vessel, in addition to pilots and various other supernumeraries.

The deck crew were an unsavoury lot, such that you would not want to meet on a dark night. The captain when asked to motivate them into a little deck sweeping or just ceasing to hang their washing over the side rails would commiserate and say "They are so rough, what can I do?"

Just like Maung Maung Lay this captain's mission was to extract as much cash from us as he could. The notion of a fixed monthly salary did not appeal. They wanted cash in hand, almost up front, before doing anything. Talk of a generous share of tips at the end of the voyage was met with a general air of disbelief. As ever in Burma faced with the choice of $1 now or $100 tomorrow, nearly everyone would opt for the former.

Captain Nyunt Wei, though he had no experience of foreigners, soon worked out that the one thing that is really important to a foreigner is time. Such a concept is quite alien to many Burmese. Time for them is a metaphysical concept, tied up with astrology and numerology. It is not something to be kept. Normally a voyage of a ship of the Pandaw's type from Mandalay to Bhamo might take weeks, even months. The crew stopping, sometimes for several days at a village where there might be the prospect of a pagoda festival, or a visit to one of several wives, friends and relatives, or simply to moor up against other ships of the line for a jolly.

Though head office would publish official schedules and even a pamphlet containing timetables this was a largely academic exercise, blindly continuing the traditions of the pre-war IFC without recalling what they were for, like the obscure rites of an old regimental mess, their origins and significance long forgotten but still solemnly continued. On the river 'schedules' were unheard of.

Each evening we would seek a meeting with the Captain to discuss the day ahead. The captain proved elusive. He would seat himself cross-legged in the bow of the ship, at the front end of the single plank catwalk that extended from the bridge to the flag pole and pray. This was a point where it would be impossible to get in front of to attract his attention and as even Hamlet conceded one cannot creep up behind a praying man. He would sink into a deep mediation, with the occasional chant flung off into the night, a sort of figurehead or mascot, ensuring the well being of ship and crew.

The spiritual responsibilities of a captain were not new to us. Any leader in Burma, whether in business or service takes on some of the function of a high priest and benefactor, responsible for placating spirits and the accumulation of merit points essential for the success of any undertaking. In the same ways generals piously meditate for the well being of their divisions.

Returning later we would be told that the captain had retired and was asleep. Thus any discussion of the next day's start time and running distance would be procrastinated. I would rise at five when I knew he would be up and about, to initiate discussions. Sometimes it was necessary to wake the crew and be present in the engine room for the firing up of the engines. After chugging an hour or so the sun would rise and then came river mists, condensation rising from the cool waters as the sun warmed them. This was an excuse to stop engines and down anchors. Discussions would then ensue as to when we could up anchors and continue. Thus a voyage would pan out in interminable negotiations, promises and restatement of promises from both sides. Somehow we got there.

Crew issues came to a head in a general mutiny over the distribution of tips at the end of the voyage. The IWT marine crew accused the hotel crew of short-changing them. I complained to 'emdee' and he rather dramatically fired the whole lot so now we had no deck crew at all.

Only one lad stood with us against the mutineers, the bosun Ko Maung Naing. Without him we would not have managed to sail the ship. Not surprisingly Ko Maung Naing requested that he join the company and resigned from IWT. He rose high up the organisation and later transferred to Cambodia earning an international salary. He is back now in Burma as a full purser on one of our larger ships. His daughter is studying marine engineering at Mandalay University and it would be an honour if she one day joined the company.

A younger more malleable crew eventually arrived who settled in fine. Only the captain mourned their loss, coming to me in tears and wailing 'what have you done with my children?' A Fagan dispossessed of willing urchins.

More challenging was the issue of 'bunkering' or refueling. Fuel was like liquid gold and control of fuel was the ultimate power. This was the requisite of the engineering department and to fill up our ship every two weeks filled them with dismay and consternation. A thousand gallons being pumped from their precious fuel barge into our tanks caused considerable hurt. The dollars we paid went to the central exchequer and not to their pockets. This was pain *in extremis*. Though there was a clear bunkering schedule we had to work long and hard to achieve this. A couple of days before, we began calling MD and all senior IWT officials to remind them.

On the day a girl from our Rangoon office would station herself in the lobby at IWT headquarters to further remind them. The day before a senior person would be dispatched to the fuelling station to stand by and treat the officials to tea, cakes and various other goodies. He would make sure the relevant officials were on site. A common trick was for a key person to go off on leave, or be ill, or on an official trip, and therefore not able to sign the relevant forms.

Then I, the menacing and intensely irritating foreigner, would turn up and hover over them, shaming and embarrassing them. It soon transpired that MD had very little control over the fuel distribution. This was the reserve of the DE who effectively could control all shipping movement through the supply of fuel leaving MD quite powerless. No wonder the DE at the time of our refit had proved so arrogant. He had been removed, which showed them the power of the foreign investor, for they had been commanded by on high to earn dollars and we were their only earner. How they must have hated dishing out all that fuel but the alternative was rustication.

Between voyages we would fly back to Rangoon, often accompanying our groups of passengers to see them off at the airport and welcome the next group to escort them back to the ship. I would use these occasions to visit IWT to plead for parts or fuel or to resolve crew issues. The splendid office never officially opened before 10am and if I attended then I would be shown into the board room and have to sit through the rigmarole of a full meeting with endless banter and a general avoidance of decision.

I discovered MD lived in an apartment above the office and worked out that if I came in and sat in the lobby at about 8am he would come down his private stair and have to walk past me. Thus we could have a cordial chat and resolve any issues between us. This is how government business is done in Burma. You go to the back door and sit round the kitchen table and work things out. Formal meetings are meaningless..

In a way this is one of the reasons why the Chinese "won" in Burma and the West lost. They can sneak round to the back door, in local disguise, blend in and get things sorted. Westerners are too conspicuous and like to do things properly. Consequently government officials tend to clam up and steer things down the official road, where nothing will ever happen.

Following the maiden voyage to Prome we attempted the Upper Irrawaddy to Bhamo once again. It was over two years since our third failed attempt on the Princess. The Pandaw had the shallow draft but as we had discovered lacked power. We realised that there was little chance given a late monsoon spate of getting up there in a week from Mandalay.

We settled for Katha, a favourite spot and once home to George Orwell and the setting for his 1934 anti-colonial novel *Burmese Days*. We soon arranged a 'literary tour' visiting the main sites described in the book: the jail, the club, the race course, the golf course, the bazaar, etc. Some speculation remained as to which of the many dilapidated dak bungalows Orwell had occupied. From Katha a fast local boat was hired to take passengers on to Shwegu with its island of a thousand pagodas and riverbank potteries.

Katha was the final resting place of the Irrawaddy Flotilla, in 1942. This was as far north as larger ships could sail in the low water season. Here they were scuppered, their hulls holed by their own officers using Bren guns or 'gun cotton' explosive devices. Here the Siam, Java, Japan and India – the four great Siam Class ships, each 326 foot long (exactly the height of the Shwedagon Pagoda) and built by Denny of Dumbarton lay in their watery graves, soon to silt up and transform into midstream sand islands. Their ship's bells can be seen hanging in the Katha fire station, the brass polished brilliantly by bored firemen.

Who would have thought that these shimmering islands, populated in low water by fisher folk in makeshift shacks, entombed such maritime treasure?

In the late 1990s with free enterprise and perhaps the availability of the equipment necessary, entrepreneurs were busy salvaging these vessels. Not just in Katha, but up and down the Irrawaddy. However Katha was the main hub of salvaging activity and dozens of vessels were raised, whole or if their backs broken, in part. Great pumps shifted the silt from around the hulks and from within the hulls too. Divers were sent down, their snorkel masks linked by garden hoses to air compressors, swimming deep inside the holds and inserting great air bags which once inflated raised the hulls. These were impressive operations with hundreds of men crawling over the mounds. It was exhilarating to be standing on the main deck of the Japan, the Flotilla's flagship that had carried royalty and their viceroys. To see the paddle housings and great boilers. To experience the sheer vastness of these great vessels. All woodwork had long since rotted away yet there were many finds that I picked up for free or for a small consideration. IFC cutlery and tableware, a ship's bell, Bren bullet casings lying on the floor of the vessel. I even have an original rivet. But best of all a diver presented me with a real paper ticket from 1942. They had prised open the ship's safe and found tickets, sealed safe and dry. Many of these ships were re-engined and now sail again. Sometimes you will see a cargo ship with the old name and Glasgow, its port of registry embossed in steel on the stern. Broken sections, particularly of larger ships, became barges, with new bows and sterns welded on.

I found a working vessel called the Braco, named after a Perthshire village near where I lived. Looking this up in Captain Chubb's book on the IFC I discovered that the Braco had been a creek steamer from the Delta. All the creek steamers ended in 'o' – there was a Plato, a Cato and even a Pluto. It is rather wonderful to think that the flotilla has sailed again.

The Pandaw was very much part of the river scene. In one village I got talking to an old lady who asked me how we all got there. By the Pandaw, I said. "Ah! They have fixed her at last." Villagers fondly know each of the 'line ships', their captains and crews, and can name any one at some distance. We would meet other P class vessels on the river and often swing alongside to allow the captains to exchange news, pilots to be swopped, and all manner of banter and barter and between the crews.

On routine services, passengers going up would know passengers going down and there would be an excited flow of information. There was a similar frenzy of excitement as our passengers waved and chatted to Burmese passengers on an adjacent ship, temporarily rafted alongside. Then, the moment over, the ships would disengage waving each other off to pursue their own voyages with parting toots of the horn.

There was this sense of being part of a very rich river culture. Each day of cruising sprung surprises. A pagoda festival here or religious procession there. Every trip ashore had an adventure in store. Life on the river was of unceasing interest. Floating cities of gold panners – half a mile long of rafts and boats, pumps churning the sands day and night. The teak rafts, some occupied by several families in mini villages of bamboo, all to be dismantled on arrival at Mandalay where they would be broken up and the logs shipped on by motor vessel to the great delta saw mills. Boat building and ship repairing, activities found on the edges of the great forests – where good timber could be had cheap without the need for government 'paper'. The famed fifty-gallon pot, lashed into frames to create rafts the size of football pitches, were sent off to southern markets, carried by their own buoyancy with a hut for a polesman.

Up till then it was cheaper for a Burmese to buy a handmade clay water pot than a plastic China-made container. So long as the labour cost remained low and materials remained abundant this rich domestic economy could continue. Yet alas, sitting mighty and sinister astride

Burma's great rivers, once pulsating with domestic industry, China is now flooding this valley with shoddy plastic goods, overnight killing millennia of craftsmanship and ecological self sufficiency. At the time of writing Burma seems to have has emerged from half a century of military rule, and almost immediately an ancient way of life, traditions of artisanry and craftsmanship disappear. The new prosperity brings a cash economy and with that choice and thus a preference to plastic over clay, metal roofing sheets to woven palm. The owner class is abandoning its villages and the traditional industries that had once made them prosperous for new exciting lives in cities, abandoning generations of experience and expertise. Another couple of years from now and I doubt if pots will still be made around Thabeik-kyin unless viable export markets are developed to supply them to Western garden centres.

Our passengers were in awe. No travel agent's brochure could begin to convey the timelessness of this scene, the sense of amazement we all felt whenever on the river. Fortunately the sort of people who would book a holiday to Burma were the sort of open minded, highly cultivated and very travel experienced people, who would appreciate the uniqueness of the experience.

Initially, another professional manager had been appointed, a rather scary Anglo-American lady who had been a tour leader for an upmarket American agency. Alas this appointment proved a disaster. Used to hectoring Americans with an endless flow of banal information, our European travellers preferred to be left alone and do their own thing. Complaints were received particularly about the way she handled the crew in front of the passengers. Kyi San, the housekeeper had his revenge when apparently in a sort of ritual involving several members of the crew, bleach was splattered over her best (designer) cocktail dress. She soon left.

Roser and I were back on board full time now and spent most of that first year on the ship, going up and down. I would boast that I could wake up anywhere on the river and look out the window and know exactly where we were. I had taken over the guiding, having got fed up with 'official guides' who had never been beyond Pagan or Mandalay and spent most of the voyage hiding in their cabins or guzzling in the kitchens. Guides would eat six meals a day, three with the passengers and three with the crew. I loved taking our intrepid passengers ashore and introducing them to a real Burma. Visiting monasteries, farms and workshops. Then in the evenings we would have a briefing and talk about what we had all seen and done. On three or four evenings I gave more formal talks illustrated with slides from a rickety projector onto a bed sheet pinned up over the bar. Sometimes I was so exhausted I would get my talks mixed up and thus my polite audience expecting to hear about 'the Life of the Buddha' might get 'A brief history of the Irrawaddy Flotilla Company'.

Indeed, playing 'mine host' can become debilitating. The endless dinners, the drinks, the same conversations repeated voyage after voyage. After a couple of months of this we decided to take a break and go to Bangkok for a bit of high life. I think we slept more or less continuously for three days and then went back to work.

We met interesting people among our passengers. Many were distinguished in their own fields and remain in touch; a number have become lifelong friends. Amongst them were film directors, industrialists, bankers and high court judges not to mention dukes, earls and once a prince.

As a humble ship manager I can conclude one thing from meeting so many of the great and the good: in life the more successful a person is, the better he treats his fellows and those working for him. The more mediocre and unsuccessful, the greater the disdain for those at his service.

Thus I discovered a very interesting test of character. I would meet the passengers on arrival at Rangoon airport. They would come off

83

their flights and see me with a 'welcome' sign board. I would introduce myself and shake hands with everyone. They would see a slightly fat, very sweaty, person in his late thirties with a bit of a of posh accent. Here was one of life's losers; a remittance man washed up in ahole like Burma. I found that cultured people would treat you as if an equal whilst the newer money was disdainful.

On the bus to the hotel I would do my spiel into the microphone and no doubt the poor first impression would be reinforced as I waffled away. Only a few days later, once settled on the ship, would they realise that I was the owner. Then attitudes would change and the previously disdainful would shifted to charm mode with varying degrees of subtlety.

After a year of this we realised we could not continue to be so hands-on. Burma was still at the stage where you needed an expat manager. The crew also liked an expat, often telling us that a Burmese manager would cheat them and treat them badly, whilst an expat would be fairer and more reasonable.

The problem was finding expats who were not crooks or incompetents. This is a problem that we face to this day. We found that if we left the ship for twenty-four hours we would often come back to mayhem. The decks would be unswept, the kitchen disgusting and the crew back wearing sports shorts and singlets, uniforms long abandoned.

John a young Australian hotel manager living in Rangoon was introduced to us and we came to an arrangement of sharing the task, alternating cruises between us. Back then we were offering a short cruise between Pagan and Mandalay to fill in the gaps between our epic longer cruises. John was affable and pleasantly laid back so got on with both crew and the passengers. When he was on duty we took care of administration and sales from our Inya Road home-office.

One evening John called on a portable sat phone we had clandestinely brought into the country. A worried voice advised that they had lost the anchor and the ship was adrift on the river.

"Then start the engines". The engines would not start. The guests? Thirty French having dinner, oblivious to their fate as they drifted downstream towards the oblivion of the Indian Ocean. I suggested that when they swung close to the river bank to get a swimmer ashore with a line and then get a hawser round a tree or something. An hour later we got the call that this had been achieved. The thirty French never even knew a thing about it.

At this time most of our passengers were British, with the occasional very intrepid American and a smattering of French, Germans and Swiss. However by the late 1990s we were beginning to get the odd 'led' American group.

There is nothing worse than 'led groups' and, with the exception of charters, when they have the ship to themselves and can do what they like, I now refuse to carry them. The tour leaders tend to be prima donnas who interfere with the ship's running, usually to the disadvantage of their clients who are forced to see and do things just so their group leader can exercise his will or ego over ship managers – who actually know what they are talking about.

Such a nightmare was with an American tour group led by a retired marine corps colonel called Charles. He was a crew-cutted caricature of such a figure, straight out of a movie. He even dressed in sort of battle fatigues adapted for tropical travel. Charles actually ran his own agency and brought with him about a dozen elderly Californian ladies. One of whom informed me that she was not here to see Burma, she was here for Charles. Charles's groupies followed him everywhere, from Mongolia to Moldova. He could have led them into Afghanistan.

Now Charles was a highly restless and neurotic type of person. Rather in the way I would try and pin down Captain Nyunt Wei to discuss scheduling issues he would try and pin me down, endlessly trying to negotiate "greater value" as he called it for his clients. Unlike me with the captain, Charles had no compunction about disturbing meditation or repose. Often at midnight there would be a rasping knock on my cabin door.

"Paul we need to talk". There would then ensue a thirty minute discussion on why there would be no walk ashore after lunch.

"Because it is 40 degrees centigrade and your clients are all in their seventies and eighties."

"Paul, they are Americans, they can do it".

And so they did heading off down the gangplank into a furnace of an afternoon. I handed each a bottle of mineral water.

"Christ Paul, what are you doing? They got bladders like sieves".

After two years on the old Pandaw we had developed a very happy, homogenous crew. They were all taking home enough to provide for extended families. Everyone earned the same, there was no hierarchy as is common in the East with supervisors and managers and the rest of it. Everyone had the same pay and status and got on very well with each other. There were few jealousies and fewer attempts to domineer.

Sadly this all went sour when one of our key people Khin Maung San, the butterfingered but much-loved waiter, announced that he wanted to go to Rangoon and attend the waiter course at the government hotel school. We thought it a bad idea as he would learn more with us, but he was so keen and such a nice guy we thought why not? and sponsored him. A month later he returned brandishing a certificate and very pleased with himself. Around the same time we needed an additional waiter and he produced his brother, Ko Soe Myint. Khin Maung San then began to insist that he receive a higher level of pay than the other team members. Why? Because he had a diploma and no one else had one.

Absolutely not, we are all equal on the Pandaw. There upon he gave up any serious work delegating all tasks to his brother who effectively became a personal slave with Khin Maung San hovering behind his back supervising his every move. Alas Khin Maung San did not last very long whilst his brother fifteen years later is still with us in a senior position.

Then we nearly lost our cook Saw Thar Gay, who it will be recalled joined us from the Chinese restaurant at Prome. One evening the boys announced that they were going ashore to a pagoda festival. The sounds of pop music having enticingly wafted across the waters. A canoe was summoned and, being overloaded, capsized mid stream. Saw Thar Gay, a Karen Christian, could not swim and proceeded to say the Lord's Prayer as he sank into the depths. Fortunately he was rescued by crew who could swim and was dragged ashore. After that Saw Thar Gay and any non swimmers were sent on a swimming course.

Ours had become a fat ship, the stores well stocked, the galleys bubbling with activity. The crew all became quite plump enjoying several meals a day in true Burmese fashion topped up with the leftovers from the passenger galley. The rats also became fat and the objects of envy from the rats of our sister ships. One night, tucked up in bed, there was an urgent knocking on the door and I was confronted by a couple of sailors asking me to come quick. On deck they shone their torches onto a hulk we were moored up against. There in the dim torch light you could see hundreds, maybe thousands of little eyes all lit up. It was a gathering of rats waiting to board our ship whilst the thirty passengers slept unwittingly in their cosy berths. What to do boss? They asked. There was no way we could fight them off and there was not enough time to wake up the captain and crew, start the engines and move off. I told them to go to the galley and bring all the bread rolls they could find. We stood there flinging the rolls onto the hulk's deck and the rats were placated and we bought enough time to get under way.

Poor U Hla Shwe toiled in the Engine Room. Several P class ships had been taken out of service, their Hydromasters cannibalised for spares. At one point even vessels in the Arakan were taken out of service to keep the dollar-earning Pandaw running. I had made contact with Dorman in the UK who had supplied the original Hydromasters in the 1970s and ordered an extensive range of spare parts which eased the problem.

However the greatest accolade must go to U Hla Shwe's wife who would board the ship each time we moored at Mandalay and see to the coconuts, perched on each engine. These were key to the success of our venture. Coconuts, arraigned with flowers and banners are an essential offering to any nat and in our case the engine room nat. This was an entity more vital to our success than even my closely guarded store of spare parts. I was amused to see that once finished in the engine room Mrs Hla Shwe proceeded to U Hla Shwe's cabin which she would search for bottles, on one occasion she was seen shouting at our poor chief as she brandished an empty rum bottle.

U Hla Shwe's stress must have been awful and one could easily forgive him his nightly tipple. On one occasion things came to a head. Moored off Pakokku, we were enjoying our sunset cocktails on deck when one of the passengers asked me what was going on up the river bank. A procession had formed bearing a recumbent figure on a sort of bier.

"Ah! A Burmese funeral" I cried. "Very interesting. Everyone, look a Burmese funeral".

The bier was borne along the riverbank towards the ship which seemed strange as this was the wrong direction for the town cemetery. Then it turned towards the ship and proceeded up the gangplank. This was no corpse, it was our chief engineer comatose but contented.

42a Inya Road

Whilst in Rangoon we lived in a reasonably smart hotel, but life there soon became tiresome. Even in upmarket hotels, personal space is confined and one quickly tires of all the characterless "comforts" and petty luxuries that make one upmarket hotel as bland as another, wherever they may be.

Also living costs were high – laundry, meals and drinks at hotel rates soon mount up. After a couple of months of this we were keen to find our own place, preferably one that could double as an office.

Indeed, the hotel laundry cost was so high that it was cheaper to buy a locally made new shirt than to send an old one to the laundry and in Burma you can get through three shirts a day. Roser took to smuggling great bags out of the hotel to a Chinese laundry round the corner. One day bearing sacks of shirts she bumped into the general manager in the lobby, her embarrassment added to our resolve to quit our gilded cage.

We started going round prospective houses with various property agents. Rangoon at that time was probably the most interesting city in Asia to live in. Nowhere else was there such a vast and various housing stock. Mostly there were colonial-era houses, tranquil islands of nostalgia set in broad gardens – neoclassical in style in the city centre, mock-Tudor in the secluded suburbs.

The year 1998 was the year the international oil companies came back to Burma. France's Total alone had over three hundred expatriates in the country all looking for an idyllic colonial house. The great perk of a hardship posting like Burma was that you could expect to live in the sort of house only millionaires could aspire to elsewhere, complete with a team of domestic servants to caring for the house and its inhabitants. Landlords were quick to catch on and within a year a house that had rented for $300 was now going for $3000.

We were not subsisting on an oilman's budget and soon became disappointed. Even the meanest of bungalows became beyond our reach as Rangoon's property owners cashed in on this bonanza, often failing to draw a price distinction between a derelict wreck and an ambassadorial mansion, assuming that all foreigners were equally gullible anyway.

Our financial parameters meant that we were shown the rejects – staff flats over garages and unwanted annexes, to which take-it-or-leave-it landowners would nevertheless demand astronomic sums. Because of usual Burmese 'face' issues — especially to the fore when dealing with foreigners — such rents were seldom negotiable.

Then we found Ko Oo, or rather he found us. Ko Oo was the son of the Ne Win-period construction minister, who had retired to salubrious Inya Road as ex-ministers invariably did.

Ko Oo had an empty, near-derelict building in his compound that once housed servants, garages, store rooms and offices with a large apartment above.

Ko Oo was one of the highest-camp Burmese we have ever encountered. He talked in a girlish shriek and had a tendency, at one moment, to fits of giggles and at the next, hysterical screams of wrath.

We secured these lodgings for $200 a month, I think because no one else could handle such a landlord. Even the most sycophantic of house agents were overwhelmed by his wild oscillations of temperament.

As part of the deal Ko Oo promised to fix up the apartment and get the place cleaned up and painted. We paid the first installment and were to return in two weeks.

The big day arrived, and full of excitement we went round to the Inya Road house to find that nothing had been done at all. We were dismayed. Roser was in tears: there was no way could we sleep in such a filthy dump. A huge row then ensued. Roser shouting at Ko Oo and Ko Oo screaming back, "How dare she speak to the son of a minister like that!"

With Ko Oo and Roser eventually pacified, we considered it best to cut losses and undertake the clean up operation ourselves. We called in staff from the ship and they brought in friends and family. In no time the place was liveable, with a new bathroom and a simple kitchen situated in a strange kind of sentry box out on the veranda. A basic office was installed on the ground floor and we had a three-room flat above.

It was our own space at last and, despite the general ugliness of the 1960s concrete frame building, it was home. No colonial mansion perhaps but the place was fine.

Importantly in Burma, we had a reliable power supply off Ko Oo's house; ex-military and government people were well taken care off even in retirement and guaranteed electricity day and night. A phone with a very basic early version of email was soon installed. We were in business.

The two important things to remember about house-hunting in Rangoon are as follows:

Firstly, when choosing a location to make sure there is a general, or minister, or someone else very important next door to ensure good services. Its not where you live that matters but who you live next to.

Secondly, ensure that there are no monasteries nearby as — particularly in Buddhist Lent — monks tend to chant twenty four hours a day and broadcast it at high volume through tannoys for the greater spiritual edification of all within earshot. A good night's sleep in Burmese Buddhism is considered a slightly decadent indulgence.

Inya Road was considered a VIP area and the main road was lined with enormous British-built mansions set in one-acre compounds. Here the heads of trading companies, banks and senior colonial government officials once lived in splendour, attended to by small armies of servants with all the comforts of the English country house, combined with the solicitous service only to be found 'Out East'.

Lanes led off the main road to further houses and we were on such a lane, just behind St Augustine's Church, said to be the oldest Catholic church in Rangoon. Next door was a more modern home that served as Rangoon's Korean church.

Every morning at six, shortly after the St Augustine bells rang for mass, the Korean pastor would embark on some epic hymn, sung at the top of his voice. Otherwise he kept to himself through the day and we never actually met him. On Sundays the entire Korean Christian community would arrive, clutter up the street with their cars, and spend the entire day there singing such hymns, one after the other from dawn to dusk.

Amazingly we got on quite well with Ko Oo, who took to crossing the compound from his house to visit us at least three times a day. His house was a great 1960s pile that had fallen into hopeless decay. Broken windows had not been replaced. External doors hung half-rotted off their hinges. Mosquito netting flapped tattered in the wind. The garden had been long abandoned to tropical profligacy. Fruit rotted on the ground about riotous trees. In the evening I would forage for limes to put in my gin and tonic, and mangos for my breakfast.

Ko Oo lived together with his ancient father. I met this gentleman only once, an educated former colonel who, as mentioned, had served as minister of construction under General Ne Win.

His house, constructed for him of course by his ministry, had been built to incredibly high standards of strength and robustness. It was like a bomb-proof bunker. Concrete-framed, the piers could easily have carried a dozen stories rather than a mere two. When the time came to knock down walls when we redeveloped our block, the builders could not believe how overbuilt it was.

Clearly the minister had to have a model house, a benchmark by which all of the nation's housing could be measured. Neglected it may have been, but it was certainly not going to fall down.

The Minister spent most of his day in meditation and would disappear for indefinite periods of time to monasteries and mediation centres, where he could aspire towards enlightenment undisturbed by the vagaries of his son's behaviour. Servants were few and never lasted more than a matter of days. Ko Oo would from time to time recruit some strapping lad as cook, or gardener, or driver but these appointments tended to be short, usually ending in a scene, and the boy being thrown out amid threats of the police being called for. The boy meanwhile would be running down the street, relieved to have escaped, preferring life in a shanty to the caprices of his employer.

Ko Oo would be left shaking his head saying "No good" and other variations on the theme of "You can't get the staff these days".

Otherwise Ko Oo and his father would rattle round the vast house avoiding each other. Most of the rooms were filled with clutter and junk. The Burmese, particularly during the years of the Burmese Way to Socialism, never threw anything away and great mountains of newspapers and magazines from the '60s and '70s were heaped in wobbly towers, coated in dust and fenced by great cobwebs.

The place had been colonised by rats. Often when I would pop into Ko Oo's kitchen several of these rodents, the size of small cats, would scatter before my approaching feet. Unable to keep a cleaner, Ko Oo would never stoop himself to the menial chores necessary for basic hygiene. I don't think the kitchen floor had been swept in years. Scraps of food lay everywhere in decomposing heaps, a bountiful Buddhist donation to the rat population who did the service of vacuum cleaners.

Ko Oo would waft in and out, immaculate in a pastel shaded *longyi* and flowery shirt, checking his coiffure with delicate hand movements (he attended the Tony Tun Hair Salon twice a week) seemingly quite oblivious to the house's other inhabitants..

The problem with the rats was that they tended to spill over to our house. Annoyingly, each morning when I went to shower the soap would have disappeared and I would have to unwrap a fresh bar. I blamed Roser for removing the soap. She blamed me back. After several days of this I found a half chewed bar on the office floor below. We were amazed that rats could scale a ceramic-tiled wall to remove a bar of soap in a dish screwed to the wall. They were, we found, capable of almost anything.

One day my favourite shoes were half-eaten. I got up in the morning to find only the rubber soles were left, the leather uppers were all gobbled away. The rats would get into my desk and eat my stationery, even plastic pens. In fact rats love plastic — they have a tendency to nibble away the shrouding of power cables and electrocute themselves, which is good, but also cause blackouts, which is not so good.

Eventually I called the pest control company who took care of the rat problem on board our ships. They gave me bars of bait and explained that if I just leave it out it would be too obvious and the rats would not fall for it. The trick was to tuck the stuff discreetly under furniture or hide it at the back of wardrobes, to avoid insulting their intelligence.

For the next few days I would awake to find a carpeting of dead rats on the kitchen floor or lying half way down the stairs, each the size of a rabbit, with sleek coats and tails like whips, in a state of rigor mortis. I soon found a tong-like implement with which to eject them out of the window into a roadside ditch. Local insect life would take care of them more effectively and quickly than Rangoon's sanitary department.

Rats were not the only form of animal life to impinge on general wellbeing at Inya Road. Ko Oo kept, or rather failed to keep, a pack of dogs. These were no cuddly domestic pooches. They were rabid-looking street dogs that for some reason had attached themselves to the Ko Oo compound. Occasionally fed, they and were at least more efficient security guards than Ko Oo's underpaid retainers.. Mangey, scabby, many with disabilities like lost ears or eyes, trophy wounds from vicious street fights, these proprietary curs spilled in and out of the house as they pleased.

They only answered to Ko Oo who would snap at them in his high pitched voice, and they would in turn cower deferentially. No one could say how many dogs were in the pack, but it was at least a dozen. Sometimes they would all settle down outside our front door and it was necessary to clear them with sticks and shouts when persons tried to enter or exit. Forever at war, there were times when a dying dog would whimper in pain all night not far beneath our window. We would lie in bed at night, forced to listen to the sounds of a dog's slow death. Ko Oo would be approached on this subject in the morning and would merely giggle, as if the dog was up to something naughty. Being a devout Buddhist there was of course no way could he put it down.

Eventually a neighbouring watchman was tipped to deal with the problem. A couple of times dogs actually did died in proximity to the house and nothing was done. The smell, accelerated by tropical speeds of decomposition soon filled the house, whether the air conditioners were switched on or not.

Again Ko Oo would be somewhat lackadaisical in dealing with this nuisance, but he would eventually oblige. Had we not raised the matter, the dead dogs would have simply been left to let nature take its course.

Around this time we employed a secretary who had seemed capable, a middle aged lady called Ma Thanda and she found us a car and driver. Ma Thanda enjoyed long discussions with Ko Oo on his morning visits and they would chat happily about hairdressers and pop stars.

Office business moved at a snail's pace. Just to pay a phone bill would involve visits to two or three departments situated in different locations around town. An employee and a car could be gone all day just settling a bill or applying for one of innumerable licences and permits. Public transport had decayed to the point of near non-existence and the current boom in cheap second hand car imports was causing the first signs of congestion in Burma. Getting anything done at all had become a test of endurance.

Ma Thanda was mainly taken up with running such utilitarian errands and, elegant, refined and gracious, she was rather good at charming a certain type of official. It is amazing to recall that when you went to the Post Office to buy stamps you had to bribe the clerk to sell you them. When you went to the bank again you have to tip the teller first, and that was to pay money in.

Alas, Ma Thanda's time with us was short-lived. We sensed all was not quite right and then one day three foreigners came to the gate. Did Ma Thanda work here? Yes, Why? They came in and explained themselves. They were Czechs and had had a company in Burma for many years, Czechs being fraternal socialist allies allowed to trade here during the Ne Win era. Ma Thanda had worked for them for over ten years and taken care of all their administration work. She had even been to Prague to stay with their families. So close had they become, so trustworthy and reliable had she seemed, that they bought a house and a car putting both in her name, foreigners not being allowed to own such things in Burma.

All was fine and well and they returned to the Czech Republic for holidays. When they returned they found the house sold and the car missing. The driver, one Ko Ronny, had disappeared with the car and had later turned out to be Ma Thanda's lover. What happened to Ma Thanda's husband remains shrouded in mystery.

I took this delicate matter up with Ma Thanda asking her if this was true. At this time with more and more foreigners coming in, reports of this kind of episode were not unusual.

Ma Thanda immediately grew hysterical, claiming that the Czechs were disgusting brutish foreigners who made her sit in an office all these years surrounded by pornographic calendars (no doubt the ones featuring tyre companies) and she was a respectable Buddhist lady. Without addressing the substance of the accusation she made it known that if they made trouble she would denounce them to the police as trying to corrupt her.

This course of action was deployed against many a foreigner who, for whatever reason, fell out with his Burmese secretary – they were denounced as a seducer assaulting the innocence of Burmese maidenhood. I knew someone who went to jail after such an accusation. Ma Thanda resigned not long after this. She could anyway see that there were thin pickings to be had at Inya Road and she set her sights elsewhere.

One of the families I knew well from Pagan suggested that their daughter come down and help us out. A charming, well-educated girl in her late teens, innocent of the vices to which Rangoonites were prey.

Ma Yin Yin proved excellent at computers and took care of reservations. Another girl called Ma Cherry joined her and took care of book keeping and accounts.

The crew on the ship felt we needed a watchman-come-runner and our famous housekeeper Ko Kyi San sent a lad down from his village near Prome. Kyi San came and stayed for a week to train him. The boy, one Lin Lin, did not seem too sharp, but Kyi San drilled certain basic duties into him like polishing shoes and placing a jug of cold water by our bedside each night. He would spend most of the mornings sitting on the steps polishing my shoes to a state of brilliance.

One of his duties was to set two glasses of drinking water by our bedside each night. On one occasion whe we retired for a siesta after lunch in he glided bearing a tray.

Lin Lin fell into bad company and started drinking hooch with the Korean pastor's watchman. We would come back from dinner out to find him sitting stoned, with bloodshot eyes.

After a couple of warnings he was sent back to his village, genuinely amazed that we paid him what he was owed plus a month's extra. Often servants do not get paid in Burma, it is considered sufficient to have a place to sleep and leftovers to eat.

Another lad was dispatched by the crew, this time the brother of our bosun from a village near Sameikkon in central Burma. Maung Kyaw arrived with his mother and, aged only, sixteen seemed very young. The mother, a big jolly country lady typical of that region, set about cleaning up the watchman's hut and setting up a small kitchen with an electric ring for her son. It did not look like a viable arrangement, but we wanted to help the family as the brother was a dependable part of our team.

Maung Kyaw proved us wrong by being very reliable and was soon going around town on various errands. He enrolled in night school and took a computer course. Before we knew it he was working in the office, speaking and writing English and proving handy with computers. He took care of the little garden, kept the house clean and did the shopping. Maung Kyaw now manages our Mandalay office.

Unfortunately for all concerned, while we were on holiday Ko Oo made his move on Maung Kyaw. New clothes were bought for him, and he was taken to restaurants frequented the great, good and glamorous of Rangoon society.

They went out and about everywhere together in Ko Oo's little Toyota. Ko Oo announced that he was going to formally adopt Maung Kyaw and make him his legal heir. Maung Kyaw, from a simple village family, was soon overwhelmed by this high life existence, which needless to say ended in melodrama, with Ko Oo calling the police to have him evicted from the compound.

Fortunately our cruise manager was staying there at the time and a foreign face, not to mention the general atmosphere of farce, persuaded the police that there was literally nothing to be gained by their intervention.

K o Oo's mother had been a Shan princess of considerable wealth and fame. His father a successful colonel promoted to minister. The family were the apogee of elegance and sophistication during the Ne Win era. But in the 1990s with a new elite in power, Ko Oo lived like a relic of the *ancien regime*. He subsisted by selling off his parents heirlooms – jewellery, antiques, Shan royal regalia and costumes — to pay for the high life he enjoyed. By the time we took the house there was little left to sell and Ko Oo depended on our rent more than anything.

One rent day he insisted on taking us out for dinner at one of his favourite restaurants, an episode that sticks in my mind as illustrative of the excess of certain parts of the Burmese elite.

Off we went in the little Toyota, Ko Oo in a state of high excitement talking rapidly in his high voice, to arrive at an enormous emporium on the banks of the Kandawgyi lake. A gaggle of doormen surrounded the car and deferentially assisted our transit from vehicle to vestibule.

Clearly Ko Oo was an old and favoured patron. The main dining hall was as big as a movie theatre, decorated in a gilded and Burmanised sort of rococo complete with monstrous chandeliers.

A pop band blared away on a stage at one end and at the other a buffet counter ran the width of the room, people jostled to get to the chaffing dishes, normal rules of decorum and etiquette seemingly abandoned in the rush for food.

Great matrons, swathed in diamonds and rubies, young bucks their belts hung with two or three mobile phones (each worth a thousand dollars in Burma's burgeoning grey market), obese children in western dress elbowing their way through a sea of *longyis*.

On closer inspection the contents of each chaffing dish spilled into the other as the hungry crowd swiped and stabbed with the great paddle-like serving spoons. Each bore off from the melee a mini-mountain of congealed goo: oily Burmese curry mingling with Chinese stir fry, Indian samosas floating in pools of noodle soup. Burmese buffets were all about quantity rather than quality.

Ko Oo seemed to know everyone here. He pointed out ageing film stars, the wives of colonels, the mistresses of ministers. The music was deafening and Ko Oo would shout at the waiters to bring beer and whisky. The owner made much of Ko Oo constantly nipping over to check things were to his liking.

Here the SLORC smart set mingled with the stars, everyone knew exactly who everyone was. Amazingly Ko Oo, emerging from the decay of Inya Road, proved himself to be a celebrity, known to all.

After some months at Inya Road we decided to improve the house. Though we had painted it up, the apartment above was dark and dingy, the windows too small, the rooms too plentiful. I mentioned the idea to Ko Oo, and as I was offering to pay for the works, he was enthusiastic. A builder was found and it was decided to knock down several walls in the office and above in the apartment to make bigger open plan spaces.

Windows would be knocked through the walls to let light in and the kitchen tower would be razed and a broad deck extend over the front door from the apartment above.

All this was done for a few hundred dollars and for this we got a new kitchen actually *in* the house, teak parquet floors, and lovely big teak framed windows all making it a very attractive place to live and work.

On one occasion works were interrupted by the arrival of a gaggle of officials, recognisable by the *taipon* jacket only officials wear – a badge of authority and symbol of all that many people in Burma learn to hate.

Where was our building permit? Works would have to stop. We would have to put the house back the way it was. Ko Oo was called. He turned red and exploded. Did they have any idea who he was? The son of a minister! Get out and never come back. Off they went and we never saw them again.

The Burmese elite, even impoverished members of the ancien regime, do not pay taxes and manage to bypass all the petty extortions that are a daily reality for ordinary people.

W e lived at Inya Road from 1997 to 2000 and thereafter we kept the place on as an office till 2002 when Ko Oo decided to sell it. He asked us to move out but then failed to make the sale. Life during this period was not unpleasant. Roser and I spent our winters in Burma, which was the tourist season, and returned to Europe for the summer.

We had the best of both worlds. During this period we hired a succession of professional cruise directors and we spent a good deal of time up country training new managers, overseeing the operation or running cruises when managers were off on leave. It was a good balance between river life and town life. Being on the ships where the fun and action was, and being ashore taking care of things like reservations, sales and marketing. I would fly up to Pagan or Mandalay for weekly short visits to the ship, constantly applying pressure and checking for higher quality. The main management dilemma was not the very eager and obliging Burmese but the often uninterested professional expat hotelier.

Life in Rangoon in the mid to late 90s was fun. The economic depression that came with regime ossification and the effect of sanctions had yet to be felt. General Khin Nyunt was still the front man, full of energy and ambition, encouraging foreign contacts and trade. The tiny expat trading community were made to feel welcome. A club met at the Trader's Hotel on Tuesday nights, called the Tuesday Club. Foreign investors would come and meet key regime figures.

At this time there were still generals who were educated and who spoke English. People like the Sandhurst-educated Anglo-Burmese General David Abel were wheeled out to charm and to offer help to businessmen. Grievances and annoyances were aired publically and noted down by the charmingly urbane Colonel Hla Min, who usually followed up with prompt actions. Irritations like a car stuck in customs or the inability to get a mobile phone were sorted fast.

Social life was a whirl, almost a replay of the last decade of colonial rule before it all fell apart. Charity balls, society weddings, dinners and endless parties. Surrounded by golf courses, expats used their hardship posting to hone their golf skills. Entrepreneurs came in and opened restaurants and night clubs. New bars and bistros abounded. You could eat classic French at Le Planteur with fine wines or pasta and pizza at L'Opera. Anything imported was ridiculously cheap as the government had yet not cottoned on to the idea of duty and tax. Wines, spirits and all the essentials of the good life could be had for very little. People came to Burma for a week and stayed a year.

With the exception of the oil companies and their salarymen, most of the people who came in were entrepreneurs like us. This was a new country opening up and opportunities abounded. Only the seriously inept could fail to make money in this environment.

The reality was that after thirty years of Ne Win the Burmese simply could not appreciate business realities, and it was easy for the western expat or Chinese migrant to step in and seize opportunities.

As with any gold rush the carpetbaggers follow. Conmen and dreamers would hang around the expat bars lying in wait for the new kids in town to be persuaded to invest in wonderfully lunatic projects – a ski resort in the Burmese Himalaya; shark-feeding cruises in the Mergui Archipelago; a flying school in the Arakan.

The favoured tippling place of the true carpetbagger was the Savoy, presided over by Ghilberto, an Italo-Scot who would volubly harangue the staff, much to their amusement. He would later join our team.

I would often be asked if I "had a home for a million" or other such patter from these opportunists. Here one would meet gun-runners, drug-dealers, white slavers, all buccaneers of a lurid sort, all landing in Burma, the golden land of golden opportunity.

My favourite character was a former gun runner, a Glaswegian, wanted in several countries, who had been lying low in Burma and whose tourist visa had run out ten years previously. He was to provide invaluable assistance to us when we most needed it.

B y 1999 the writing was on the wall. The good days were over and the carpetbaggers had all left town. Likewise the big Asian investors – the South Koreans, Singaporeans and Malaysians were pulling out too. There were two main reasons for this collapse in optimism.

Firstly, the glory days of the Khin Nyunt renaissance were well over. It became clear that his power base was now restricted to a few minor ministries, like Social Welfare or Religious Affairs.

Government had more or less ceased to function as the rift between General Khin Nyunt and General Maung Aye grew. General Maung Aye came from the "real army". These hard-faced reactionaries were a foil to all of Khin Nyunt's grand cosmopolitan designs.

Within the military, factionalism grew, and it was out of this murky background that General Than Shwe began to make his first appearances.

Up till then a shadowy, almost mythical figure, nothing was known of this emergent dinosaur. His rise coincided with the increasing perception that corruption had become endemic and that Khin Nyunt's Military Intelligence Service or MI had disintegrated into a vast mire of dubious business ventures and protection rackets.

Working in Burma at that time, it became very difficult to get things done. No-one in government was making decisions any more and everything seemed at a standstill. New projects and ventures remained incomplete or unopened. Internecine gulfs tore the country apart. It was into the resulting political vacuum that the Chinese were to move. They would find rich feeding grounds.

Secondly, sanctions began to bite. Tourism had already been badly affected. The five hundred-room hotels stood all but empty, some were never completed and remained concrete hulks used by the army to quarter secret battalions.

With our little ship we were small and specialised enough to weather the storm. It helped that there were enough of old school folk out there who were not going to be told where not to go by *bien pensant* editors at the BBC. Aung San Suu Kyi's call to boycott Burma during Visit Myanmar Year in 1997 had been picked up by the international media and the "ethical" foreign policies of the Blair-Clinton axis.

The British Ambassador, only the previous day a friend and guest aboard our ships, hauled us in and read us the riot act. Having previously encouraged our venture, he now asked us to go home, and simply abandon a huge investment of time and resource that the day before he had supported.

But the real impact of sanctions was not on tourism but on Burma's nascent manufacturing industry. In the early 1990s a series of enormous textile plants, each employing several thousand workers had been set up in the Rangoon and Pegu areas. Burma at that time boasted cheaper labour costs than China, yet these new factories still paid a wage far beyond what an agricultural labourer might ever hope to achieve.

Families moved from rural areas to be close to these new facilities which mainly employed women who were the sole supporters of extended families. The closure of the textile plants, one by one as sanctions hit, caused a staggering amount of hardship and suffering amongst the Burmese working class.

At the same time that western agencies continued to deny the country any form of humanitarian aid. Aung San Suu Kyi had asked western aid donors to stay away and not to 'support' the military regime. This was all very well but it meant that there was a staggering twenty years between the withdrawal of aid donors in 1988, following the massacres, and their return in 2008 with Cyclone Nargis.

Some agencies managed to sneak in through the back door. I knew the International Red Cross people and they told me that their operation was unofficial, almost clandestine, defying the diktat of the Nobel laureate. As a consequence Burma, already an economic basket-case, received none of the basic healthcare and immunisation programmes that any other developing country could expect. People died as a result of this pig headedness.

The power and influence of Aung San Suu Kyi was immense. But however good her intentions, a few words of hers could mean that thousands became unemployed and an entire generation would go without basic health and education support. Burma went back deeper into the dark ages than ever before.

The irony was that the generals, instead of suffering as Suu Kyi intended, continued to get richer and stronger during this period. Their fallback ally was China, or if the Chinese would not help, North Korea would. Sanctions and the denial of aid served to entrench Beijing's influence deeper than ever before.

Even more ironic is the fact that, if Khin Nyunt had received the support of the West against the might of Than Shwe, in other words if he had been allowed to deliver the goods whilst he had the chance, and brought in the investment, tourism and aid that could open up the country, then Burma would not have become the effective Chinese colony it is today and the Burmese people would be much further down the road towards democracy.

All this time, Than Shwe remained in the background. No one we knew had ever seen him. He did not appear on the TV or in the papers. Few foreigners living in Rangoon had even heard of him.

An early glimpse of his power was given on the Myat-thanda. A never-ending issue between successive captains and myself had been over crew uniforms.

As IWT had no money we had fitted out the crew with fine new uniforms. However these were only worn on special occasions like passenger embarkation or disembarkation. The rest of the time the crew dressed in a motley collection of tattered *longyis* and old football shorts.

A second set of workwear uniforms was invested in. These consisted of a sort of blue football strip with big numbers on the shirt backs. The crew seemed to like them. The compromise we reached was that when the ship was in a major port like Mandalay, crew would wear dress uniforms, image being important.

I arrived one day in Mandalay to find all the crew, officers and captain dressed in civvies. I complained. "Orders from Rangoon". The wearing of any uniform other than military dress had been banned throughout the country. Why? Blank expressions hinting at some deeper cause.

Later, I learnt that General Than Shwe had been invited to the naval academy passing out parade. Seeing the ranks of handsome young naval officers, kitted out in their elegant new blue uniforms, the general went into a fury as the navy uniforms were so much smarter than army issue. He stormed off, announcing that he never wanted to see any uniform other than the army uniform on anyone ever again.

The next day the police, customs, navy, air force and of course IWT received the order to wear only civilian clothes. This order lasted only about three weeks until everyone reckoned that the general had forgotten about it. Thus inadvertently, we learnt of Than Shwe's rise to supremacy.

The entire country was run on such whims of iron. It was around this time motorbikes and scooters were banned from the streets of Rangoon. Apparently because some boy on a bike scratched Madame Khin Nyunt's car at the traffic lights. To this day the ban remains in force, if only everyone zipped around on scooters as in Saigon, things would get done much quicker. Actually a more plausible reason for the bike ban was that biker gangs had been forming and had become highly dangerous. These were not disillusioned kids from ghettos, rather these were the 'SLORC brats', the children of the generals – spoilt rotten and above the law they were wild on booze and drugs, untouchables leading a high life beyond police control.

Another aspect of Rangoon life in the late 1990s was the predominance of the Wa. Known as the 'Wild Wa', this hill tribe had never been tamed by the British Raj, who, given the tribe's natural bellicosity, had sensibly left them to their own devices. After Independence the Wa had all signed up to the Burma Communist Party, its materiel supplied by China, with which they had maintained a thirty year armed conflict with Rangoon.

In the late 1980s the Wa had, had enough of Marx and Lenin and overthrew their Burmese cadres, opting for a more profitable and softer life growing and trading opium, protected from state interference by the threat of latent insurgency. Khin Nyunt had miraculously managed to deal with the Wa who were now left alone to get on with the things they do best – smuggling drugs, guns and girls.

The problem was as that as a result of this unexpected peace dividend the Wa decided they too wanted a slice of the high life in Rangoon and with their prodigious, ill-gotten wealth started buying up property and businesses. Almost inevitably they came to control the city's prostitution and drugs trade, not to mention money laundering and a variety of other shady enterprises.

Khin Nyunt could not interfere. Peace hung by a thread. On one occasion a police station was shot up after an over-zealous brothel raid, on others there were gun battles between various Wa groups in Chinatown. The Wa have gone now, they departed along with Khin Nyunt in 2004. Yet at the time they were very much part of Rangoon's rich tapestry.

During this time of tension, Rangoon itself became a hotbed of 'security alerts'. We would come home from a night out to find soldiers with metal detectors checking the roadside ditches. Whole regiments would camp out in people's gardens. Convoys would move through the night shifting troops around the capital. Yet life went on and we danced till dawn in an endless round of parties, the mysterious workings of the military the butt of jokes.

One would take a short cut down an alley to find hundreds of soldiers lying in wait. This was not as intimidating as it might sound. One would wave and smile and the gnarled old soldiers, wearing the red scarfs of shock troops, would wave back with the sweetest smiles and even the odd wink.

Around this time Burma acquired some T56 tanks from the Russians and these were rather ostentatiously parked outside the entrance to the War Office compound on Shwedagon Pagoda Road, their commanders ready in the turrets. I don't think the tanks ever went anywhere: they were very much for show and show alone served their purpose.

At moments of high tension the tanks might reposition to the front of the town hall, such posturing reflecting a state of affairs within the regime rather than any popular movement or other external threat. One might surmise from this that the regime's enemy was the people. On the contrary the enemy was within the regime. Within the army each faction saw itself as surrounded by hostile forces.

Indeed, the enemy had been the people in the late 1980s, but the people had long since been defeated. Both the army and the people knew that there would never be any hope again of a mass rising like in '88'. For one thing, after '88' the army had more than quintupled in size. It had re-equipped itself with latest technology from China and Russia. Cities had been redesigned to allow the military to move at speed whilst hindering any form of public gathering. Parks and boulevards had been enclosed with wrought iron fencing. Universities were closed for a decade and then relocated to obscure sites far from urban centres, with the majority of students enrolled in what they called 'distance learning' — correspondence courses designed not to let any number of students congregate on a campus for any length of time.

The split between Khin Nyunt and his MI and Maung Aye with his field forces has already been mentioned. There were other fissures. Regional commanders had evolved into virtual warlords.. Their armies were essentially private militia, paying only lip service to Rangoon command.

They would pay and finance their troops from commercial activities within their regions – the farming of taxes and border imposts, opium trading if in the north or piracy in the south, extortion and rackets. And of course there were the Chinese. By 2000 the Chinese were flooding into Burma. Mandalay was already a Chinese city with all important businesses, factories in Chinese ownership. The Chinese paid their dues to the military commanders in return for peace and protection.

Every few months the capital would brace itself for a Regional Commander's meeting. Each general would arrive in his helicopter with a private army for his protection and proceed to his own heavily guarded compound. It was every regional commander's nightmare that he would go to Rangoon but not come back and thus the personal protection was against seizure and arrest by other junta members.

At such times security reached a fever pitch. In the elite Inya Road area where we lived there were any number of military owned 'safe houses', enormous mansions, well maintained and heavily guarded. When things got tense, the city filled with a half a dozen private armies, it was said that Khin Nyunt slept in a different house every night.

There was the strange case of General Tin Oo, the Secretary Three (S3), who was on a helicopter trip to the southern city of Moulmein when the crew attempted to throw him out the door as part of a planned assassination. The general's bodyguard then exploded a hand grenade within the helicopter downing it with the loss of several lives.

Such were the tensions within the Slorc. Every so often such and such a minister would be arrested, ostensibly for corruption. Such rises and falls followed a formula – a general would be rewarded with a ministerial post, he and his family would get very rich very quickly, then they would get too full of themselves and start showing off.

I got the impression that the liquidation of corrupt ministers was a sort of cash flow stopgap. When the exchequer got low they would identify a particularly fat and juicy victim and plan the dawn raid. One general was discovered to own over a hundred land cruisers (each then worth about \$100,000) and twenty houses. His daughter was flown to Singapore with a couple of security men who escorted her to the bank to withdraw his ill-gotten savings and bring them back.

This, then, was the strange world in which we had chosen to live. To some outsiders Burma was a sinister military regime along the lines of North Korea, to others a nutty kleptocracy like Zimbabwe. On the inside, it was a remarkably pleasant place to be with its cocktail parties on the lawns of graceful colonial houses and we worked easily with an energetic and enthusiastic people, full of fun and humour. There was a sense of being in the right place at the right time and being part of a progressive momentum that was both benign and meaningful.

For the first time there was peace in the hills and trading in the towns. A new urban middle class was emerging intent on making up for the lost time of the Ne Win years. Looking back, perhaps we were suffering from a mild form of Stockholm Syndrome, identifying too much with our 'captors'. Later we were to pay the price for our naivety.

Business prospered and our little ship the Pandaw was almost always full. It chugged up and down the Irrawaddy between Pagan and Mandalay four times a week and at other times set out on our ten-night expeditions when it was high water on the Chindwin, Upper Irrawaddy and at low water in Middle Burma between Prome and Mandalay. The crew settled to the point that they knew the schedules off by heart; IWT was now groomed into a state close to the cooperative.

Life was settling down to a balanced routine dividing our time between the office in Rangoon and the ship with John the Australian filling in for us when we were in the city.

Office life was not exactly pleasant and much of my time was spent trying to placate the nasty Swiss travel agent ladies, who were used to dealing with empty hotels, and unable to understand that we were fully occupied, in both senses of the word. These so called 'Destination

Management Companies' or DMCs, would be contracted by the tour operators at home to book hotels, tours, guides, cars and other peripherals for them.

Their business model is one of very tight margins and very high volume. Fortunately, as sanctions hit, this model could not be applied to Burma, and we can at least thank both the generals and The Lady for further preserving the country in its pristine beauty for a further twenty years.

The development of tourism had and has great potential in Burma, with its thousand-mile coastline of beaches, its mountain ranges, great rivers and its two millennia legacy of Buddhist treasures. But the Pandaw vision was at odds with the new "destination management company" vision.

These mainly Swiss-owned DMCs wanted to do to Burma exactly what they had done to Thailand thirty years previously. Essentially this was to trash the place with hotel complexes, coach tours and bottom-end leisure tourism. The Pandaw vision was one of quality rather quantity. Low environmental impact, sensitivity to local culture and respect for religious traditions. The big Swiss companies saw a village monastery as a selling point in a trip itinerary. We saw it as a chance for integration and shared understandings.

Very fortunately these predators were thwarted, ironically by Daw Aung San Suu Kyi who had asked tourists to stay away. But now that the country is opening up again and mass tourism once more rears its ugly head.

On the Run with Toni

Roser and I had been unable to have children. Roser was keen to adopt a baby, I was not so keen, being more content with our childless state and its compensating freedoms. I agreed to look into it, more I admit, to humour Roser than anything else, and we arranged visits to one or two orphanages in and around Rangoon.

Expat friends had fostered a little boy and were familiar with the various orphanages, a few privately run by mainly Christian charities and the majority by the state.

What we saw on these visits was horrific. Burma was at that time going through a change in social norms, and with this loosening up of "morals" young people were enjoying a freer lifestyle. Unwanted pregnancies were rife. Even middle class girls would have their babies in the hospitals and then just walk away, leaving them to the care of the nurses. The babies would then be transferred to the state-run orphanages. We found whole rooms with row upon row of cots.

State policy was against foreign adoption for perverse face-saving reasons. Though there was nothing in Burmese law against foreign adoption, only General Khin Nyunt had spoken out against it in the wake of a scandal where babies had allegedly been sold to Singapore for re-adoption.

Burma in the 1990s received virtually no aid despite epidemic levels of poverty and an absence of any form of basic healthcare. This denial of aid together with a vicious regime of sanctions preventing any form of inward investment were inspired by the NLD. I thought these were naïve and misguided.

Burma by now was so poor, thanks to the sanctions and the denial of aid and investment, that employers had long since given up paying their workers. Two meals a day and a bit of floor space to sleep on were considered sufficient recompense.

The effect of sanctions on social services was scarcely imaginable, and to this day has never been properly scrutinised by journalists, NGOs or scholars. Orphanages could not feed these infants and many simply died of malnutrition and other related diseases.

You would enter rooms where up to fifty toddlers would sit listless, eyes glazed. The pervasive smell was of urine. What food or funds that were   delivered to the orphanages went to feed or pay the staff, themselves existing on the poverty line.

We would take bananas and cake and make sure they were distributed to the children in front of us, as we knew that otherwise they would never receive them. Every child was crying out to be adopted – they would grab your legs, desperate to be picked up and cuddled. There would be scrummages of toddlers fighting for your attention.

It was in such a room at the Shwegondine orphanage in Rangoon that I was struck by a bolt of lightening. Of the fifty-odd two-year-olds in this room, there was one very small boy who did not join the scrummage, who held back and who avoided my gaze as if aware of forces beyond his comprehension. I walked over, picked him up and his little arms circled my neck and locked on. It was a lock that was to prove hard to prise off. I was overcome with joy and certainty. This was meant to be.

We went to see the head of the orphanage who told us the child's name was Lin Lin Htun and looked up his file. There were no known parents, he was a foundling handed into the Parami District Council office, a few miles from the orphanage, at the age of six months. This was unusual. As said previously, kids are abandoned at birth. There was clearly a story here but we would never know it.

The orphanage head reaffirmed that foreigners could not adopt, but I was blasé, I had powerful friends and connections.

We were warned that he was not an easy kid, why take him? He was difficult. If we really wanted a baby why not take one that had just been handed in before the paperwork was done?

I was very confident that my connections would help. After all, I had twice been summonsed to formal audiences with General Khin Nyunt, not to talk about river cruising but about our publishing programme. The general loved the books I had produced on Burmese culture, in particular the magnificent eight-volume *Inventory of Monuments at Pagan* that my firm Kiscadale had published with UNESCO.

Had he not had said at each meeting that, in gratitude for the work we had done promoting Burmese art and culture, if I ever needed help with anything we should contact him? His right hand was the urbane Colonel Hla Min and I had the colonel's phone number.

For two months we visited the orphanage every day, sometimes twice a day. Roser took to spending the entire day there, having carved out a little corner in the nursery where she sat with the child we were to call Toni. He was all we talked about, all we thought about. We went to India for a week's vacation but could not sleep at night for thinking of him and came back more resolved than ever.

The colonel promised to do what he could. I was to write to the general stating our case, which I did.

Nothing happened. Weeks went by. A kind friend engineered a dinner one night with the colonel and his wife, who reassured me that the general was aware of the case and trying to help. Fortunately the Social Welfare Ministry, which ran the orphanages, was one of the ministries that Khin Nyunt controlled. We met the minister and they offered us a 'fostering agreement' whereby Toni could come and live with us but would never be allowed to accompany us abroad. We rejected this.

The only Burmese legislation on adoption matters dated back to colonial times and was about protecting the inheritance rights of adopted children. There was nothing in law to say a foreigner could not adopt, it was common enough amongst Burmese, though often wealthy ladies would adopt cute little kids as play things and spoil them rotten and when they got to puberty and became bolshy teenagers, they would return them to the orphanages.

Other Burmese would 'adopt' in order to get free servants — effectively slave labour — for their house. The residue of unadopted kids, if they survived, were sent to be soldiers if boys. Pretty girls were dispatched to sleazy nightclubs and the less pretty ones became unpaid labour in sweat shops.

Months passed. The uncertainty and anxieties were intolerable. I was told that it might help if I was a practicing Buddhist. I arranged a formal induction ceremony in an important state-controlled Buddhist monastery that was to be witnessed by a number of senior government officials, sympathetic to our situation. This was photographed and my 'conversion' publicised. Still nothing happened.

Christmas loomed and the thought of Toni all alone in his prison became too much. We approached the head and asked if it might be possible to bring him home for a week or so over the Christmas period. In fact we were scheduled to be on the ship over the Christmas period. The lady in charge who like everyone else involved genuinely wanted to help, agreed. Kids clothes were borrowed and we drove over to Shwegondine and prepared him for his exeat, removing his ragged institutional clothes and dressing him in nice shorts and t-shirt.

Off we went in my little green Volkswagen beetle. Sitting on Roser's lap Toni was very excited to be seeing the big wide world for the first time, pointing in amazement at all the cars, lorries and buses. U Zawta, my monk friend from Mandalay had called that morning to let me know he was staying with a brother monk near where we lived so we called in on the way, euphoric with our new son.

U Zawta looked at me and shook his head, *'pyatthana sha de'* which translates as 'looking for trouble'.

Once back to our house in Inya Road, Toni whizzed round exploring everything. He was like a little bomb going off in successively timed detonations. Half an hour before he had been docile to the appoint of appearing sedated, and now he exploded into a whirl of activity. We managed to get him into the shower to hose him down and get the orphanage smell off him. He loved the shower and could happily have spent the whole day there.

We tried to feed him but most of the food went everywhere other than his mouth. That night we put him in a cot in our bedroom but he tossed and turned and would not sleep, such was his excitement.

We brought him into our bed and all night he kicked and punched out. We got up the next morning bruised and shattered. A visit to the doctor indicated that he had TB but that it was treatable. We had to start him on a light diet, as he was unused to rich food, gradually building up the proteins. He got better very quickly, putting on weight, and getting more colour in his cheeks.

The energy level was incredible. We had had no idea he was so extrovert, so talkative, so outgoing. He spoke a little Burmese, but his speech development was well behind average for a two and half-year-old. I was 'Pay-pay' and Roser 'May-may'. On day one he had worked out how to put a CD on the player, having never seen this done before. Quickly he became almost parrot like mimicking my words and mannerisms. The watchman happened to be cross-eyed and one day I caught Toni in the act of copying him, doing a brilliant cross-eyed impression. That was to be discouraged.

As planned we flew up to Pagan to join the Pandaw. On Christmas day we had the boat to ourselves and had a delightful Christmas lunch cooked by Po Ko climaxing with a cake. Toni's first Christmas was spent on the Pandaw, as have been many a Christmas since.

It was not all easy. Toni had a lot of anger bottled up inside him. There were rages and tantrums that went beyond the norm for a two year old. He had a lot to get out and was on a very fast learning curve, catching up on everything he had missed in those crucial first two years, all the cumulative experiences and lessons of early developmental life.

Helpful life lessons, like not sticking fingers into electrical sockets, had to be learnt.

On returning to Rangoon we decided to try and postpone returning Toni to the orphanage. A message was sent from the office saying that we were delayed in Mandalay. The head said that was fine, he was not missed.

A week went by, then a month, and no one called asking for him back. A month became two and then three. Meanwhile I working assiduously at trying to regularise the situation. Various charlatans would appear, offering to 'fix' things for us, usually requiring absurd sums of money. Some genuinely tried to help out of kindness, and everyone was amazed at the brick wall we had come up against.

In some senses, Burma is one of the most flexible and easygoing countries in the world, exceptions to any rule are plentiful. In this case the agents of the military regime, rather than being draconian, were perhaps being the most flexible of all.

After several months our friend the colonel took me aside and explained the problem. Khin Nyunt's power base was wobbling. He was under direct attack from Maung Aye and beyond him, Than Shwe. His every move was watched. Every decision vetted. Khin Nyunt, once the great hope of a new Burma, had been reduced to ceremoniously opening pagodas and feeding monks. Yes, he was still prominent on the TV and in the media, but his remit was confined to sport, culture, religion and the charade that passed for foreign affairs.

Than Shwe was more concerned with procuring and financing defence equipment, while letting Khin Nyunt carry on as a frontman. The matter of Toni's adoption, which loomed so large for us, was merely chaff, caught up in the much bigger, grinding wheels of the politics of the day.

Looking back, our failure to make the headway I had complacently assumed, was our first intimation that Khin Nyunt's game was up. It was not till 2003 that he was finally toppled in a putsch, brutal even by the standards of the Burmese military. He and his family were imprisoned, and our colonel friend disappeared along with so many others who had once been counted the hope of Burma.

I went to the British Embassy. In the old days I would have been ushered straight in to see the Ambassador. Now, as I was contravening Foreign and Commonwealth Office policy by doing business here, I was a pariah, somewhere on the scale of lowlife between a drug dealer and a white slaver.

I was taken to see a large English lady of middling rank in the Embassy pecking order. She immediately started taking me to task for promoting tourism. I pointed out that it was a former British Ambassador who had actively encouraged me to start my tourism business. I also pointed out that I was not an 'investor' in the pejorative sense she implied. Any money we had put into the business had been made in Burma and had stayed in Burma. We had started with nothing.

When it came to the issue of Toni I was clearly not going to get any useful help. I would need to go back to the UK and complete a home study report with a social worker, before they would consider issuing a passport to Toni.

The average duration of such home studies and the permit for overseas adoption in the UK was then five to eight years. Then we would have to have legal agreements from the Burmese authorities. In other words, forget it.

A Glasgow Irish friend, despite a rather dubious past as an arms dealer and said to be wanted in several countries and therefore lying low in Burma, was also a pious Catholic with good contacts within the local hierarchy.

He suggested we go to Bangkok and talk to a couple of priests he knew who could arrange passports and get people out. Off we went to Bangkok and met Father Dan and Father Mike who operated out of a sort of Aids hospice- cum-refugee centre in the 'Little Burma' area of Bangkok. We told our story which did not surprise them at all.

Irish Americans in origin, they were frontline priests used to dealing with the lost and the stateless, the dissident and the persecuted. Getting people out — or even getting them in — was what they did.

So it was just a passport for the kid we wanted? No problem at all. Father Dan called in a little Burmese sidekick and explained our situation. No problem. We gave him our Rangoon address details and he told us to go back and someone would contact us. That was it.

Sure enough a couple of days later we were approached by a man whose business card bore the motto 'Think First'. Think First as we called him explained the process and the costs involved. The passport department kept spare passports that were sold on the black market.

These were the real thing and would be signed and stamped by the right people but they were never entered on the register, so did not officially exist. All was arranged and Toni was photographed. Things then happened astonishingly quickly and within twenty-four hours we were told the passport would be ready. First he needed a birth certificate and one was arranged from the Hpa-an hospital in the Karen state, someone being sent up there on the bus to collect it. Hpa-an, then a couple of days by car away, was considered too remote for anyone to check.

The next issue was the visa. Clearly the British Embassy was not going to issue Toni a visa. Spain, Roser's country of origin, has no consulate in Burma, being represented by the French.

We knew the French ambassador and his wife socially. The French had none of the selective scruples of the British and they were by then major investors in Burma. The oil giant Total lead the field and the French had the largest number of tourist visitors.

I called the French Ambassador and explained our situation. Like many others in Rangoon's small foreign community they knew about Toni and had been very sympathetic. He told me that as soon as the passport was issued I was to come and see him.

That afternoon we received the passport and I went to the embassy. The consular staff raised various technical objections, but *Son*

The early ships 1995-1997: Irrawaddy Princess (top) in the Myathanda bar with Captain Maung Maung Lay to the right (middle), Roser, Paul and the Pandaw I crew with Chief U Hla Shwe (left) and Capt Nyunt Wei (right), 1998.

Pandaw I in 1998, five of the crew pictured are still with us twenty years later.

Paying cash for Pandaw II, the Inya Road office staff,
Pandaw II under construction and Toni arrives at Inya Road for the first time with U Zawta.

Life on board with old and loyal crews and Toni in discussion with Purser Neville.

On the Mekong where the fleet rapidly grew by the mid 2000s.

In Borneo on the Rajang River, dancing with the Iban under the influence of local rice wine and many a navigational hazard.

India: A recce on the Jamuna River led to the departure of Pandaw 4 under tow;
if only we had seen that sign!

Work of the Pandaw Charity – schools, clinics and relief work
during the 2008 Cyclone Nargis.

Excellence smoothed things over, personally signing the visa. As our projected route to Europe was through Charles De Gaulle airport, he even issued a letter to the French frontier police asking them to offer us every assistance.

It was now about 6pm. The Bangkok flight left at 8pm and I had already booked tickets with Thai Airways to Bangkok and Air France to Paris and then Barcelona. With a French visa under the EU's Schengen rules we could visit Spain where we had a home and family.

We knew we had to get out as quickly as possible. Burmese officials can be very fickle. Minds change, policies change, people change. Other than Think First not a soul knew what we were doing. Servants, office staff, everyone gossiped about everyone and everything. The fact that there was no press or media to speak off meant that people were often better and more speedily informed of anything than they would have been if there had been a free press.

Returning home our Karen cook served up a meal as per normal. I had asked our nice Australian manager, John, to come round and we explained what we were doing. He agreed to take over the office and I would be in contact once abroad. We hastily packed a couple of bags and John drove us the airport. We left everything behind, the plates on the table, our books and CDs, our clothes and personal possessions. The house staff did not even know we had gone.

At the airport Think First was waiting in the car park. He grabbed Toni from us and told us he would be returned to us air side. Once through border controls. Roser and I were, to say the least, jittery. We said good bye to John and passed through the many checks and controls smoothly.

In Burma then there was always someone watching someone else. An MI man would be watching the immigration officer and someone else would be watching the MI man. The whole atmosphere was terrifying. We were sweating heavily in the heat and trembling all over. My face was known to most of the officials and we were soon nodded through.

Sure enough, once on the other side in the departure lounge Think First sauntered in, bearing Toni in his arms. He was handed over without a word and that was the last we ever saw of Think First. The lounge lighting was dim, the place shabby. We found a corner, partly hidden from view behind a concrete pillar. There were several people we knew on the flight, Burmese and expats. There were even a couple of the nasty Swiss travel agent ladies. Everyone, it seemed, knew of our plight, so anyone could blow the whistle.

We had opted for business class as economy was frequently overbooked and passengers were always getting bumped. We hurried onto the plane, hearts pumping, adrenalin kicking in, trying to look nonchalant.

But even on the plane we could not relax. Just as we were about to take off a white French Embassy car drove up to the gangway. What was this?

Then I recognised Philip, an old Anglo-Burmese friend who had been arrested and imprisoned a year before on some trumped-up charge. Philip had a French passport and the embassy had just got him released. Like Toni he was on the first flight out before anyone changed their minds. It had been a busy day for the French Embassy! Once on board, Philip recognised me and would not stop talking – delighted to see a friendly face after his year in hell.

It was only when we landed in Bangkok and were safely ensconced in the Air France lounge with a glass of champagne that elation hit. We had done it. We had got Toni out. Toni also sensed the excitement but was perhaps more preoccupied by the novelties of a big airport.

We flew on to Paris and then Barcelona without incident ready to start a new life in Spain. Clearly returning to the UK would be impossible but Spain had a very strong overseas adoption programme, and regarded such cases with a more humane perspective than the ever-bureaucratic British. It took a further two years to normalise Toni's status and eventually he was naturalised Spanish citizen.

We had left everything behind. Not just our personal possessions and a whole way of life but also a thriving business and a rather beautiful little ship. Australian John had agreed to caretake the office and it was June so we were not in our sailing season. But I expected that once the news became known we would be closed down pretty quickly, the ship confiscated, our business finished. It was only a matter of time.

We had a holiday home in Spain, a farmhouse in Catalunya, which over the past few years when not cruising the Irrawaddy we had been doing up. We moved there and I set up a little office. By 2000 we all had email so communication with the Rangoon was relatively easy.

A month went by, and then another and another and nothing happened. There were no phone calls and no visits from the authorities. Toni had been forgotten, accidentally or deliberately.

We had taken the problem away and that in Burma amounts to a solution. Friends, expat and Burmese, assumed that we had got permission legally. In Rangoon where no one ever really knows the true story, an assumption can very quickly become reality.

After three or four months I went back alone to test the waters. Clearly Roser could not bring Toni, that would be madness. For the next few years, until Toni got his Spanish passport and we felt confident enough to bring him in, all my visits were alone, sometimes for several weeks leaving Roser and Toni behind, which was not easy.

At time of writing Toni is seventeen and goes to my old school in Scotland which he seems to enjoy far more than I did. Unlike me is rather good at sport, a keen rugby and hockey player. Like me he is a keen sailor, skier and climber. He does not speak much Burmese anymore but he loves Burma and all things Burmese, and we visit and spend time there every year. Toni knows Pandaw ships and their crews inside out, and is probably second only to me in understanding how it all hangs together. Though he has lived most of his life outside Burma, in Spain and Scotland, he has not lost the humour, with occasional little gems of wit and a mock-bemused glint in the eye that only the Burmese possess.

Pandaw II

Back in Rangoon in September 2000 I was in the shipyards again. Business had grown and demand was high, we needed another ship.

This time we decided to build a new ship rather than restore another old one. It is not that there were not plenty of available antiques to adapt, but as with houses a new build can be cheaper, quicker and more efficient than a restoration.

By 2000 IWT were becoming more and more difficult to work with. There were the first signs of corruption and it was hinted that if we put the MD on a monthly retainer things would go more smoothly for us.

As it happened at the time they were making things more and more difficult for us and there was huge resentment that what they saw as a joke ship like the old Pandaw could have been so successful. With its foreign earnings it made them more money that the entire IWT fleet of five hundred ships put together (most of which were laid up with broken engines). Of course they resented us.

After the educational experience of the first Pandaw refit, we now had the confidence just to go out and build a ship for ourselves. No one had ever built a cruise ship in Burma before. There was a good local tradition of barge and tug building, and some blue water fishing trawlers. But even in the 1930s heyday of the IFC, ships were still built in Glasgow and shipped out in parts for reassembly at the company dockyards at Dalla. As far as I know Dalla only ever produced one ship on its own and then the Second World War put an end to dreams of a local ship building industry.

I had many friends in the local marine scene and there was a terrific pool of talent to draw on. There was also no shortage of small dockyards along the Rangoon River. Many of these were state-owned from the Socialist period and, though by now long defunct, and littered with broken-down machinery, their slipways were still usable.

Only three things are needed to build a ship – a place where you can launch, lots of people and materials. You do not need much static plant and equipment. If a crane is needed to lift in an engine or whatever, a mobile one can be hired by the day. Welding sets are mobile and can be powered by portable generators.

Our naval architect was one 'Newcastle Charlie', so called as he had studied at Newcastle University in the 1960s. Uncle Charlie was an old Burmese friend who I had known well in Mandalay when he had supervised the IWT shipyard there. U Charlie was something of a Burma marine history buff and we had enjoyed many a discussion on IFC lore. U Soe Naing, who had restored the original Pandaw for us, was persuaded to take on this project and found a disused yard at Dawbone, belonging to the Directorate of Marine Administration, keen to rent it out.

Plans were drawn up. These tend to start with me doing a back-of-envelope sketch and then U Charlie and his team interpreting this into a general arrangement drawing. Once that had been agreed, technical drawings would in theory follow.

I did find that technical drawings, required for the vessel's official classification, often followed the build: first they built it and then they drew it.

I grew up in shipyards. My father was a ship builder, the fourth generation of his family to work in the Clydeside shipyards. Like his father he had worked at John Brown's Shipyard, famous for building the Queen Mary and the two Queen Elizabeths. As a boy every Saturday morning my father used to take me down to Clydebank and we would walk round the yard. At that time in the mid-sixties they were building the QE2 and I have memories of scaling the great bronze propellers, lying on the quayside awaiting installation. The half built cruise liner was the ultimate play park and I would explore the decks with cables, trunking and pipework coiled all around.

Back at in the Dawbone shipyard, it all came back to me – the shipyard smells of oil and grease, burning metal, sweat and grime. Building little riverboats can in no way be compared with building great Cunarders but the same atmosphere prevailed. This was compounded by the passion felt by men who work on ships. It is an extraordinary thing, hundreds of men working to produce a creature that will one day pulsate with vitality and then just sail away. Fights would break between our squad and the workers on a ship on an adjacent slipway, the squads jealous of each other, passions running high. Ships do that to you.

U Soe Naing, at heart a very typical Burmese of the type you would find in any village, saw his role as shipbuilder as spiritual as well as temporal. The initial keel-laying was elaborated into a religious ceremony with monks and nuns chanting as the welder made his fist join. As owner, I was required to take on a priestly function, sprinkling both the steel plates and the assembled workers with holy water, cast from a sprig of laurel.

At each stage of construction monks and nuns would be invoked, either at the yard or in their respective religious houses. U Soe Naing was a devotee of one nun, or *sayarmagyi*, who was known to be something of a seer. Sayarmargyi was consulted on a near daily basis on all aspects of construction, engineering and shipyard management. Of course U Soe Naing deep down knew what he had to do but he lacked the confidence to be decisive and Sayarmargyi could see into his mind and put him on track.

The general arrangement of the ship followed the traditional IFC colonial design that we had reinstated on the old Pandaw, now known as Pandaw I. That is with the cabins, now twenty-four of them, ranged around open promenade decks. This arrangement had proved popular with passengers and eliminated the need for a corridor running down the middle of the ship. The Schottel type propulsion system was ordered from a company in China and the engines from Caterpillar Marine.

Financing the construction of the ship was not easy. Nobody used Burma's state-owned banks as they took a 10% flat fee off any inward transaction, so we had to pay in cash. I would fly out from the UK with $100,000 or so in cash in a money belt. On arrival I would go to a little grocery shop called Ma Khin Aye, near the Myinegone market. Ma Khin Aye was one of the most admired and respected people in Rangoon in the 1990s. Behind the front of a little grocery store, she ran a banking empire. The nationwide exchange rate was set daily, not at the central bank, but here in a humble shop house. Everyone went to her to change money.

Every so often the government tried to close her down, if only to control the falling kyat, the local currency. It was simple enough to arrest Ma Khin Aye and stop the currency slide. But then people needed to change money, the economy required foreign exchange, pressure would build up and she would be released.

In some senses Ma Khin Aye, a simple and Burmese shopkeeper had more power than the finance minister or state bank. She was iconic figure loved by all – expats and locals. My old *hsaya* (master or teacher) U Than Htut, who lived round the corner bewailed the demolition of Rangoon's old Myinegone district, as pretty wooden houses gave way to ugly apartment blocks. He told me that he and his wife was only staying on because they loved their morning shop and chat with Ma Khin Aye. Burma then had virtually no street crime. My secretary could go up and change a few hundred dollars and walk back to the office with clear plastic bags filled with kyat without a second thought.

I could walk into Ma Khin Aye's shop with $100,000 in cash and not an eyebrow was raised. Follow me. Round the corner, I was led up the stairs to an apartment. An old lady, perhaps an elderly aunt, opened up for us. She was alone in this big apartment stacked with cardboard boxes filled with kyat. It was a sort of cash stockpile. Indeed, there was probably more money here than in the state bank. I was left to load a number these boxes into the car — $100,000 converted into Kyat was equivalent to an estate car crammed to the brim. I then drove across town and handed over the boxes to U Soe Naing at his office where half a dozen or so of his accounts ladies sat for an entire day counting the money right down to the last kyat. Thus it was that the steel plates were purchased.

There were questions about how legally to operate a privately-owned river vessel, as no one had done this before. IWT were approached but they were uninterested, until the promise of a dollar based service contract, whereby they would allow us to use their jetties and pilots, won them over.

Meanwhile it was necessary to get ministerial clearance. The fighter pilot minister had long been 'retired', I forget in which corruption scandal, and we were now dealing with the deputy minister. I was summoned to the same great chamber where I had received my dressing down from the fighter pilot minister.

The deputy was a very small man in his sixties who spoke good English but did not seem to be very decisive. He talked about river conditions and navigational matters, having previously headed up the waterways department. I could not steer him round to the issues of licencing and permits for our tourists to travel.

Throughout the meeting a young uniformed army captain, sat at the back and it seemed that the minister took his cue from him – waiting for a nod, or some form of eye contact before pronouncing on anything. After the audience, when the minister had been duly escorted out with all necessary pomp, this captain came over and shook hands, gave me his business card and told me to come and see him at his office.

This was over the Citimart Supermarket at the Aung San Stadium and it was from here that the *bogyi*, or captain, ran the affairs of the ministry. His official position was PA to the deputy minister but his private company took care of all the applications for licences, permits, shipping registrations, and other business of the ministry. Applicants paid a fee, Bogyi's team facilitated matters and the minister did the rubber stamping.

Somehow one got the feeling that Bogyi was the main beneficiary of this system and the deputy minister received a lesser share of this largesse.

There is a *bogyi* in every minister's office in Burma, it works well – the ministers are often doddery old generals who do not have a clue about anything much, and these smart young PAs take care of the humdrum routine stuff out of their hands. This Bogyi was clearly prospering – he sported an enormous ruby ring — and he invited me to dinner that night along with U Soe Naing.

We met at a nightclub somewhere in the suburbs where Bogyi appeared to be well known. The room had a stage at one end and the air of a village hall decorated for Christmas festivities with tinsel and fairy lights everywhere.

A bottle of Chivas Regal appeared and Bogyi proceeded to get very drunk. U Soe Naing, ever the pious Buddhist, refused a drink, and thus I was compelled to keep Bogyi company. It was a long night. Dancing girls gyrated before our young captain who would ecstatically festoon the prettier ones with flowery garlands, the cost of which was added to the bill. Towards the end of the bottle Bogyi put his arm round me and with genuine tears in his eyes told me "How I love my country. This is the best country in the world. Look at these girls, this food, this place. I love my Myanmar more than anything". Who paid for all this? I wondered.

A t the time of writing Pandaw II is now fourteen years old, still young in shipping terms. Many of our regular clients, all Pandaw aficionados, tell me that it remains their favourite Pandaw. One retired lady doctor from Blackpool actually came to live on her, spending several winters cruising up and down the Irrawaddy telling me it was preferable to a care home and cost about the same. Dr Kay became something of a ship's mascot, the adopted granny for many of the crew. Her cabin (201) remains to this day a hallowed place.

Being a new build we improved lots of things from the Pandaw I design. Hours were spent hammering out solutions to technical issues. U Soe Naing's team and I were learning as we went along. Of course there were teething problems that in later builds we managed to iron out but fundamentally very little has changed in design and concept between the ship we designed and built in 2001 and the ships we are building today.

As the vessel neared completion the intensity of U Soe Naing's religious activities increased, directed by Sayarmargyi. Offerings were made in various parts of the vessel. The nats had to be placated in addition to the Buddhist merit accumulated. The ship had its own karma that would guide it through the waters, whilst the nat spirits of the river and of the ship, not forgetting the supremely important nat of the engine room, had to be propitiated.

All this was done with great solemnity. Prior to the first test voyage monks were offered food and recited the *paritta* or prayers of protection. In Burma these protective prayers were not just against the forces of nature but against the evils of government, for in Buddhism the Four Great Evils are: fire, flood, wind and government.

I was required to make offerings to the river nats, casting water pots filled with offerings overboard from the bow. There were further sprinklings of holy water over the ship and crew and U Soe Naing was satisfied that his ship was ready to take to the rivers.

The first trial was a euphoric experience. All the workers brought their families along so we had a full complement onboard. We took off down the Pazundaung Creek heading for the Rangoon River. However when we hit the mainstream something went badly wrong. The ship started spinning on the spot, as if caught in a whirlpool. No one knew what to do. The captain fiddled with his joystick. Calls on the intercom were made to the chief in the engine room. Several minutes passed and it looked like we would be whirling around for ever. It was then discovered that one of the outboard rudder propellers was set higher than the other causing these extreme revolutions. With these readjusted we continued down the river to do speed tests on a measured mile.

There was a terrific sense of self-congratulation. A historian had got together with a housebuilder and with no previous experience had built a 50 metre-long, triple decked, luxury cruise ship from a pile of steel plate and a load of teak logs. This was all in well under a year, well ahead of schedule and on budget too.

The maiden voyage was planned for early October. Fortunately, over half of the passengers booked were old friends who had travelled with us before. They understood the eccentricities and idiosyncrasies of travel by Pandaw. I had taken the ship up to Pagan as part of a shakedown cruise, testing and re-testing the services which included checking that loos flushed properly and showers did not drip. Cleaning and re cleaning each cabin several times after the filth of the shipyard. Pandaw II was looking great when our forty-odd passengers joined.

We were to proceed upstream to Bhamo. None of our ships had yet made it that far. What with strong currents and weak engines, Bhamo remained an elusive dream though we did once get a group there by chartering a small hovercraft, then operating out of Mandalay. Truth to tell we found the place a bit of an anticlimax.

Unfortunately the deputy minister of transport had taken an unhealthy interest in our project. He was forever 'inviting' me to his office to discuss the project, a somewhat bazaar experience as a large TV would play Spice Girl videos as we sat around the tables discussing kedging techniques. The deputy minister would send two of his 'best' pilots with the vessel. It turned out that they were desk-bound office pilots from Rangoon who had not been on the river for years. The IWT pilots were much better. They were beat pilots, who changed over every couple of days and who knew their sections of the river intimately. But we were not to get them.

The Irrawaddy's channels can change on a daily basis, particularly just at the end of the monsoon, when the river can fall by two feet overnight, and when and no one yet knows just where the channels will emerge.

Following the inaugural celebrations we proceeded up river swimmingly. We had just emerged from the third defile and as the river widened and grew shallower we ran aground. Groundings are par for the course on the Irrawaddy and no voyage is complete without one. Going upstream you are less likely to get really stuck than you are when proceeding downstream, when the force of the current can run you up on a sandbank.

This time we were going up, but somehow none of the usual techniques of wiggling and backwashing the sand from under the hull, using the 360-degree, rotation of the Shottel propellers, seemed to work.

The river was falling fast and within a few hours we were well and truly stuck. I got onto our illegal satellite phone and called the deputy minister requesting tug assistance.

He was loath to send tugs (not wanting to pay for the fuel) offering instead to send several more pilots. Over the next few days a variety of officials arrived by launch or steamer to 'advise'. The higher the rank the more useless they were. We were on our own.

By the second day it was possible to disembark and wade round the ship in ankle deep water. We were beached on a midstream island as the river fell away all around us. There was little chance of a rise, or not till the next monsoon several months off.

It seemed we were finished. Future cruises would have to be cancelled and deposits returned. The loans I had taken out with the Yoma Bank could not now be repaid and my own home, pledged as collateral would be taken from us. Roser and Toni were back in Spain and I dreaded breaking the news of inevitable bankruptcy.

In the days of the Irrawaddy Flotilla if a captain grounded a ship he had to stay on board for the duration. There were a number of cases where a captain would spend up to nine months sitting in the middle of some sand island in a remote and forgotten part of the country. Most captains were then Scots who are not especially good in the heat so imagine enduring the hot season where temperatures hit the mid-40s. Some planted little gardens round their ships to grow fresh vegetables. Such thoughts were running through my mind as I vacillated about what to do.

The first step was to evacuate the passengers back to Mandalay, find them hotels and try and arrange tours by coach or car so they could at least complete their holiday in Burma. A meeting was called and the passengers assembled in the saloon.

Up till then the mood had been quite good, and no doubt the dispersal of free drinks from the bar had helped. In some trepidation I broke the news of the abandonment of the expedition.

There was a stunned silence, then murmuring and then visible anger. I was thinking in terms of compensation, how would we find the money to refund them all having spent every last penny on the ship? Then Mickie Allen, one of regulars, called out:

"I don't know about the rest of you but I am staying with Paul". Then another said "me too" and then another and then another and then the whole room broke into spontaneous cheering and clapping. There were tears in my eyes and I tried to explain that it might be a long wait but no one was having it. There had to be a way off and they had the confidence that we would work it out.

Later one of the crew, Ko Nan Myint Oo, came to me with an idea. Upstream there was a gold panning operation. This was no bunch of hillbillies with hand-held pans but rather a fleet of boats with massive pumps on board that would suck up the river silt which would then flow down conveyor belts. This technology is homespun – massive old lorry engines mounted on wobbly little boats – all very Heath Robinson and all very Burmese, but it worked well.

Nan Myint Oo's idea was to take a boat up there and see if we could hire some of these to come down and pump the sand around

Pandaw II and see if we could float her off. It seemed far fetched but anything was worth a try. By evening of day two on the sandbank, we had half a dozen of these pump boats ranged around the mother ship. Great tubes, sucked up the sand and made mini sand dunes in a circle about us. The noise was terrible but no one worried. The passengers watched fascinated. Trips to local villages had been arranged with country walks and the atmosphere on board remained almost festive.

It began to appear that this might just work. A basin was being created about us and gradually under us and water was flowing in. With any luck we might just float again. However once afloat in our basin there was a distance of about a hundred feet to the main shipping channel. It was so close, yet so far. It would be necessary for the pump boats then to carve a canal to connect the two. As night fell the pump boat crews got tired and cold but were persuaded to continue all night with bottles of rum and more cash.

Work continued through 'Sandbank Day Three'. Passengers continued to visit the nearby village, two walks a day, but I felt this could not continue and again offered to evacuate people to a Mandalay hotel. This time half a dozen or so passengers decided to go, quite rightly in my opinion, but not in the opinion of the remaining diehards, with murmurings of 'wimp' or even 'traitor'.

A launch took them off that day and we settled for another night of thudding engines. By this point we were most definitely afloat again and the pump boats were working on cutting a channel to get us out. It seemed much further than we had thought and progress was painfully slow.

On 'Sand Bank Day Four' we decided to try and break through, got about two thirds of the way down the newly cut channel and got stuck again. We were within spitting distance of the main channel but could not get over the last hump. I recall the early morning, thick mist around us, as the propellers spun, and every last one of us on board silently willing all 850 tons of Pandaw to break through.

Then out of the mist a foghorn sounded. Seemingly floating in the air the figure of Captain Nyunt. He stood before us in a sort of mystic apparition. It transpired that our old Pandaw I captain was stood in his favourite position at the front of the catwalk that extends from the bridges of the old P class steamers.

He had been transferred back to a line ship after a couple of years on Pandaw I. He called out "Is this Mr Paul's ship?", Yes! "Normally I would not stop but as it is Mr Paul we will stop to help". Cables were attached and his steamer spent much of the morning pulling as we pushed back with our engines. But it was to no avail and apologetically the good captain had to return to his schedule.

The pump boats continued all day working away at the channel and by evening we were confident we could break through if we could get a tow. The river was busy but no one was going to stop, grounded ships are a daily occurrence and someone else's bad karma. The minister had indeed failed to send a tug and we badly needed a tow. A couple of our lads took a tender out mid channel and flagged down a passing tug pulling a great raft laden with logs downstream. Persuaded with more bottles of rum for the crew and wads of kyat for the master, they dropped their raft alongside the opposite bank and chugged over. By now night was falling, steel hawsers were attached to the towing gear on the tug and round the capstans on the Pandaw's foredeck. As darkness fell the wires heaved and strained. The Pandaw captain had his engines full on and so did the tug, so small yet full of power and traction.

I was on board the tug and using a sort of semaphore (like satellite phones, radios were banned by the military regime) I directed our captain. We inched forward. An inch became a foot and a foot a yard. We stopped, revved down and then revved up again. Further motion. Then over the final hump we were in the channel – free at last!

I gazed up in the darkness to the saloon windows over the bow, lit up and aglow, passengers heads surrounded by a warm glow. There in the midst of the central window was Mickie who raised a glass in salute as all around cheered and clapped. That night we had a big party on board and it is the only occasion in Pandaw history that I have allowed piped music through a ship – in this case the band of the Black Watch, appropriate to the Scot's resolve that had seen us through the crisis.

Clearly Bhamo was out, but we managed to reach Katha, as mentioned, my favourite Burmese town and onetime home to a young Assistant District Superintendent policeman called Eric Blair, aka George Orwell.

I had taken to arranging literary tours round Katha and in the Penguin edition of *Burmese Days* there is actually a town map and you can today trace the principal buildings mentioned in the book – the court house, the jail, the bazaar, the civil lines with their splendid dak bungalows and of course the club, now the Katha Tennis Club.

After such excitements we returned to Mandalay several hours late and found ourselves in real trouble. A very unpleasant Swiss millionaire had chartered the ship for a bunch of would-be investors and was deeply upset.

His party had no understanding at all of what we had just been through. The fact that we were well covered for such events in our terms and conditions made little difference and he later hounded us for compensation. Such is the lot of a river ship operator.

Beyond Burma

By 2001 it was clear that the dream of re-establishing the Irrawaddy Flotilla in Burma, with a great fleet of river cruise ships, was not going to happen. Sanctions were starting to bite and Burma was simply not on the radar of the chattering classes who thought what their often misinformed media, told them to think.

Only the determined and independent-minded travelled to Burma. They were the kind of people who were not going to be told by politicians or journalists where it was acceptable for them to go, and which destinations they should snub. They would make their own decisions based on what they saw and experienced. Mercifully these were, and remain, the best sort of people to have on board.

Pandaw had become an established name. We were respected in the market as people who understood rivers and the appropriate naval architecture. We had got the formula right technically and also stylistically with just the right balance between comfort and adventure. Our passengers may have shrunk from words like 'deluxe' but were not going to be denied home comforts, most of all a decent drink at sundown.

I think the reason it all worked so well was because we were so much in tune with our passengers. We had set Pandaw up the way we liked things ourselves, not the way hoteliers or travel agents think they should be done. The satisfaction levels were enormous and the high repeat rates spoke for themselves.

A desire to grow is a very human impulse, and anyway, businesses that do not develop tend to stagnate. There was no demand for more ships in Burma, indeed with three on the river by 2002 we had overcapacity.

I started to explore other areas – Thailand, India and the Mekong between Vietnam and Cambodia. Each country required extensive research and reconnaissance. Laws regarding foreign investment,

139

import of ships and inland water policies varied hugely from country to country. In some cases there were no policies at all on foreign-owned ships operating on inland waters as there was no precedent. Wherever we went we were always the first.

Thailand would not have been our first choice for a river cruises but a Swiss-Thai travel company we had a relationship with was keen to set something up on the Kwai. Headed up by a famously flamboyant, carefuly coiffured 50-year-old Swiss called Tootzi, they were desperate to be the first to run river cruises in Thailand. I travelled to Bangkok and joined Tootzi and his lovely Thai wife on a river recce. This involved driving at high speed up roads along the side of the river and stopping periodically to measure bridge heights and wade in to measure river depths.

I was well equipped with a box of tricks, which included ropes, measuring tape, and the other bits and bobs necessary for a river recce. It was never hard to find a length of bamboo and mark up lengths on it. We also hired boats, superbly designed local long tails with Toyota car engines which were just as fast as any car.

The river was astonishingly pretty and full of variety and interest with loads of sightseeing potential. Kingfishers abounded, the water being so clear you could swim anywhere. Waterfalls tumbled over cliffs into the river as it wove through jungle-clad mountains. The Thai villagers and fisher folk we met along the way were charming and very friendly. Tootzi's business partner had pioneered floating river lodges where we stayed and I found most of the employees were Mons, an ancient ethnic group staddling Burmese border with whom I could converse in Burmese.

It was some weeks after this trip when a friend asked me archly how I got on with the lovely Mrs Tootzi? I was eloquent on her charms. My friend stared at me incredulously. Had I not realized? Realized what? That she was a he.

The Kwai was lovely, almost the perfect river but the challenges were great. The duration of any cruise would be limited by navigational constraints: there was simply not a lot of river to ply. There was a low bridge just below Kanchanaburi, not to be confused with the notorious wartime 'Bridge over the River Kwai' which was a little upstream of the town. This would reduce air draft resilting in an open upper deck without any fixed accommodation. Our length could not exceed twenty-five meters due to sharp bends in the river. This would result in a smaller and less profitable ship.

There was also the question of whether our core Pandaw passengers would want to go to Thailand, which had developed into a familiar and even tacky destination. They all wanted frontier stuff.

Tootzi was not to be deterred by such pedestrian concerns and was anxious to rush ahead. He would scoff at any of my worries, ever the positive thinker. What about the big rocks in the middle of the river at mile 78? No problem — we blow them up with dynamite. What about the sand bars on the estuary? No problem we get bulldozers on barges. At one point he was gently dissuaded from delivering the vessel overland from Burma by lorry. What about annual dry-docking? We construct a dry dock. As it turned out (apart from the overland delivery) he ended up doing these things, such is the power of positive thinking.

A deal was struck whereby the three of us, Tootzi, his Thai business partner and myself would invest in the build and delivery. Given the success of Pandaw II it made sense that the ship would be built with U Soe Naing in Burma and sailed round to Samut Songkram, the estuarial port for the Kwai rivers just south of Bangkok.

The ship had to be ultra shallow draft – well under a metre and had to get under a bridge with an average clearance of four metres. This was a real design challenge. We had to get ten cabins to make it commercially viable. Back at the ship yard in Rangoon U Soe Naing and I worked on a new design, based on the old IFC K class that could operate year round on the very shallow Chindwin river, drawing just 50cm of water. There could be no accommodation on the upper deck as everything had to fold down to go under the four-metre bridge. Even the tables and chairs folded up. The handrails were all hinged and the awning structure was designed to fold down, controlled by the anchor windlass. This, it turned out, was not very successful but the Thais later improved on the design.

I made a couple of further trips back to the Kwai to satisfy myself that it was a goer. The challenges were huge. Could a twenty-five metre boat really get over rapids and round dog-leg bends with rocks all about? Could you really dynamite an entire river, which after all was supposed to be a national park? But Tootzi was keen to press on and an itinerary was planned from the mouth of the river at Samut to high into the hills, we need as long a cruise as possible for our passengers to get their money's worth.

Over the years I had got to know an Irish sea captain who had been working in Rangoon restoring a classic yacht built by the great turn-of-the century Scots yacht-builder William Fife. 'Captain Rob', as he was known, certainly knew his stuff and I had hired him as a superintendent for the yard during the build.

Red-haired, red-bearded and red-eyed, the Burmese found him a terrifying apparition, the ultimate foreign devil. That Rob could not speak without shouting and that every second word was the F-word shook them deeply.

I had hoped that his uncompromising approach might make the Burmese a bit more pro-active, rather in the way Ghilberto had turned our hotel operation around with his very Latin histrionics. Rob was a great lateral thinker, full of innovative ideas. But the more he shouted the more inert the Burmese became. They froze into a state of cowed inactivity.

On one occasion during a test run on the Rangoon river with Captain Rob at the wheel, the steering cables broke and not a crewman was to be seen to deal with the crisis, they were all hiding in some distant cabin. It was just Rob and I in the wheelhouse drifting off on the tide towards the Bay of Bengal. Fortunately we were soon picked up by a tug.

On another occasion the entire workforce walked out, with the active collusion of the management.

Rob would bark an order and then go home for the evening. Overnight the workforce were indeed galvanized. They sprang into action and would work all night to do the exact opposite of what he had ordained, meaning that he would return in the morning to a little surprise. The Burmese call this *pyinya-pei-de* or teaching a lesson.

By December 2001 the ship was ready and it was decided that Captain Rob would sail her round to Bangkok.

The notorious pirates of the Straits of Malacca were a serious concern to me, but Rob was fairly blasé about this risk, claiming to have shot a few in his time. Fire hoses were rigged either side of the bridge rather like Gatling guns.

To our knowledge, no ship had ever been exported from Burma before, and the paperwork was excruciatingly complex. It took several weeks to find a way to obtain all the necessary permits and we had only been issued with port clearance up to Kawthaung, the last port in Burma to the south. No one in Rangoon was going to give us clearance all the way to Bangkok. I think the idea was to get us of their hands and let the decision rest with the authorities in Kawthaung. Then there was some official issue about the voyage being too risky for Myanmar seaman, and we had to fly in a Thai crew who, once at sea, got on very well with Rob.

The ship sailed. I had supplied Capt. Rob with a clandestine satellite phone to call in an emergency.

Rob is one of these sea people who are a disaster on land (discontented ex-wives, financial foul-ups, failed businesses, and all the rest of it) but masterfully competent on water. I was confident that he could do the job. I was not allowed to accompany the boat as I did not have a "seaman's ticket" — the mariner's universal passport — and instead arranged to meet Rob in Rannong, the first Thai port over the Burma border, across the Kra River from Kawthaung where we had clearance.

A week or so went by with no communications and I was beginning to get quite nervous, sitting in a rented apartment in the nearby Thai coastal resort of Phuket where we had decided to base ourselves for the winter. Eventually I got the call from Rob's Thai mobile phone that he was approaching Rannong. I jumped in a hire car and raced up there eventually finding Rob in a bar near the docks. Amazingly he had made it out of Burma going non-stop from Rangoon to Rannong, without bothering to stop at Kawthaung. Tootzi would take care of port clearance from here. After a couple of beers Rob insisted that I come out to the boat as he wanted to make a test run and show me some issues with the steering. We took a water taxi out to the mooring.

Rannong is a rather seedy border port, with a mix of Burmese refuges and illegal 'guest workers' coming over to work in Thai sweatshops or as cheap crew on Thai fishing trawlers. It had been a smuggling centre and through the 1970s and 1980s one of the main lifelines to Burma, western goods going in and white powder coming out.

In Rannong you are always looking over your shoulder and at same time minding your own business. The Kra estuary is a labyrinth of creeks, canals and hidden channels straddled by a stilt city, pungent with rotted fish and other tidal detritus.

Rob and I took the Kwai Pandaw out for a run in the main river and were making a series of manoeuvers mid-stream when suddenly out of nowhere a grey Burmese naval patrol gunboat appeared, machine guns manned, and we were ordered to hove to.

We were boarded and ordered at gunpoint to proceed to Kawthaung on the Burma side. Over we went and moored against the main jetty. The ship was searched and we were hauled off to the port office where we were interrogated and the ship's papers gone through. Rob, his red complexion flaring up, became angrier and angrier at this intervention, and I had to send him away to continue negotiations on my own.

The situation was unprecedented. Here was a passenger cruise vessel with port clearance only up to Kawthaung. We had to apply for the next clearance to Bangkok. The Burmese authorities had no idea what to do.

The day wore on and in the evening I was told that, as I did not have a seaman's book or Burma visa I would have to return to Thailand for the night and report back in the morning.

I was sped back across the river, which is at least a mile wide, and to the comforts of a decent Thai hotel, leaving Rob to stew on board.

Returning in the morning the officials were clearly more stressed than ever. The issue was now Captain Rob, who had set himself up in the port office, rolling cigarettes and haranguing the port personnel on aspects the finer points of the International Law of the Sea.

The officials were looking tired, even jaded. A decision had to be made by the local military commander and a delegation of port officials were camped out in his office discussing the case. Another day went by and I took to exploring Kawthaung, a really very pleasant port town. That evening I was sent back to Thailand once again.

On the third day the harbourmaster appeared brandishing the necessary letter containing port clearance. A decision had been made.

In a way this way had proved easier than doing it through Rangoon as regional commanders at this time were virtually autonomous, effectively local warlords, living off the land to pay and equip their troops with little interference from or recourse to Rangoon.

The harbourmaster took me aside and told me how happy they were that we were going. They were all terrified of Rob, and the military commander had no wish to have Rob on his hands for a prolonged period. There was a final inspection when a customs officer found a twenty foot sailing yacht I had had lashed under a tarpaulin on the sun deck and accepted that this was a lifeboat. And when he found several antique Triumph motorbikes that Rob had collected in Rangoon, he declared that they were second hand, with no customs value.

It was evening as we cast off and crossed the Kra once again to the Thai side and decided to put into an unused jetty just up stream of the town. Lines fast, we were just settling down for a drink when we heard the chugging of a boat's motor. Suddenly another gunboat appeared out of the haze, bristling with guns manned by smartly uniformed sailors. It was the Royal Thai Navy.

Rob emerged from his cabin into the glare of the searchlight, splendid in only a pair of yellowed boxers, his red chest hair matted, his beard ragged and his orange face pierced by the great red orbs of his eyes. He yelled:

"Will you all just feck off and come back in the morning." And they did just that, terrified, as if they had seen a demon from the deepest and darkest of Buddhism's five hundred hells. The gunboat edged off and returned to the darkness of the river never to return.

The voyage continued and the Kwai Pandaw delivered to Samut Songkram. After weeks at sea she would need repainting and various mechanical repairs. By now Tootzi had assumed command of the operation and I found myself sidelined. Tootzi saw the whole thing as a publicity stunt to get media attention for his travel company and moreover for himself. He would operate the ship and take over the marketing. I was not against the idea as I had gauged from our Pandaw passenger response that river expeditions in Thailand were not of great interest. Our kind of passenger had "done" Thailand in the 1960s and '70s: Thailand was *passé*, it was for the package tourist not the adventurer.

At the same time the Bangkok metropolitan authority decided to dam the river and take most of the water flow off for the city's water supply. This meant that there was no water on the lower river, which would half the itinerary in time and in distance.

Tootzi bought out my third of the business, for which I was grateful. I remain filled with admiration for the Thai partner who got the cruise up and running, dynamiting their way up river, shifting sands, building dry docks. Rob stayed on to work for Tootzi but almost inevitably there was a falling out. I have been back a number of times and it really is a miracle. I still cannot believe that they manoeuvre this large floating object up a tiny river, over rapid, through gorges and round the tightest of bends. She draws only about sixty centimetres which I think was more a fluke than a clever feat of naval architecture; we have never been able to achieve so shallow a draft in subsequent builds.

A rather nifty little tug launch accompanies the ship and helps pull her round at tricky points. It really is a class operation and, amazingly, everything does fold down when they go under that bridge.

India was next. In 2002 I travelled to the north east state of Assam with a Mr and Mrs Sprott, high-end English travel agents who specialised in the Subcontinent. Mr Sprott had followed the development of Pandaw in Burma and was convinced that the same formula could work on India's mighty Brahmaputra. Mr Sprott had little experience of shipping or river navigation and was keen to have me along to explain something of the logistics and challenges involved.

The trip was hopelessly organised and Mr Sprott, an Old Etonian, spent much of the time bickering with Mrs Sprott, who made sure everyone knew that she was a general's daughter. When not bickering with each other, Mrs Sprott harangued the poor guide or anyone else who came within her orbit. They seemed quite content to run around tea estates, reveling in the residual vestiges of the Raj, and showed little interest in actually going on the river. Eventually I forced the issue and we found a 'country boat' for hire and we sailed from Tezpur to Guwhati.

Conditions on the Brahamaputra did not seem so different from the Irrawaddy, only everything was on a far grander scale. However, overall I was disappointed. First of all it was quite difficult to find the river, which might seem strange as it was clearly visible from the moon at the time of the Apollo missions.

Roads did not run parallel to the river and the crossing points were few. Once found, though beautiful and teaming with wildlife there was little human interest. Human interest is what Pandaw does best – the rivers we work on are buzzing with people fishing, trading, travelling and worshiping. On the Brahmaputra we did not see a soul. The main attractions were the wildlife parks, the principal being Kaziranga where we saw wild elephants and rhino. We visited several of these but they all seemed the same to me. Great for twitchers and wildlifers but I doubted if anyone would ever see the promised tigers.

Cultural sites, with the odd temple or ruined fort, whilst quaint enough, were not what you come all the way to India for. Logistics on the river would be difficult and the cruise would have to double back to Guwhati, the Assami capital, as water levels would not enable passage to Dibrugarh higher up and the obvious end point of such a cruise. Most of Assam, including all the parks, is flooded for about seven months a year, which makes for a short season. Then there was the fact that Assam was in a state of marital law following recent terrorist outbreaks. We were given an escort, armed with Lee Enfield 303 rifles, and the highways, bridges and airports were heavily patrolled.

Despite many a reservation however I remained cautiously enthusiastic and the plan was to build a boat in Burma and bring it in, local shipbuilding being of rather shoddy quality. Mr Sprott had brought me along on the understanding that we would be partners in such a venture so I was a surprised to receive a trade announcement some months later stating that he was going ahead himself, converting a local hulk that belonged to the Indian Inland Water Transport department. They made the best of a bad job and these cruises have been quite successful, if only because there were no alternatives on offer. I would return to India, but first the Mekong — 'the mother of waters' — beckoned and was to occupy time and energy for the next few years.

L ike Burma, Vietnam and Cambodia were by the late 1990s emerging from decades of political turmoil and isolation. I made my first recce there in 2001 and found the atmosphere very different from Rangoon, which by then had sunk into a torpor as a result of political division within the military, coupled with economic sanctions by the West. Saigon by contrast was abuzz with investors and opportunities. Doing business here seemed easier than Burma, there were clear roadmaps on how to do things, unlike in Burma where no one could make a decision and no one knew how to get things done.

I had been introduced to a potential local partner, a rather scary Vietnamese lady called Madame Thuy who was forever starring deep into my eyes and inviting me out for little suppers, something I skillfully evaded. Behind the elegance of the silken *ao dai*, (the long Vietnamese tunic, and trousers), there was a chilling asperity.

Saigon in 2001 was a city of bicycles. By 2010 it was a city of scooters and, at time of writing, it is fast becoming a city of cars. Great logjams of bikes gridlocked the city's principal intersections and taxis were strictly of the motorbike variety. To the city's credit it has retained a Frenchified colonial elegance, with splendid *belle epoque* public buildings like the General Post Office and the Opera.

Saigon remains a lovely city, perhaps the least architecturally debased of Southeast Asia's cities, more so even than Rangoon of which very little of the grand Victorian and Edwardian port I once knew and loved nowadays remains.

In business terms, it was all very unlike Burma. Ms Thuy had appointed a 'runner' called Mr Dong to take care of the project. Mr Dong was a person of dazzling efficiency. A fat file was produced showing research undertaken. Which ministries had to be involved (several), which authorities, agencies, and along the proposed river route, the local communist party offices, 'People's Police' units, tourism boards, and many other players. There was a sort of itemised checklist with price tags for each approval.

There was also a clear timeline. This was another world from Burma where, if bribes were to be paid, it was to ensure that the minister would not get involved, in other words 'paws off'.

The extraordinary thing is that fifteen years on I have yet to meet a Vietnamese general, minister, high official or indeed any official of any sort. Everything was taken care of by the ever-diligent Mr Dong at a fixed cost and on time.

I set off from Saigon on a speedboat hired for a few days so I could tour the Delta and connect to Cambodia. This was terrific fun and I had my bag of tape measures, knotted ropes and other bits of survey kit. Forgetting to pack a hat or sun block by the second day I was truly lobstered. The key thing was to find a routing and work out what design of ship would best make the passage from Saigon to Siem Reap.

No one had — at least since French Colonial times — linked the two countries by ship. Cambodia and Vietnam had been at war with each other in '70s , and in 1979 the Vietnamese had invaded Cambodia ousting the psychopathic dictator Pol Pot and his henchmen.
That was only fifteen years previously and the river border had remained closed to shipping, though tourist speedboats were just beginning to make the crossing.

Back in Saigon nearly everyone I talked to said such a project would be impossible. Relations between the two countries remained frosty. A protocol for river transport had been drafted but never signed. The border formalities would be insurmountable. The Vietnamese would never co-operate with the Cambodians or vice versa. It was impossible, even insane.

Exploring the delta backwaters, I worked out a route through avoiding low bridges, mainly made from American runway tracking and bits of tanks dating from the Vietnam War. There was only one bridge that was problematic, over the Cao Gao Canal. One would have thought that a foreigner going around photographing and measuring bridges would arouse suspicion but no one asked me anything. I was largely ignored as the Viets whizzed past on their bicycles going about their business.

Phnom Penh was very different and delightful. In the early 2000s most emerging Asian cities had very few cars and you could get about really quickly by cyclo, tuk-tuk or motorcycle taxi. Nowadays, whether in Saigon or Rangoon, Phnom Penh or Mandalay, it's all traffic gridlock, pollution and noise.

I met with our agents and various ministers. They were all very easygoing and said yes to everything but clearly were not going to do much, either to impede or encourage our project.

In Burma they would with glowing warmth, sincerity, and helpfulness say yes and then behind your back cause as many problems as possible simply in order to make a fortune by "fixing" them.

The Cambodians by contrast seemed too naturally comatose to get up too anything of that sort. Allegedly Cambodia has more generals than any country in the world, also more princes and princesses than any other monarchy, and no one has ever counted the number of ministers. In the Khmer elite anyone who is anyone gets a top government job and has to be addressed as 'Your Excellency'.

I still have lots of fun writing letters to the port agent addressed to 'Your Excellency'. At meetings you would be introduced to the assistant to the special advisor to the deputy minister's head of staff's personal assistant. Needless to say these government posts were not taken very seriously and office attendance was rare, if it happened at all.

Such appointments and titles, with their respective emoluments, resembled the offices and pensions handed out as part of a patronage network in old monarchic Europe, or the patron-client networks of the Roman Empire, where large chunks of a potentially troublesome population were happily maintained on hand outs It is not so very different from modern Europe with our socialistic bureaucracies, where

151

people have elaborate job descriptions but not much to do, so-called 'public service' being a kind of dole for the intelligentsia. It's the same old problem of what to do with a class of people who are educated but non-wealth producing.

I stayed in a concrete complex called the Cambodiana Hotel. It had been a Sofitel but the French hotel operator had long since 'de-flagged' as they say in that industry. It was very grim and populated by extremely shady characters, not the jolly carpetbaggers of Rangoon but rather sinister misfits from the Indochinese underworld.

On the river bank a great hulk of a ship lay moored. Now abandoned it had been a floating casino. Well, I thought, if they could get that up river to Phnom Penh there would be nothing to stop a Pandaw.

The days of the 1992-93 UN 'transitional authority' in Cambodia (UNTAC) were a recent memory. One friend told me that when she first opened an office there she had been advised to get a gun. When she told her boss she was a rotten shot he turned up at her apartment with an RPG launcher and told her that if someone came in just to point it in their general direction and fire. I asked where it was now and she said she chucked it off the Mekong Friendship Bridge.

Hold-ups in the street in the '80s and '90s were quite normal. Another friend was held up and asked for his wallet, then his watch, then his shirt, then his shoes, then his trousers and finally, yes, his underpants.

The real achievement of the UN was in disarming an entire population – giving boys bicycles and girls sewing machines in return for handing in their Kalashnikovs.

In Vietnam, the government official's first question is "What's in it for Vietnam?", while the second question would be "What's in it for me?" Always the greater good of country and people came first. In Burma, the first question would be "What can I avoid doing so I do not get into trouble for it later?" In Cambodia it was simply "What's in it for me?"

The Mekong was perfect for a river cruise with good end points at Siem Reap for Angkor and Saigon, both of which have airports. There was much of interest to visit along the river with some good excursions and the scenery was interesting. A two-country cruise linking two major tourist destinations had to be a winner. We would sail from the Saigon River all the way to Siem Reap across the hundred-mile wide Tonle Sap lake. We would confound the skeptics and chalk up another first. It was back to Rangoon and back to the drawing board to design the right ship.

With one bridge to get under we had to go for the Kwai-style fold down sun deck but the bridge was higher so we could have an upper deck. U Charlie, the naval architect, used a modern Chinese hull design, used on the old Myat Thanda, which had proved very efficient. In fact this ship remains our fastest ship and can hit 25kmph on flat water. U Soe Naing quickly had the hull laid in the shipyard at Thein Byu where now we had three hulls under simultaneous construction – Hull P3 to be launched as Pandaw III nearing completion for Burma, Hull K1 to be the Kwai Pandaw half-built and now Hull V1 which was to become the Mekong Pandaw.

There was a whirl of activity as several hundred workers hammered away, sparks flying from the welders.

As mentioned, I had spent a lot of impressionable time in my childhood in the shipyard where my father worked. The sights, sounds and above all smells are amongst my earliest memories and now flooded back, particularly the smells of oil and grease and burnt metal and brackish water. How I wished my father who died in a fire months before the maiden voyage of the Irrawaddy Princess had lived to see this. I had been told shipbuilding was dead and to go off and do something else. And here I was surrounded by ships under build, part designed by myself. I felt very proud to be the fifth generation of my family to be building ships, though the first not on the Clyde. My great-great grandfather had made the journey from Forfarshire to the Clyde to make his fortune about one hundred and fifty years before. My great grand father Robert had started at Fairfield's shipyard as an apprentice at twelve and ended up a director building battle ships for the Royal Navy.

All of Robert's brothers went to different parts of the world and ended up running shipyards: in Ireland, America and Australia and one remained in Scotland with Robert a fellow director at Fairfield's. Both my grandfather and father had been directors at John Brown's, my father ending up as chairman.

As for me, with a degree in history, my only training had consisted of those Saturday morning trips to John Brown's yard. Lack of formal training apart, it was in me – that gut feeling, the instinct of what is doable or not, when it came to ship design.

Back at Thein Byu, U Soe Naing's management systems were not coping to well with so much activity. Burmese shipbuilding was only financially viable so long as there was a plentiful supply of cheap labour. One could see that the moment labour costs went up, even fractionally, it would all fall flat. (This is exactly what had happened on the River Clyde by the mid twentieth century.) For each worker actually working there would be three or four overseers. One man would be welding and four watching. Other watchers would be watching the watchers. Thus in the shipyard you had a microcosm of the Burmese state.

Theft was a major cost, the most common form being welding rods hidden down worker's *longyis*. One welding rod was worth more than a day's pay. Get several out and you were onto a winner. (This was not unlike Clydebank where most families managed to get a new carpet when they were fitting out the QE2, in this case carpet rolls were rolled up inside trouser legs.)

There was a bizarre attempt at strip searches at the yard gates that proved rather half-hearted. Another problem was power, the city supply was erratic and inefficient and U Soe Naing had several generators running to power the welding machines. This cost a fortune in fuel. I asked U Soe Naing why he needed so many managers and other hangers-on who did not do much and he came up with a very Burmese explanation. If you are an owner in Burma you have to take care of all around you, your relatives, your friends children, even their nephews and nieces, you cannot say no to anyone. Thus any enterprise in Burma becomes a little welfare state of its own, again a microcosm of the state itself. I do not think U Soe Naing made a lot of money out of these builds, but that was not the priority.

This business model might be compared with U Win Pe and the Irrawaddy Princess, but in U Win Pe case it was about domination and exploitation. U Win Pe model reflected the Burmese Slorc military government's exploitative style whilst U Soe Naing's was rooted more in the more socially equitable times of the Burmese Road to Socialism.

In between meetings, I would wander off and explore the shipyards that strung along the shore of Strand Road. Ours belonged to the Port Authority and here lay a graveyard of abandoned vessels: tugs light ships, pilot ships and yards full of buoys as big as cars left to rust ashore. Sheds lay full of long abandoned machinery, plate rollers and cutters, I think all dating from Burma's brief economic resurgence after the War.

These yards were living again, heaving with workers, many were boys in their early teens that seemed to be the brightest, keenest and most able. It felt like being transported back to the time of my great-grandfather on the Clyde, the banter of cheeky apprentices and the curses of the gaffers. There is a fantastic sense of camaraderie around building a ship: the pride is palpable.

By the summer of 2002 V1, or the Mekong Pandaw as she was to be named, was finished in record time and I flew out for trials. It was decided to take her up to Prome and back, and to fully test her before sending her across the water.

What could have been a relatively pleasant three-day cruise across the Irrawaddy Delta became something of an endurance test as our hotel director Ghilberto announced he was joining us to check on hotel fittings.

As with Pandaw I, II and III, the Mekong Pandaw made a stately progress through the Twante Canal that divides the vast 1,000-square mile Delta between the Irrawaddy and Yangon rivers, under the direction of U Soe Naing, stopping at shrines great and small as instructed by Sayarmargyi back in her Rangoon nunnery in a sort of Buddhist route map, a riverine path to banking higher levels of karma for the benefit of ship, crew and all who would sail in her.

In addition to religious observances there was a great deal of testing to be done. The engineers fine-tuning their machinery and Ghilberto checking the accommodation and hotel side.

G hilberto was an Italo-Scot who had joined us the year before from the Savoy Hotel in Rangoon. He had come to Scotland in his teens to work at the famous Gleneagles Hotel and stayed on. I am not sure how he ended up in Burma but he joined us at a key juncture.

As the ships were getting better and better in terms of design and quality the service side had lagged behind. Various expatriate hotel managers had been tried and found wanting, unable to cope with the general eccentricities of Burma or the isolation of running boats up river. Ghilberto had a way with the Burmese that I have never encountered before or since. He broke every rule in the book – shouting, swearing, punching, slapping, kicking — and they still loved him. If any other foreigner behaved like that they would be on a plane out of the country, assuming they escaped a long stretch in a Burmese jail.

And Ghilberto got results. He inspired the Burmese. He was their *sayar* or teacher. For many of our crew who were trained by Ghilberto he remains their *sayar* to this day. They often ask me about him, and I tell them that he is retired now and living near us in Edinburgh.

156

Short, almost as wide in girth as he was tall, unlit cheroot in slobbering mouth, he would stomp the decks chiding the crew, lavishing insults on all within range, moaning about the uselessness of all things Burmese. The crew would watch filled with awe and admiration, as if he was some nat or spirit god incarnate who was there to be propitiated.

Of course he was a relatively benign nat, outstandingly generous and giving away half his salary each month on presents and entertainments for the crew. They knew there was no malice in his ranting, rather it was all part of the great theatre of life.

Over and over again I have had managers come in and try and introduce modern management systems. It just does not work. Manuals and handbooks to the Burmese are merely symbolic. Instead they respond to charisma, generosity and the example of excellence. Your MBA types may have all the answers but they are not going to work in a place like Burma. The ancient business model of sayar surrounded by his disciples, an extended business family, bonded through affection and admiration is the only way to get results.

Roser and I started this way, Ghilberto brought in the polish, and still to this day with a dozen ships we follow the family model that inspires such loyalty. This is how we have achieved such inspirational levels of service and devotion to the task.

A week on the ship with Ghilberto was something of a challenge. For one thing his monologues could go on uninterrupted for several hours at a time. One morning he stomped into the dining room, where he had set up a temporary office with all his lists and papers, lit his smelly black cheroot and embarked on a monologue that continued unabated till dinner time, I think nearly ten hours in all, with a couple of brief visits to the loo. A system of acolytes had developed whereby there would be a respectful crew member at his side nodding and every couple of hours they would swap over.

"Now Ronnie, he was room service manager, he took the tea to the Arab sheikh in the morning and the sheikh he say where is

157

Ghilberto? so Ronnie come and get me and I take tea to his highness then he give me a gold watch, look I wear it now... What the fuck are you doing you little shit? No not there over there.... Anyway the bastards wanted to put microwave in the pantry, I say you do that I resign, matter of principal, so I resign and go to Africa where I sleep with 1000 women, I was there six months so do the maths....Switch of that fucking machine and get out. The bloody Burmese totally useless every one…" and so on.

Ghilberto's main side kick was one rather creepy Burmese called Kyaw Kyaw Zin who handled his book-keeping and ran circles round him with the creative accounting. There was a famous moment when Kyaw Kyaw Zin was being particularly irritating and Ghilberto threw a massive punch and then somehow mid air remembered that he should not be punching a colleague and diverted his hand down to the table breaking his wrist on impact.

Thus we chugged across the Delta towards Prome: U Soe Naing spending most of his time in prayer, meditation and trips ashore to make offerings at key shrines and Ghilberto thumping about, intermittently moaning and shouting and rambling on.

Things were going well. The trials had been a success, the ship – our first with inboard engines – achieving good speeds. We reached Prome and it was time to take our leave, Ghilberto would bring her back to Yangon and prepare her for passage to Saigon and U Soe Naing, his team and I were to return to Yangon by road. The office had sent up a comfy air conditioned car for me and I offered U Soe Naing and his brother seats. U Soe Naing stood on the river bank, holding a sort of plastic mesh shopping basket in which you could see his tooth brush, wash kit, and a couple of spare shirts and *longyis,* ever the humble village Burman, and looked disapprovingly at my car. "I must return with my children by bus", he said as he humbly pointed at his motley bunch of engineers, carpenters and one crewmen returning home. Put to shame, I felt it was not very comradely to jump in my car (a thirty year old Toyota and hardly a limo) and said I would come with them and the car went back empty.

At the bus station there was a great choice of companies offering a service from Rangoon to Prome. Needless to say U Soe Naing went for the cheapest. This was an old Japanese bus with plate glass windows that would not open. Inevitably the air conditioner did not work and it stopped everywhere and took ten hours instead of the usual five.

Captain Rob had been contracted to arrange delivery to Saigon and flew into Rangoon to prepare the ship. Having already exported the Kwai ship we felt confident now on the procedures and the Ministry of Transport were more confident as well. The documentation this time went quite smoothly. However at the last minute a huge fuss was made about the dangers of the voyage.

What if the Mekong Pandaw were to sink in the Rangoon River and block the channel? Actually the channel is about half a mile wide, but in the end I was persuaded to sign an indemnity for twenty million dollars, thankfully without collateral. Then, as with the Kwai ship, they refused to let a Myanmar crew go with the ship. It was too dangerous to endanger Myanmar lives. Considering that every day thousands of Myanmar sailors put out to sea in rickety fishing boats, rust-bucket coasters and sundry unseaworthy craft, this did seem like rank hypocrisy.

Rob, returned to Thailand and managed to put together a crew of 'old mates' mainly Aussie yachtsman up for a bit of a challenge. For navigation Rob had a compass and a hand held GPS, and for communications a hand held VHF radio and a portable satphone, that I had smuggled into the country.

They set off and I was home in Scotland sitting by the phone day and night in case he called. In the first week Rob called in regularly, mainly to get me to go online and relay weather reports. Then there was a silence. A most dreadful silence. I would lie awake all night

159

waiting for the phone to ring. After a few days I began to panic. I put out the alert and started calling harbour masters in ports along the Andaman coast. I tried Rannong, Langkawi and eventually they were sighted moored in Chalong Bay in Phuket. Rob and his mates, being paid on a daily rate, had decided to stop off there for a bit of R&R, on expenses.

After many a pleading call they were all located in assorted bars and nightclubs and persuaded back on board continued the voyage. They reached Singapore a week later where the engines broke down and expensive repairs had to be undertaken. Eventually, a month after departure heading up over the South China Sea, the ship limped into the Saigon River.

On the Mekong

We had planned to moor alongside in the city centre, a short stroll from the main hotels, shopping and restaurant areas. Instead we found ourselves up against a great concrete wharf in the international container base. When the tide was out it was necessary to descend down rickety ladders and enter via the sundeck. Overshadowed by bulk carriers at either side we seemed to be lost in a dark canyon. The port authority had decided that as we were flagged Burmese we were an international ship and put us in the container base some distance from the city centre.

The majority of passengers booked on the Mekong Pandaw's maiden voyage were Japanese as one of the investors was a Japanese travel corporation. Carrying Japanese passengers is never easy as everything has to be planned to the minute and if something goes wrong they tend not to take it in their stride, and end up demanding massive compensation.

In frontline environments like Burma, Cambodia or Vietnam this is a recipe for disaster. The other passengers booked were an English tour group who had not been told that this was an inaugural cruise that had never been attempted before. Readers can guess where this is going...

Pottering around, the passengers not due for another half hour or so, the crew off on one of their union regulated breaks (Communist Vietnam had very strict working hours that did not apply well to ships) I was suddenly confronted by the arrival on the wharf of a coach of mainly elderly Japanese ladies. I picked up the intercom and called – no one came. I tried the Tannoy — no one came. I attempted calling out — no one came.

So there I was on day one of the inaugural voyage personally helping these fragile ladies on board down wobbly ladders, seeing to the baggage, handing out room keys, and getting very flustered. Sorted,

161

the crew then appeared from their break and seemed quite oblivious to my predicament. First lesson learnt: the Vietnamese are not the most flexible of people.

The other passengers arrived and we were all set to go. We had planned the entire voyage and designed the ship around setting out from Saigon city port down through the Delta canals to join one of the Mekong's main channels at My Tho. There was one bridge that caused concern but I had twice visited it at low tide and was convinced that we could get under. No one had really believed me and when we reached the bridge the captain refused to pass beneath it. Again indemnities were signed in which I agreed to take full responsibility on pain of all I owned, or at least life imprisonment in the 'Hanoi Hilton'. Low water was at dusk and I went up with my measuring rope and checked once again and was reassured we would get under. The fake funnel was dismantled, as intended, to reduce airdraft and the ship made ready to pass under the dreaded bridge. I went up onto the road bridge with a walkie-talkie to direct the captain and the ship edged forwards. What I did not tell the captain was that the Mekong Pandaw just scraped under with about 20cm to spare. He still does not know that.

The Mekong Pandaw was already exhibiting engine troubles, the strain of the sea crossing on a poorly designed inboard propulsion system designed for a river navigation had been too much for her. By the end of that first season they had given up the ghost and costly tugs had to be contracted to pull us along. New engines and shafts were then installed in the rest up period and the ship has run well since.

On leaving Saigon we had gone through elaborate port formalities as if we were a ship departing on an international voyage as in theory the Mekong had been designated an international waterway. There was port clearance, immigration, customs, quarantine, deratting, safety inspections and other formalities normal for a ship's departure – at some point dozens of uniformed officials had over run the vessel and several hours later we were allowed to sail.

162

Three days later here we were on the Vietnam-Cambodia border and the entire process was repeated, again dozens of officials appeared and at one point the Mekong Pandaw, moored mid stream had a flotilla of launches moored around her. All these people needed to be entertained to drinks in the bar and meals in the dining room and expected to walk off with cartons of cigarettes, bottles of whisky and nice fat brown envelopes. We were a whole day on the Vietnamese side when amazingly we were cleared to cross over to the Cambodian side.

At this point we lowered the Vietnamese courtesy flag and raised the Cambodian one. Being quite organized we had purchased a Cambodian flag from a flag shop in Rangoon and were feeling rather smug about our efficiency. However when the first batch of Cambodian officials came on board there was some consternation. Apparently this was the old Khmer Rouge flag. For short time we were flagged as a vessel of Pol Pot's navy.

We had moved about a hundred metres up the river to the Cambodian side of the border and lowered our anchor. We had had a team of people down on the border for a couple of days before to prime the officials and get them ready.

It had been important to get the day right. Imagine if we had crossed on one of the 100 (or so it seemed) gazetted public holidays in the Cambodian calendar – that tend to become long weekends. We might have been stuck on the border for several days.

Then the first boats appeared, not the mere flotilla of the Vietnamese with perhaps half a dozen or so, but a veritable armada of various craft, large and small, bearing a full task force of Cambodian officials high and low. The Viets seemed minimalistic by comparison. The ship was over run by inspectors and officials of every conceivable department. Busloads of these functionaries had been transported down from Phnom Penh to the border in anticipation, a sort of civil servants works outing. They took over the entire dining room, each table turned into a desk so the place resembled a Cambodian government office. I sought sanctuary in the ship's back office only to

163

find the French manager comforting the Vietnamese secretaries who were all crying hysterically with the trauma of it all. Passengers were getting restless and free drinks arranged on the sundeck that the abstemious Japanese disdained and the Brits helped themselves to copiously, though it only seemed to make them grumpier than ever.

One issue was that, as the river border was then rarely crossed other than by the occasional intrepid backpacker, the Cambodian immigration officials only kept a small number of visa stickers in the little hut that acted as border post. A man had to be sent on a scooter to Phnom Penh, at least four hours away, to collect more.

By the end of the second day, the ship's stocks of whisky, cigarettes and brown envelopes near depleted, we saw them off. The Japanese investor glared at me for my hopelessness. A meeting was demanded in which humiliated, I was to apologise and then bow in accepted Japanese style, presenting a small gift from the ship to each passenger. I managed to evade that one.

The Brits gnashed their teeth and grimaced at my inefficiency. I felt strangely elated.

The ship's company had been much augmented at the instance of various Cambodian officials. There was a group of pilots who spent most of their time eating and sleeping. An unarmed police escort also spent most of its time eating and sleeping and various 'advisers' were seconded to assist us in planning and logistics who also spent most of their time eating and sleeping. The channel from the border to Phnom Penh is deep and well marked so we made a quick night passage and arrived in port first thing. This was a big moment and again elation was in the air. The passengers were keen to get off the ship and explore after two days stuck at the border. Then horror of horrors we espied another great swell of officials, in their much-decorated uniforms, milling on the wharf waiting to board.

These were the exact same ones who had held us at the border and had been whisked up by over night coach to receive us in Phnom Penh International Port. Thus the nightmare began all over again, the dining room converted into a Kafka-esque government office – the quarantine, the de-ratting, the customs, immigration, port authority, police, pilots, etc., etc., all over again.

Thus it was on one voyage from Saigon to Phnom Penh we had four sets of formalities to undergo. This remains the same to this day but we have speeded them up considerably and at one point sponsored the re-equipping of the Cambodian border post with a fax machine so we could send them passenger lists in advance and mobile phones so we could call to get them all ready as the ship approached. These days we are over the border in a couple of hours, not a couple of days.

Tensions on board ran rife. The Japanese investor, a minor shareholder at that, insisted on lording it over crew and passengers. The elderly Japanese ladies, many of whom seemed in some way related or connected to him did not seem to mind his imperious attitude. But when he deliberately dropped his napkin on the floor as the German chef came past and told him to pick it up the German chef not surprisingly and in no uncertain terms told him where to go.

Whereas I, the majority shareholder, toiled night and day to keep the show on the road, coaxing a reluctant captain and doubtful engineers, the Japanese investor insisted on VIP treatment. This thoroughly infuriated the British, who were after all paying guests.

The Brits became more and more disgruntled as each day passed and it turned out had not been primed by their tour operator that this was an 'expedition' in every sense of the word.

They could not understand why scheduling was well nigh impossible. Their collective unhappiness was exacerbated by the presence of their tour leader, an overzealous lady called Donna, who would follow me around trying to extract information as to times of arrivals to pass on to her clients.

On one occasion, as I was struggling with a chart and compass quite lost in the midst of the great Tonle Lake, deep in a heated argument with the Cambodian pilot, Donna appeared at the wheel house door and enquired "Paul, what time is the village stop?". Now in twenty years of running river trips this has been the only occasion (so far) when I have lost my temper: "Donna, will you fuck off!"

Half the passengers heard it too. In fact, as the voyage progressed and timings became more and more abstract I realized that I had become a hate figure amongst the British. They were blaming me for everything that was going wrong and giving little credit for all the things that were going right – like the ship actually doing the impossible. The young French manager proved totally useless, he spent most of his time hiding deep on the bowels of the ship where the back office was located, surrounded by Vietnamese secretaries, doing unknown stuff on the computer. It proved impossible to extract him from there so I made a mental note to fire him at the end of the voyage.

Managers glued all day to computers has been the greatest human resource challenge we have faced over the years, which is why I prefer the older generation of manager, like Ghilberto, who are out an about all day and not hiding away pretending to be engrossed in something of vital importance.

Sitting behind a computer is not going to get a kitchen clean or fix a broken engine. Sadly we are beginning to run out of the older breed. There have been times when I have removed all computers from ships so the managers can get on with the real job without distraction.

Gone then were the euphoric early days of Burma, when we were cheered on by a bunch of adoring eighty year olds who had made it through the Japanese occupation. I wish Roser had been with me but she was home in Spain looking after our four year old and I felt very alone, perceived as a conman, failing to deliver what had been promised (we had missed that village stop) and there were murmurings of compensation claims to be made on returning home.

I was confronted by an angry group of men in the bar, blamed for the preferential treatment of the Japanese were receiving, which was quite untrue, but in their feverish cabins this myth had built up as the days went by. When they disembarked at the end a number of passengers refused to shake my hand, heading off down the gang plank with angry shakes of the head. Clearly my people skills had taken a turn for the worse.

Wistfully I recalled those early maiden voyages of seven years before on the Irrawaddy and Chindwin – the three cheers for Paul and Roser, the presentation of a souvenir gift after a whip round by grateful passengers, once home the dozens of adulatory letters that fell each morning onto the doormat. It felt like a huge failure, I was depressed and deflated – so much hard work and effort by so many, so much risk (my own home on the line once again).

All of that angst disguised the reality: that it had been an enormous success. We had cracked the border and got a ship from Vietnam into Cambodia confounding all predictions. The twin evils of Vietnamese red tape and the Cambodian mafia had been overcome. A flat-bottomed ship had been built in Burma, sailed all the way round South-East Asia under its own power and all the way up the Mekong to be the first large vessel ever to cross the hundred-mile Tonle Lake. All this with a 'work to rule' crew, a captain who said no to everything and pilots who did not want you to go anywhere, oh and constant engine problems.

At the end of the cruise I fired the French manager and the German chef walked off in huff. Not surprisingly, I felt like doing the same myself but unfortunately could not. I was stuck on a floating nightmare. Here I am at the time of writing still stuck twelve years later with variations of the same nightmares.

We needed some quick fixes. Clearly the Vietnamese with their union rules and inflexible working times were not suited to run a hotel — ship. I called Ghilberto and got him over to Phnom Penh as quickly as possible with a team of key Burmese. They soon slotted in and took over the running of the ship and almost immediately things improved. At the same time most of the Vietnamese hotel team were dropping out, unable to take the stress and daily trauma. Quite how they won three wars, successively against the French, the Americans and the

Chinese, remains a great mystery. Clearly the Viets had softened since the days of Dien Bien Phu or the Ho Chi Min Trail.

In their place we hired Cambodians who are more flexible and service-orientated. We found the Vietnamese made good deck crew and engineers and thus evolved our tradition on the Mekong of Khmer hotel teams, Viet marine crews and Burmese managers who, being neutral, held it all together. Again people said that the two traditional Indo-Chinese enemies would end up killing each other but other than one occasion, when a rather large Cambodian house keeper punched a rather small Vietnamese captain for changing the mess TV from a Khmer to a Vietnamese station, tensions have been low. On a ship the ship is your country and other loyalties soon fade into the background.

Cambodia was of course a democracy of sorts, not like the military dictatorship of Burma. As a democracy it seemed to get unlimited aid and the entire economy fed off the NGO gravy train. As a result most people had given up doing anything, even fruit and vegetables were shipped in from Vietnam or Thailand. They made nothing. Smart new highways were constructed by guilty donor countries but they had little traffic on them as the Khmers conducted little business.

Sanctioned Burma by contrast was a hive of activity as people fended for themselves. They grew things still and made things too. In the Phnom Penh of the early 2000s, where the bulk of traffic seemed to be UN agency land cruisers, 'the economy' amounted to whatever trickled down from aid workers. The average NGO expat cost about $250,000 per year (even then) to maintain, and this went on chauffeurs, servants and secretaries.

We had a real recruitment problem as the educated classes were used to unrealistically high NGO salaries and to not doing very much to earn them.

Ten years on this has all changed as the Chinese have arrived and are now running everything, they have been far more efficient at firing up the economy than the NGOs with their gravy train. Now its all gone 'modern' with unfinished high rise flats and traffic jams. Real progress.

Cambodia's democracy consisted of a highly venerated and largely ceremonial constitutional monarchy and a strongman leader, Hun Sen, who is of course democratically elected in periodic free and fair elections monitored by any number of UN and EU agencies.

His popularity is evident from the fact that his party always wins and he has been in continuous power now since the 1970s when an invading Vietnamese army ousted Pol Pot and put him in power, apparently forgiving his youthful indiscretions as a Khmer Rouge cadre himself.

Because Cambodia has free and fair elections it gets lots of aid and other help. After the rigours of Burma, how free one felt working in a democracy. Any democracy has of course a free press with nosey journalists. One night in port there had been a minor fire in the galley, the fire brigade were called, came very quickly, and demanded an enormous sum of money to put it out so instead the crew very efficiently dealt with the fire whilst they watched from the pontoon.

Then a car full of journalists arrived, no doubt tipped off by the fire brigade, they also demanded an enormous sum of money or they would print the story.

On another occasion a thief was caught on board and the police were called. The police said it was really none of their business and the crew should deal with the thief how they saw fit. At this point the story becomes confused but it seems that the thief, whose hands had been bound, jumped over the side of the ship to try and swim for it. Other versions say he was pushed. In any case, he washed up on the riverbank the next morning drowned. This time the police did arrive whisked away the body and collected hush money from a terrified crew.

By the time I heard about it a few hours later and demanded from the port police a full investigation the body had been very speedily cremated. The purser, a Karen, then behaved very suspiciously and fled the country, so there may well have been something in the story that he was pushed rather than jumped. We will never know, but the finger of suspicion pointed at that purser.

Staggeringly, the very next day there was a further trauma when, moored up at Kampong Cham, and in the heat of the afternoon the crew decided to take a dip in the river and a young cook was swept away.

That was a very painful and distressing episode, and it has happened again in 2012 in Burma to an experienced engineer who likewise took a quick dip at Katha and was washed away. This is why we are strict on not allowing either our passengers or crew to swim in these fast and dangerous rivers.

Cambodia, with its army of expat advisors, had introduced international style labour laws intended to protect employee rights. These were based more on the French model where labour rights consist of the right to a job for life from which you cannot be sacked. As in France, in Cambodia if you tried to fire anyone they would go immediately to a labour tribunal and bring the wrath of the government down upon you.

The only way out would be to not only pay the employee off, but also numerous officials. A fairly normal claim would be for several years' salary, holiday pay, legal costs, compensation and penalties. Thus an employee earning say $12,000 a year would put in a claim for over $100,000. One such case went on for five years and ended up in the high court with a sort of silent auction as to who would pay the judge most, which was obviously intended to be us.

We got round this eventually by signing all crew to our Singapore management company. Clearly French-style employment laws are a barrier to entry for any potential investor. For that reason, if you were going to build a factory somewhere Cambodia would be your last choice.

The Cambodians are the most charming and pleasant people on the planet though in some cases just that little bit too charming. One season we lost a number of waitresses to single male travellers, mainly

Australians. These girls had a full week to work on an array of 50 or 60-something travelling divorcees, followed up by correspondence and further visits.

After this experience we tended to employ homelier types. One such was the large housekeeping lady who had slapped the Vietnamese captain. She spoke very good English, and as a housekeeper had a good contact with passengers as she made up their rooms and could linger on chatting away. There would be a long tail of woe of how she came from a poor family, wanted to go to university and get an education, and to get away from this poorly-paid job on Pandaw (actually we pay more than any of the hotels).

Nice gullible travellers would come to an arrangement to sponsor her through university for the years to come. I believe that at one point she had several monthly remittances coming in and most certainly did not relinquish her supposedly ill-paid post on a Pandaw.

Then there was the guide I overheard, rather shabbily dressed with unkempt hair, who as the end of the tour gave the group a heart rendering tale of woe, poverty and the struggle to educate her children, of being a single parent and victim of Pol Pot's terror squads. There would be a whip round and a very generous honorarium presented. I watched her shuffle off to the car park in her tatty sarong and fish out of her handbag the keys of a brand new Land Cruiser.

Worst of all was the case of the orphanage at Kampong Cham. We were keen to find a project to support and involve our passengers in as we had done in Burma. We approached any number of NGOs who would disdainfully tell us that they had enough funding thank you, so awash was Cambodia in donor cash. We found an orphanage just outside Kampong Cham. The director had a number of projects that he needed help with – a new accommodation block, a water tower, a basketball court to name but a few amenities, all of which we agreed to fully fund. Despite this, we could never persuade him to put up signs saying things like "Donated by Pandaw Passengers".

Then we found other organisations sponsoring the orphanage who had donated a new accommodation block, a water tower, a basketball court, etc. In fact I think each of these projects were sponsored several times over. Meanwhile the director was sporting a brand new Rolex of the non-fake variety, and had a latest Land Cruiser outside his house.

Such is the story of aid in democratic Cambodia. Meanwhile in non-democratic Burma none of the big charities or aid donors would go in, largely because they were encouraged to stay away. However, the Cambodian experience suggest that might have been a good thing as it made people become creative and productive, an interesting case of good motives having bad effects that in turn lead to good outcomes. Such is the moral minefield which we have tried to tiptoe through for the last 20 years.

By the end of the first season on the Mekong (2002-03) we had worked out our routing and stabilized the bureaucracy, or rather the kleptocracy. A dozen years on and we still have the same problems of four sets of formalities per voyage, police escorts, expensive but useless pilots and all the other Cambodian turns of the screw designed to extract money from us. In fact after that maiden voyage such things were set in stone and it has proved impossible to renegotiate them.

The real issue was what to do about our Vietnamese partner Madame Thuy. Not content with providing various profitable services, she had moved to impose an exorbitant administration fee. At the same time she was constantly intimidating the Vietnamese crew who seemed to live in fear of her. No doubt this was to ensure she got a cut in on all the scams going on. For example, the very communist split of fuel money – the supplier would bill us for 12,000 litres but only deliver 10,000 and split the profits with the captain and chief who would then give a share to every member of the crew. In Burma they would never be so egalitarian, but then scams there were on a less ambitious scale. Madame Thuy wanted her cut of this and the food budget and many other things, which included a percentage of every crewman's salary. She would come down in her limousine and harangue the crew. Not being a Vietnamese speaker, I still do not know what she would say to them but there was terror in their eyes.

Clearly if we were to make a success of the Mekong operation she had to go, but how? With so complex a web of permits and contracts we were well and truly ensnared. I struck on a plan. The ship had been only temporarily registered as Vietnamese yet remained officially registered in Burma under a Burmese flag and the ownership of our Burmese company. We had discovered that the port authorities in Vietnam and Cambodia treated us as an international shipping line. They were only interested in collecting their port dues and as the Mekong between Saigon and Phnom Penh had been designated an international waterway a ship flying any third country's flag could ply it. In fact there was no need at all for the joint venture and many permits and licences that Madame Thuy and her then sidekick Mr. Dong had collected; they were superfluous.

By this point Mr. Dong had fallen out with Madame Thuy and we let him in on the plan and he agreed to co-operate and smooth over any issues with the port or other authorities. We waited until the last cruise of the season to reduce the danger of interruption and sent the order to change the flag back to Myanmar and appointed another company to take care of the ground handling services.

I expected a bad reaction from Madame Thuy but nothing prepared me for quite how bad a reaction. The ship was about to sail and the port authorities had given us clearance, which involves submitting a crew and passenger manifest. Once that has been submitted it is not permitted to change any crew or indeed passengers. The vessel must arrive on the border with the exact same complement as on manifest as when it set out from the port. Madame Thuy moved fast and we suddenly found ourselves without a captain. Without the listed captain the port authorities would not let the vessel sail. We had fifty passengers effectively trapped onboard.

It turned out the captain had been kidnapped and was being held in an apartment in downtown Saigon. His mobile went unanswered and his wife with no idea where he was. Madame then called me and demanded $100,000 for his release. I refused. A day went by, the passengers were getting very restless stuck on a ship that was going no where, moored up in the insalubrious My Tho industrial port next to the Fosters brewery.

The Americans on board were calling their consulate demanding to be rescued. Visions of a special forces-style rescue mission loomed. Madame Thuy was becoming incoherent, her calls hysterical and garbled. What we had not planned for is that in Vietnam if you make someone lose face it is tantamount to assassination, a public humiliation from which there is no going back. Confronting the Vietnamese, as twentieth century history has shown, is not a pleasant prospect. Pick a fight with a shrew of Madame Thuy's stamp and the ensuing conflict is going to be formidable. Fortunately our old friend Tootzi, Madame Thuy's nominal boss in Bangkok, got involved and negotiated a lesser pay off that would save face. The captain was returned and the ship sailed. Just before sailing our nice Austrian manager walked off, stressed to the extreme and unable to take any more.

Despite all of these challenges we could see that the future was on the Mekong not in Burma and it was decided to send Pandaw III over in April 2003, this time by tug: I could not face further Captain Rob dramas. The tug delivery went very smoothly and worked out a lot cheaper than Captain Rob and his merry gang of Phuket pirates.

Meanwhile the Mekong Pandaw had to be re-engined and we began to discover that the Vietnamese shipyards were technically very able to do high quality work, on time and on budget. Mr. Dong transferred to us full time and remains with us today taking care of the engineering and shipyard side of our operation. After an inaugural year of hell we discovered that Vietnam is a brilliant place to get things done, thanks to an innate efficiency. It seems that any new investor is made to run the gauntlet and the Vietnamese, from high official to shopkeeper, will do their best to fleece you and chase you out penniless. Survive, and you have earned their respect and they will take good care of you. So it is for us today. Likewise Vietnamese employees will regard the foreigner as a fool until he or she has proved their mettle, then they will be very loyal. In Burma the opposite was true, and foreigners put on pedestals in perverse parody of colonial-era racialism, this time imposed by the Burmese on the foreigner, so that responsibility can be abnegated to the ever-expendable expatriate.

To this day the Mekong, a two-country operation (and two very different countries at that), remains a daunting administrative challenge. Fourteen years on and none of the issues of that first cruise have been fully resolved. It is a human resource challenge too as, being so complex an operation, managers tend not to last long but we have evolved a system of employing very good local managers who tend to carry the expats. It works, and numerous other companies with ships of their own have copied us. Infuriating as this is, there is something to be said for the annoying platitude 'imitation is the highest form of flattery'. At one point we had five ships on the Mekong and there must be another half dozen competitor ships. Some of these are really very nice and do justice to the Mekong and others are hideous, catering for a cheaper middle market, which brings the destination down. We have to stay one step ahead and come up with new ideas and itineraries but the pack is always hot on our tail.

Dramas and adventures still pop up from time to time. There was the case of the sunken fish farm when the Mekong Pandaw captain lost control of the steering on the Chau Doc canal and the ship veered off course and hit a floating fish farm, sinking it instantly with its cages of sea bass, fortunately without loss of human life. The ship was immediately arrested by the local People's Police and held pending the payment of compensation. The enormous sum of $75,000 was demanded. I put the matter in the hands of our insurers in London who very promptly sent an assessor up from Saigon. This was then a day's drive away and then a further day was spent in negotiation with the police and the fish farm owner who eventually agreed to a settlement of $25,000. Lloyds of London faxed over a promissory note for that amount and the fish farmer and police looked at this piece of paper as if we were attempting an elaborate joke. Instead we managed to ring round a few contacts in Saigon and gather that much cash to courier up the next day and the ship was released.

The passengers were amazingly understanding and there were no calls this time to embassies for heli-evacuations. I think they were all enjoying the drama as it unfolded.

In 2008 we built our first ship in Vietnam, the Orient Pandaw which was a spectacular success, project managed by the ubiquitous Mr. Dong. The build process tells a lot about how the Vietnamese go about things. We took the ship builders and showed them over the Tonle Pandaw telling them that we wanted to copy it identically. A team then went over it with measuring tapes, noting down every detail, photographing every nut, bolt and weld. They went away for a very long time and I had more or less given up on them when they came back to me with a dossier some centimeters thick with a price calculation showing the cost of every nut, bolt, and weld. It was a masterpiece of detail. On being asked if they could build a ship as good as the Burmese models, nationalist hackles rose. Theirs would be better, much better and I did not doubt them. Dong found a carpenter who could make the cabins, a Mr. Phuoc. I insisted that he build a sample cabin so we could test it for quality and accuracy of reproduction. I was taken to Mr. Phuoc's shop house in one of the remoter Saigon suburbs and there in the front room was confronted by an enormous wooden cube. I entered and there was the perfect Pandaw cabin, every detail perfect and indeed better than the original. Phuoc got the job. We have now built five ships in Vietnam and Mr. Phuoc has long since left his shop house for an elegant villa and his scooter given up for BMW coupé. That is Vietnam.

The country is of course a former French colony, and visitors love to revel in the belle epoque architecture, the survival of the baguette and other Gallicisms. France was but one of several influences on Vietnamese culture and character. The most defining is of course Confucianism from China but in the shipyards I also identified a strong Teutonic influence. Surprising as this may sound, I reckoned this came about through the close relationship during communist times with Russia and its allies, in particular with East Germany. Many of the engineers I worked with spoke German, not French, and their technical thoroughness clearly came from the German engineering tradition, training and experience.

On the river in Burma there is so much to see and discover that itineraries are pointless and you could stop anywhere and find lots to see and do. But on the Mekong there was less of cultural interest outside of Phnom Penh and of course Angkor. The real story here was the human interest, and the extraordinary contrast between two peoples – the Vietnamese in their delta busy making things and going about their business and the Cambodians rarely stirring for even the slightest activity. Such contrasting peoples is one of the extraordinary features about the Mekong, which is the twelfth largest river in the world and seventh in Asia that flows for 4,350km through no fewer than six countries China, Burma, Laos, Thailand, Cambodia and Vietnam.

You could not find six countries more different from each other linguistically, ethnically and culturally. In French colonial times it took longer for an official sent to take up duties in Laos to sail by river steamer from Saigon to Luang Prabang than by ocean liner from Paris to Saigon. Such is the immensity of the Mekong as it traverses Indochina. There is so much more to navigate beyond the Khone Falls and into Laos. Future projects beckon and in 2015 year we successfully pioneered the Red River in North Vietnam, from Halong Bay to the edge of the Tonkinese Alps and from Vientiane in Laos to the 'Golden Triangle' between Laos, Burma and Thailand. In 2016 we plan to go a stage further up the Mekong into China. More firsts for Pandaw.

Disaster in Burma

In April 2003 I was in Rangoon to see off Pandaw III to the Mekong. Following the success of our operation on that river we needed a second ship in Cambodia. This time we were not taking any chances with a manned delivery and had arranged a tugboat to come up from Singapore to collect her and take her to Saigon, a voyage of three weeks.

There was an emotional moment as I stood in the bridge, the last man on board on an eerily empty ship. Never before have I been the only man on board a ship, all systems off, the silence almost sinister. I stepped onto the Nanthida Jetty on Strand Road and she was cast off, the tug pulling her, stately and splendid as ever, into the mid channel. We had plated up the bow section and covered all windows in plywood, hatches had been sealed and all movables like furniture lashed down. I had photos of the old Pandaw boarded up on the Clyde for her sea passage to Burma in 1948 and had a good idea of how to do it. It was a sad sight to see her go, but business in Burma was turning for the worse, sanctions and 'don't go' campaigns were having their effect. We could keep going on one or two ships but there was no room for growth and thus Pandaw III became the Tonle Pandaw and fourteen years on has completed over one hundred thousand river miles on the Mekong.

At the same time the hull of Pandaw IV was being laid. She was destined to go to India where we had worked on a project to put a ship on the Ganges. We were expanding rapidly, financing these new builds from cash flow without recourse to the banks or to outside investors. We had pioneered, Burma, the Kwai, the Mekong and now India loomed. We were on top of our game, the largest river cruise company in South-East Asia. Things were good. Ghilberto, high maintenance though he was, raised standards of food and beverage service to new heights. Sadly perhaps, we were losing that quirky expedition feel for something more classic and refined.

In a customary state of ebullience I had failed to pick up various warning signs. A good friend in Rangoon over dinner warned me that there was a lot of gossip going around – that I did not pay my bills, that I treated my people badly, underpaying them, and so on. This came as a complete surprise but I put it down to little local jealousies. Lots of people had come to Burma in the mid nineties and whilst the more energetic few had 'made it', the losers were left behind propping up bars with tales of woe. I had underestimated the sheer virulence of gossip. We had no PR operation and our Ghilberto was perhaps the greatest gossip of them all. I had seen before that when an expat left Rangoon, no matter how popular he or she had been whilst there, all their supposed friends would turn on them once gone. I think this happened to us when Roser and I got out in 2000. No one liked to see a fellow captive escape, particularly if he had prospered.

Rangoon, with its heavily censored press and media, thrived on rumours. Expat gossip would spread like wildfire to Burmese friends, associates and servants. There were a number of former employees washed up in Yangon where the drink was cheap and the girls cheaper. There was Donald, a Glaswegian engineer, who in his month with us had never ventured far from a bar stool. Adriano, a slippery Italian ticket clerk, caught with fingers in the till, had stayed on, filled with dark hatred for all things Pandaw. Then there were the omnipresent and ever neurotic Swiss travel agent ladies who had long predicted failure for our ventures and were piqued at our successes.

I did not see this and went about town telling everyone about the ships were building and our plans for the Mekong and India in foolish innocence, not realizing that the more I talked the more I rubbed people up the long way.

Then there was the government itself. They did not like to see foreigners succeed. Most foreigners came to Burma, got royally fleeced by an ad hoc alliance of government and local business partners and then left. You were not supposed to succeed.

I was running ships at a profit, something the Inland Water Transport with its fleet of five hundred ships in the half a century since Independence had failed to achieve.

Whilst I thought I was telling it like it was, people took me for a braggart.

My greatest error was to fail to realize the power of envy: the most damaging of all evils and perhaps the greatest motivating force on the planet. Looking back now I can see I had my eye off the ball, the past couple of years had been almost all taken up with setting up new projects on the Kwai, the Mekong and various recce trips to India. I had ignored Burma leaving it to Ghilberto.

Sadly, the victim of this malice was not myself but one of our loyal and trusted employees. In June that year, back home in Spain, I received news that our 30-year-old office manager in Rangoon Chit Su had been arrested. I received terrified calls from her sister. She had been picked up and taken by the MI (Military Intelligence) to a safe house, no one knew where, and was being questioned over the export of Pandaw III. Chit Su had been with the company since 2000 and had been made a director. A shy girl, Chit Su was very honest and very natural, quite incapable of deceit or malice, and thus a perfect candidate for a directorship.

At that time it was standard practice in foreign controlled companies to appoint proxy local shareholders and directors controlled by the foreign investor by means of a trust agreement. That was what was done, and one thought nothing more about it.

It transpired that Ghilberto had appointed a young man called Win Zaw to the office who was said to be 'connected' which meant that his brother was an MI officer and could help with permits, licences and all the various bits of red tape that took up so much time. Every office in Burma has such a fixer. Later, Ghilberto fired him at my suggestion, as he was a thoroughly unpleasant character, pure poison in fact. I did not want his toxic presence in the office spoiling the atmosphere. The problem was Ghilberto, as was his wont, created a drama and fired him in front of the others so the boy lost face. You do not do this in Burma. In fact, you should never have to sack anyone. Instead you create a situation in which they can resign and save face, for example a hint that they might like to transfer to the dreaded Mandalay office usually did the trick.

Once I, mistakenly, switched off an office girl's email and she immediately resigned rather than face what she thought was to be a dismissal. It was with some difficulty that she was persuaded to come back.

We immediately engaged lawyers to deal with the Chit Su crisis but in military-ruled Burma no lawyer was ever going to stick his neck out or he too would be on the wrong side of the iron bars.

After a few days Chit Su was released. It transpired that when we had exported the ship one permit had been missing, the one from the Ministry of Trade. We had worked with the Minister of Transport for the export of the ship. In fact, we had been very thorough and made sure that we had all the right bits of paper including a document signed by the minister giving us permission to export the ship and a check list of permits, licences and approvals required which included immigration, customs, quarantine officers, port authority and many, many others.

All this we did. Alas, one single sheet of paper from Trade, then under the powerful General Maung Aye, had been overlooked. Transport had advised us we would not need this but feathers were ruffled at Trade, no doubt jealous that they had not shared in any largesse such an arrangement might bring.

With hindsight I think the Win Zaw plan had been a combination of vengeance and extortion. My first mistake was not just to fly out and meet with him, apologizing for Ghilberto's behaviour and giving him a nice big pay off. I did not do this. Stupidly, I came over all British and announced pompously that we were not going to respond to blackmail.

Nothing happened for months. My brilliant ruse of doing nothing seemed to have worked. Then in October that year I got a call from Ghilberto that Chit Su had been rearrested. This time it was not to a safe house for a bit of verbal bullying it was 'official' and she was in jail.

Chit Su was arraigned before a court and remanded in custody. Furthermore I had been cited and there was a warrant for my arrest. Apparently Win Zaw had now written to the trade minister informing him that we had not applied for the export permit. It was well known that the very powerful minister of trade did not like the not-so-powerful minister of transport who then proved not very helpful in this crisis.

Chit Su was released on bail and it became a matter of the size of the payoff, something the lawyers would negotiate with the judge and the MI officers bringing the case. In Burma at this time there was no distinction between civil and criminal cases. The legal code, or lack of code, consisted of a statute book of pre-war British Indian colonial laws, various Buddhist laws mainly concerning the family issues like inheritance rights, adoption and divorce, and numerous often contradictory decrees and orders issued by the generals since the 1962 'revolution'.

Even trained lawyers could not distinguish between civil and criminal law – if you made a mistake and forgot some permit or licence you went to jail. Your get out of jail card was hard cash. And with Chit Su it was all about hard cash. Then three distinct circumstances were to collide, with tragic results.

Firstly, the Khin Nyunt regime was eliminated in an overnight putsch in November 2003. As we had discovered over Toni's adoption, Khin Nyunt's power had been ebbing. The government had become paralysed by a split between Khin Nyunt and his rival Maung Aye, the aforementioned minister of trade.

Khin Nyunt controlled certain ministries like transport, home affairs and foreign affairs and Maung Aye the real power with defence and trade. Khin Nyunt had been allowed to maintain his public image, indeed it suited the real powerbrokers in the army who were camera-shy and not too good at dealing with ambassadors, visiting envoys and the international media.

They left all this window dressing to Khin Nyunt but took away his real power. However, as we had seen with the case of Chit Su, MI was clearly out of control. It had grown into a vast organization with offices in every town and village. Their officers lived off the land. Like all Burmese officials they were paid little and expected to augment their incomes through business deals, extortion and protection rackets. My impression is that the organization had become so big that Khin Nyunt had lost control of it. Rogue elements had set up all over as powerful little local mafias, and it was into one of their clutches Chit Su had fallen.

The putsch itself was not undramatic. With meticulous planning Khin Nyunt and his senior officers were all arrested at their homes one early morning. Scores were settled and a number died under interrogation. Children were also arrested. Khin Nyunt's son, Ko Ye Naing Win, whom I had known when he had owned a coffee shop, was taken in. Interrogations were about finding out where the cash was hidden. In some circumstances the children of an imprisoned officer were flown down to Singapore, under escort, and taken to a bank to withdraw funds to bring back to Rangoon in order to secure parents' release. Often the children or even grandchildren of a fallen one would be held in jail as a surety against good behaviour. That was the Burmese way.

All this affected the Chit Su case because suddenly we had no one to call – all our friends and allies were in jail too.

Out of the darkness General Than Shwe emerged. Though 'head of the army' he had stayed out of the limelight and was generally assumed to be a figurehead. Nothing was further from the truth.

Suddenly he took charge and things changed dramatically. New ministers were appointed and our man at transport disappeared. Again, foolishly, I hoped that with the suppression of the MI the Chit Su case would be lost in the mayhem. Indeed things went very quiet for a couple of months. However in February 2014 the case resurfaced and Chit Su was once again summonsed to the high court. The maximum penalty was seven years in jail, however after the transfer of fairly large sums of cash to the lawyers I was assured that it would be just a matter of in and out over night and the matter would be forgotten. Meanwhile I was advised by the lawyers and by the British Embassy not to come out. I was desperate to jump on a plane and come and resolve matters. To this day I think if I had and been seen around town and had talked to the right people then things might have been different.

With mounting pressure the situation became more and more complex. A classic case of the knock-on effect, one thing leading to another, and troubles proliferated. Key people in the company were resigning out of pure fear. No one could say who would be next. At this point our main competitor, who I will call Gin Palace Cruises, joined the fray.

We had always enjoyed cordial relations with Gin Palace Cruises who operated a rather ugly big white modern thing with shag pile carpets and windows that would not open. Despite this, there had been a lot of jealousy: we were nearly always full when they were nearly always empty. Our ships with their shallow draft could go where theirs could not. The great and the good, the smart set, travelled with us, much to the chagrin of GPC. Against this background, their Rangoon based general manager, a washed up merchant navy captain, wrote a formal letter to the minister of tourism complaining that Pandaw had unfair advantages and did not pay taxes.

Now in such cases an official Burmese reaction can be very hard to predict – either they ignore it or they completely overreact. In this case, given the fact that we were already in the spotlight, they

185

overreacted. A note was sent to all ministries opening investigations into Pandaw.

Pandaw IV, fuelled and provisioned for her maiden voyage was arrested and we had to cancel all sailings for the season at a loss of $2 million. Worse than this, we lost trade clients to our competition who to this day have not returned.

The Gin Palace Cruises letter was the second circumstance that brought us down and changed everything for Chit Su's case. Now the matter was so public, the talk of the town from tea shops to expat watering holes, discussed in every corridor of power, in every department and ministry.

Rather like the case of Uncle Leo, when the government decided to go 'official' it would throw the book at the case, with no compromises and no hush-hush cash to save face.

Naively we believed that in the words of the lawyer the trial would be 'choreographed', thanks to lavish payments from our side, Chit Su's trip to jail would be in the words of the lawyer "just an overnight stay". Chit Su herself believed this, as we did. This after all was how things worked in Burma. There was talk of smuggling her our over the border and refugee status could be sought and a job guaranteed in one of our overseas offices. But Chit Su is a very typical Burmese girl. She loved her family and her country and did not want to go into exile. The night before the trial, over a very emotional phone call, I promised not to abandon her and begged her to be brave and go through with it.

The next day in court came. The lawyers, judges and various officials pocketed our money anyway and sent Chit Su to jail for the full seven years.

The Gin Palace Cruises letter had meant that they had to do things entirely by the book. I was broken. Chit Su's family were broken. And of course Chit Su was the most broken of all. Good conditions were promised, if we paid so much she could stay in the warden's house at the Insein Jail with his family. In fact Chit Su found herself in a dormitory of similar women, receiving better conditions, who could have meals sent in from outside, but this hardly compensated.

Money could buy better food and treatment but prison was prison. I flew to Thailand and met with Chit Su's sister in Bangkok, the first of many such meetings over the year to come. Guiltily, I was relieved at how little they blamed me. If anything they were grateful that Chit Su had not been abandoned which is what any Burmese would expect in such a situation. The women's prison was filled with such cases, or even sillier cases – women jailed for not carrying an ID card when stopped in the street, women without a bus ticket, women caught with a illegal Thai lottery ticket in their hand bags.

All went to jail for terms of several years for the most petty crimes. Or, as in so many cases like Chit Su's, no crime at all, but just for falling foul of complex red tape or falling victim to the malice of the envious.

After many further discussions and further payments it was agreed with the authorities that she would only serve one year not seven. I too had been tried in absentia and had a seven year jail sentence hanging over me.

The implication was — and this was not written into any legal code — that if I stayed away for the seven year jail term I could come back after it and I would be all right. I was serving my seven years in a comfortable Spanish farm house while Chit Su's was in the notorious Insein Jail.

Meanwhile Gin Palace Cruises realized the damage they had done and, I would like to think, felt some remorse. I was courted by a wily executive, fearful that I was going to go public with the story. He invited me to lunch with their legendary owner, itself something of an experience. They expressed an interest in buying my business, though I later understood this to be a ploy to keep me quiet.

By this point, as was no doubt obvious to many, I would have sold the business to anyone for anything just to be rid of the curse. There was even the hint that they were buying us out just to close us down.

I asked them to write to the tourism minister and rescind the earlier letter, pledging their support for Pandaw. It might just turn the tide and help Chit Su. This would have cost them nothing but they would not do it. They wanted us to go down.

Back in Rangoon the rumour mill went wild: Pandaw was being taken over, closed down, nationalized etc. Against this the third circumstance that led to our downfall emerged. Our main competitor was owned by a group of cross-border Kokang Chinese who had heavily invested their profits in tourism and taken over the old Pandaw I. They had got their hands on our old ship using backdoor tactics. This was soon after I had refused to pay an enormous bribe demanded by the new managing director of IWT for the renewal of the lease.

They got the charter from IWT for one tenth of what we paid and thus we had lost our baby. They had employed Andriano, the slippery Italian I had fired the year before for misconduct, and under his wily direction his bosses began a systematic smear campaign in official circles to damage us. The plan being to have us closed down, the ships seized and then again via the backdoor, to sold on to them for a knock down price. They had done it once and could do it again.

Sure enough the tax authorities hit us with an audit and the company accountant disappeared, back to her native village in the Arakan and was never heard of again. The tax authority then demanded a six figure down payment against several years back tax, again a ploy that would hopefully bankrupt us as after paying so many bribes we were surely low on cash resources. However being savers by nature we had the funds and paid up.

Our Swiss ground handler became frightened and refused to handle our business. The shipyard where we built the Pandaws came under investigation. We were under attack from several directions. Anyone associated with us came under fire and quickly tried to break that association. The slippery Italian, fuelled with a near pathological hatred for all things Pandaw, was seen amidst his drunken friends in a Rangoon bar toasting the fall of Pandaw. I then received a death threat on my answer machine in Spain, this we traced to the Swiss home of the same travel agent who had refused our business as we were 'too dangerous'.

Feeling abandoned and paranoid, I was fast becoming a wreck barely sleeping at night and consuming a couple of bottles of wine each evening in the hope of snatching three or four hours of fitful sleep. People around me must have found my stress unbearable.

The nice English reservations manager who worked in our office in Spain resigned, but was persuaded to stay. Quite how Roser coped with me remains a mystery and a silent testimony to her inner strengths and endurance. Nearly everyone I knew in Burma had, if not turned against me, turned away from me. No one would help. Even the Chinese banker who had a year before begged me to repay a loan as he was in trouble, and I had done so out of good faith, told me he could not do anything, he had his own problems.

Old and close friends would not take my calls or return emails. I was a pariah, but at the same time many of my more influential friends had similar difficulites when the Khin Nyunt regime fell. No one knew any of the new generals and ministers brought in from the sticks by Than Shwe.

A year before I could have picked up the phone to a certain colonel and he would have fixed it all in no time. That colonel was now in jail. Many of my friends had their own problems with businesses under attack and nowhere to turn. I was angry at the time but looking back, I can hardly blame them.

Pandaw survived simply because Pandaw had money. Knowing that the environments in which we operated were high risk, we had built up a good cash reserve to take care of contingencies in addition to financing future expansion plans. We were able to buy our way out of the mess, paying off everybody, settling the taxes they were hitting us with to try and bring us down, and of course buying Chit Su out of jail after a year had to be served in order to save the face of the authorities rattled by Gin Palace Cruises's letter.

What hurt most that there were so many people, foreign and local, that we had helped over the years, given good business to and taken good care of and not one of them stood up for us. I was desperate and at one point made quite a large donation to a semi official charity but even that backfired and just made people even more jealous.

Then Maw Maw called me. Maw Maw is one of my oldest friends in Burma and I had lived with her family in the early eighties for six months at Pagan. Maw Maw asked me if I knew what people were saying about me: I had not paid my crews for months, I was an embezzler, a conman, a crook, etc., etc. She could not believe any of this of her old friend or 'brother' as one can be honoured in Burma. She would try and help me.

Maw Maw is a village girl and hardly influential but she set to work talking to her few army contacts and friends in Yangon. We set up a rendezvous on the Burma Thai border at Tachilek where I waited nervously on the other side of the 'Friendship Bridge' for her to cross over on a day pass with her husband. Maw Maw wanted to see me face to face and decide if the stories were really true and I had become the monster I was portrayed as across Burma. Amazingly she decided I was still the old me. Further meetings were arranged in Bangkok together with Chit Su's sister and another rather dramatic one in Rannong, the southern Burmese port when both our planes, mine from Bangkok and hers from Rangoon were caught in a hellish monsoon storm, circling around together, unable to land and in my case forced back to Bangkok. What we did establish through all this was a way to support Chit Su and her family and a realistic timeframe to get Chit Su out of jail. In the end this worked, and we were not duped again by the lawyers and officials.

After Chit Su's release a passport was obtained for her and she came to Bangkok with her sister and Maw Maw. I was wracked with guilt. It was my mess and she had been the innocent victim. All of it could have been avoided if I had come out in the summer of 2003 and sorted things out myself. I had become complacent thinking that problems if ignored would just go away. They do not.

My biggest mistake was lack of an effective PR operation, something I tend to dismiss as unnecessary, perhaps arrogantly. We had allowed the loser community in Rangoon to escalate gossip to the point where denial was pointless.

I stayed away for four years and returned in 2008 after Nargis. During these years I effectively disappeared from view as the Pandaw principal. New directors were appointed and with really good well-trained local managers I was soon forgotten about. I was the problem, not Pandaw.

We had also lost all our local business as a result of the arrest of Pandaw IV. Yet out of sight and out of mind all soon forgot about us and we were able to quietly rebuild our business with direct sales cutting out the local middlemen.

Over ten years on, Chit Su runs our company office in Yangon with her habitual efficiency and dedication. It is thanks to Chit Su that each year thousands of our travellers are taken care of so well from arriving at the airport to getting on a ship. She has since married and has a gorgeous little baby. She does not like to talk about that period of her life. She is yet another ordinary Burmese woman who has endured so much during the years of dictatorship. She is one of the unsung heroes who are victims of the stupidity, ignorance and ill-feeling that military rule brings in its wake.

Nargis – Our Finest Hour

Cyclone Nargis made landfall in Burma at 1600 on 2nd May 2008 with winds of up to 120mph. Reports started coming in showing the scale of devastation. The Irrawaddy Delta covers an area of over ten thousand square miles and and in the township of Laputta alone over 80,000 people died. The final count was approximately 150,000 dead across the Delta and over 2.5 million people rendered homeless, with nearly all wooden or bamboo houses lost.

With the exception of concrete frame buildings in the larger towns and brick monastery buildings, nearly every home built of wood or bamboo, had been lost. Most livestock had been killed, wells poisoned by the ingress of salt water in the successive tsunamis that swept across these flat lands. Thousands of children were orphaned.

Contrary to some reports Nargis was not a total surprise. We had received weather warnings and a message had been sent to the ships from my office in Scotland to prepare for the cyclone. However nothing prepared us for its sheer violence and scale. Pandaw IV, then resting up off-season, was moored on the fringe of the affected area at Prome, sustained some damage and Pandaw II, up in Mandalay undergoing engine repairs was unscathed.

All our people had escaped harm, except one lad from housekeeping who had returned to his delta village on leave and of whom we never heard anything again.

One's first thought was what to do? Communications were down and not much news was getting out. Media reports were confused. However we had sat phones on the ships and I was able to talk with the pursers and remarkably quickly phone lines and email contact was restored and I could talk to Nwesu in our Rangoon office.

Initially I thought of using our ships to deliver food and supplies. Then I remembered that during the War these Irrawaddy Flotilla ships had been easily converted to hospital ships. I had seen photos of them with great red crosses painted on their roofs in the hope that this would safeguard them against Japanese divebombers.

We had the hardware, the crews, and the experience of these waters, but we did not have the medical expertise. I started calling some of the major charities but was dismissed as a crank. Then a contact put me in touch with Mark Hawkins at Merlin, a UK medical charity. Mark had been in the Royal Navy and immediately understood what I was trying to get across. The Delta has several thousand creeks and channels and nearly all activity is waterborne, so any relief effort had to be amphibious.

The Pandaw ships with their own power supply, water treatment plants, air conditioning and refrigeration were the obvious way to provide medical aid and accommodate the medics. Mark was flying out that week and would visit Pandaw IV at Prome and see for himself, which he did. Instantly he saw the advantages of using a Pandaw. I called Ko Win Hlaing the purser and asked him if he and the crew were up for it. Many had lost part or all of their houses and needed to get home and sort things out. But every man volunteered to stay on board and take the ship down to Laputta, the most devastated area.

The ship moved down to Henzada, which was closer to Rangoon and practical for loading supplies and doing the necessary work to convert her to a floating hospital.

The Merlin team came on board and set about converting the big main deck dining hall into an emergency clinic with bays containing operating tables screened off from each other. A Burmese friend who owned the Mandalay mineral water factory sent a truck load of bottles of water and one of our main suppliers, Citimart, sent another truck load of instant noodles.

Sitting in my office in Scotland I became increasingly frustrated at not being on the spot and decided to go out to lend a hand. It had been nearly five years since I had last visited Burma. It was no official reprieve that brought me back from exile but rather the strong sense that I should be there.

Merlin arranged a visa, passed through the Burmese Embassy in London with a bunch of their own applications so as not to alert them. I still had my seven years jail sentence to serve but I reckoned that with the distraction of Nargis the government's mind would be on other things. I slipped in without any trouble and kept a low profile.

Our office then was at the Inya Lake Hotel and I think I was the only guest but one. It was rather like when I first visited the hotel in 1981. It was a ghost ship. Few lights were working, and the odd rat scampered down gloomy passages. The grounds were devastated with so many once gorgeous trees down.

Rangoon was transformed. With so many trees uprooted, streets were opened up to view and the architectural monstrosities of the Slorc years revealed. The city I had known and loved for so long had become ugly.

In the couple of weeks before flying out I had put out a fund-raising appeal to all our former passengers. In total we raised over $750,000. We had the company credit card facility to enable this and the clandestine means to get cash into Burma fast, whilst the major charities were fumbling around trying to get round the sanctions and get much needed money into the country. We had the money, we had the ships and above all we had the 'software', meaning highly trained and experienced teams. It seemed that the Pandaw crews had been training for this moment since we began, myself included. We had the skills to do this job. We knew how to live of the land and work the system. We could move fast, unencumbered by committees and boards of governance. After all, we had been working under the radar for thirteen years. Our people were quick-thinking and resourceful, they knew how to fix things whether technical or bureaucratic.

Whilst Pandaw IV was being made ready at Henzada we started sending truck loads of supplies down to Laputta. The markets in Rangoon had re-opened and it was possible to buy nearly everything we needed there from sacks of rice to medical supplies from India, China and Thailand. There was no need to fly stuff in as the big charities were trying — and failing — to do. In fact the week after Nargis three rice ships sailed for India from Thilawa, Rangoon's container port, laden with Burmese delta rice.

The helpful Dutch manager at the Inya Lake hotel gave us unlimited storage space for free and we were able to stockpile supplies. On the first mission two hired trucks, laden with bags of rice, visited the first makeshift refugee camps set up by the army. Then we found a monastery where several hundred people were bivouacked within the brick shells of the buildings. A Burman's first instinct in time of trouble is to go to his local monastery. Monks have the organizational skills and sense of fairness to ensure an equal redistribution of offerings. Thus we could offer a monastery a truck load of rice and know that it would be properly shared out. This is the time-honoured and surest form of social welfare in Burma and it continues to work well to this day.

The team came up with the idea of the Pandaw Family Box, a domestic startup kit with all the basics – plates, cooking utensils, candles, matches, a couple of *longyis*, a towel, a mosquito net, packets of instant noodles, a bag of rice. These were soon assembled and almost daily we had trucks rolling out of the Inya Lake hotel destined for Laputta and the worst areas of devastation. We were in there long before the big aid donors who had to contend with the government's refusal to accept aid.

The fact that the US Navy had two warships on standby off the coast, put the generals on red alert thinking they were going to be invaded and only served to block the supply of any aid further.

By June we were renting local cargo boats and sending the family boxes down river, saving on delivery costs and reaching areas that lacked roads. I was not allowed to accompany any of the convoys, the entire delta area was off limits to foreigners and I was keen to get on Pandaw IV before she left Henzada.

So I tried to drive up there dressed in a *longyi* with dark glasses and a baseball cap pulled down over my face, wedged in the back of Chit Su's tiny car between a couple of stout crewman. We were turned round at the first roadblock by a very amused young sergeant. But I did not need to go, the team knew exactly what to do and where to go and the presence of a stowaway foreigner might even jeopardise the mission. I had only wanted to see everyone and the new look Pandaw hospital ship for myself.

Pandaw IV sailed with the Merlin medical team (who being official doctors had the necessary permits) on board and with satellite communications I was able to maintain daily contact with the purser, Ko Win Hlaing. Based in our Inya Lake Hotel office, making the occasional foray into town to meet old friends and associates. As no one came and arrested me, I became braver. When I met people they generally assumed that I had been rehabilitated in some way. That a deal had been done and amnesty granted.

As mentioned, the lack of media in Rangoon means that rumours can become reality . This time it worked for me rather than against. The story went round that I was back and all had been forgiven and eventually all the ministers and government officials thought this too.

Much of my time was spent meeting and advising the big donors on how things worked in Burma. I was trying to get the message across that airlifting in thousands of tons of dried biscuit, which the rice-dependent Burmese refused to eat, was unnecessary, particularly when you could buy rice far more economically in the local markets.

I was asked by one organization to help get a ship of medical supplies in, I took them down to one of the markets and showed them that in Burma you could buy just about anything off the shelf, and cheap too, as these pharmaceuticals were made under license in India and China and retailed at a very low price. One aid donor were getting emergency boxes in and these contained a sort of airline wash kit including a razor which was caused much mirth as most Burmese do not shave.

Pandaw II was called down from Mandalay. The engine overhauls were not yet complete so she came down on the one engine whilst the mechanics finished work on the other. I had come to an arrangement with Save the Children who would use the ship as a floating base for their medical teams moving around.

Ironically Save the Children were one of the organisations I had offered the ship to back in the UK who had dismissed me as a crank. Now they were very keen to get hold of her. They did not convert her into a floating hospital, using her more as a floating base and supply centre for their medical teams moving around.

Within two or three days of sailing Pandaw IV had taken up position outside Laputta and was handling hundreds of patients per day. Four babies were born on board, which in Burma is said to be very lucky for a ship owner. They were all girls and their names all have Pandaw in them – for example Pandaw Lay, Pandaw May, etc. The operating theatres were working flat out and the expat Merlin team working alongside Burmese doctors showed an incredible dedication and capacity for hard work.

At the end of a hard day they could at least have a hot shower and an air-conditioned room, not to mention a square meal. Conditions ashore were abysmal. Whole towns had been blown away; ships beached hundreds of meters inland; both livestock and crops lost; orphaned kids were roaming lost and hungry; water supplies poisoned by the ingress of salt water from the sea.

The Pandaws with their high-capacity water treatment plants were able to make and distribute water for the local people who would come alongside in all manner of craft to fill up jerry cans, pots and buckets with drinking water. The team set up feeding stations on deck so that families waiting, whilst a family member received treatment, could be fed, mainly with the good old instant noodle in a soup.

Patients were also given a sort of goodie bag to take home with them containing basic food items. The ships were more than floating clinics – they were water points, feeding stations, and centres for the distribution of the Pandaw Family Box which were now arriving in bulk by specially chartered cargo boats from Rangoon and then taken out by the team on smaller motor boats for distribution in the remoter villages far up the back waters and creeks.

I would always ask people coming back from the area if they had seen any other aid in the villages – from the World Food Programme? From UNICEF? No, we seemed to be the first in and I fear in some places the last as well.

The cyclone struck during the tourist off-season when the ships rest up and undergo maintenance. However we had good bookings from mid September and would need the ships back on line by then. Convinced of the importance of water-borne aid I decided to use some of the funds we had raised to buy a replacement boat to continue the work after the Pandaws had returned to their cruising schedules.

We bought a 128-foot motorized barge in Mandalay and on its big flat cargo deck we built an accommodation block containing a surgery, dispensary, accommodation for medics, galley, water treatment plant, generators. There was a drawbridge-style ramp at the front so we could even carry our own car or a light truck.

The barge was purchased and fitted out within a month and she was on her way from Mandalay, laden with supplies, by September. We handed her over to Merlin who lined the holds and mainly used her for water delivery. I was a bit disappointed that Merlin did not make more use of her but by the end of the year the relief effort had moved onto the next phase, being less concerned with trauma medicine and more with reconstruction. We then loaned the clinic-barge to a German NGO who continued for several years afterwards operating her as a floating medical centre around delta villages so in the end it was money well spent.

Nargis was a wake up call for the Burmese regime. It gave them notice that the world was not going to continue to tolerate indifference to the plight of the majority of their people. The presence of the American warships had helped drive them deep into their bunker. Slowly they realized that the world was not going to allow such inhumanity and incompetence.

They were only persuaded by the arrival of the UN secretary general Ban Ki Moon who brokered a face-saving deal whereby the warships would stand off and the aid planes were allowed to fly in.

Madame Than Shwe had said publically that the cyclone was an act of karma punishing the delta people, many of whom are Karens, Mons, and other ethnic minorities and where there are sizable Christian and Muslim populations.

Nargis was also a wake-up call to the rest of the world that blindly following Aung San Suu Kyi's eccentric demand that the West withhold all aid was badly misguided. Nargis brought the aid community into Rangoon in force, and they came to stay. Prior to Nargis any sort of NGO activity had to be almost clandestine. A friend ran the very low profile International Red Cross unofficial office in Rangoon had described how despite the escalation of the humanitarian crisis of poverty and lack of basic healthcare during the sanction years, they had to work unofficially, almost secretly, to avoid international censure. No one could deny Burma aid now.

For all of us at Pandaw, Nargis had been a life-changing experience. At moments it seemed that all these years of struggle, running ships in places like Burma or Cambodia, against all the odds had been worth it, as it had prepared us for this moment, where we could do something really useful, even if for just once in our lives.

For all the team who served in the Delta the memories live on, as do the stories. All that training and experience in caring for well-heeled passengers came in incredibly useful when caring for the displaced and dispossessed.

We were not the only ones to move fast, a number of local organisations sent supplies down but they were limited by range and a limited road system, whereas we had no such limitations. Later the big aid came in, but ours was very much a Burmese effort to stop the gap before that aid could get organised and overcome all the formidable political obstacles.

What we did not realize at the time was that the Cyclone Nargis relief effort was to develop into a proper charity. We continue to support one orphanage in the delta, and as said the clinic-barge continued to operate with a German NGO. However, it was up country in our home area where we operate our ships and have the local knowledge and contacts that our NGO or charity has flourished. Prior to Nargis we had been involved in a school building project at Yandabo, where we would take passengers to the village school and collect funds for its reconstruction. After Nargis, with a formal organization established, we were able to really gear up efforts and a further twelve schools have been constructed in villages up and down river from Pagan. The main concentration is on and around Thiri Island where we have built five schools, which, though geographically close to Pagan, feels very remote when you go there cut off by the fast-flowing river and submerging completely during the peak of the monsoon.

One of the Thiri schools is a high school so kids can complete their education. Previously the nearest high school was too far away and the journey expensive and difficult so few kids got to go to high school. Each school, finished in teak and very solid and well built, could be completed for about $15,000 and take an average of 200 children. The government provide teachers and we offer additional support and training. It works well and what is pleasing is that these school construction projects are community projects, the villagers donating the land and helping out with the construction on a voluntary basis. We get these projects done because we have the local contacts (a number of our crew are from Thiri island) and can work as ever discreetly below the radar and away from official government scrutiny. The generals would do their best to block any such projects out of a perverted sense of face-saving patriotism – accepting foreign aid means accepting their own failure.

The person behind all this is my old friend Maw Maw, who came to the rescue in 2004 when we had our crisis. Maw Maw is now a very successful businesswoman running the Bagan House lacquer shop and school where she trains local kids in traditional handicrafts like lacquer making.

Maw Maw can be a rather a domineering lady, but she gets things done as only Burmese matriarchs can. She galvanizes the villagers into action and makes sure everything is billed at cost on budget. She is one of these people so open, honest and natural that makes everyone jump enthusiastically into action filled with goodwill.

In 2009 Maw Maw and I decided to build a clinic on the mainland at Gantgar but close to the crossing point to Thiri so it would be accessible to the islanders. A plot of land was pledged by the village headman and a simple bungalow constructed, two doctors were hired for a couple of days a week when we would open a small outpatient clinic. Little did we know what we had started.

Into the Heart of Borneo

Seated cross-legged on the sundeck of the Orient Pandaw, shirt soaked in reaction to the 100% humidity, before a bank of TV cameras and press photographers, a chicken was ritually slaughtered before me. Its blood was then decanted into a chalice, mixed with rice spirit, and raised to my lips amidst shaministic chants and the clapping and cheers of the audience. Thus the Orient Pandaw was blessed once again this time according to the rites of the Iban people, a branch of the Dayaks. Here we were exploring a new river in the heart of Borneo.

Navigable rivers in South East Asia are in surprisingly short supply. Indeed the sub-continent is dissected by great rivers but few of them are navigable. The Salween in Burma, one of the mightiest of rivers, and far longer than the Irrawaddy, is only navigable on larger boats for about 100 miles. The Chindwin for much of the year is too shallow. The Mekong above Cambodia into Laos is rendered impassable by great waterfalls. In Thailand, the Kwai, lovely as it is, had proved too short to be of interest, our passengers seeking longer expeditions into the unknown.

A good river is like a good story — there has to be an exciting beginning, an interesting middle bit and a climax at the end. Each day there has to be something new and different to see and do. There has to be easy access at either end with international flight connections and transfers that are neither too long nor arduous. All these things had come together on the Irrawaddy and on the Mekong but finding other rivers with the magic combination was challenging. And then there is the fact that every country has different policies on foreign investment, inland water navigation, flagging of foreign ships or in some cases no policy at all.

Borneo is the world's second largest island after Greenland. The largest part of Borneo is Kalimantan, which is part of Indonesia, then there is the oil rich state of Brunei, which is an independent sultanate, and then there is Eastern Malaysia, where we were, consisting of two states – Sabah and Sarawak. We were in Sarawak as I had long been a fan of Redmond O' Hanlon's 1984 book *Into the Heart of Borneo*, one of the funniest travel books ever written, which describes a journey in the 1980s up the Rajang River in search of an elusive white rhino.

Roser, Toni and I, after a Burma visit in the aftermath of Nargis in the summer of 2008, decided to go over there and try to follow as far as we could in O'Hanlon's footsteps. We had contacted the Sarawak ministry of tourism who were very keen on the idea of a Rajang river cruise and the minister, who was from Sibu the main city on the Rajang, was keen to meet us.

Sibu is not an attractive town, and almost completely devoid of touristic interest, yet the government were desperate to promote tourism there. I was not sure why, as the place seemed prosperous enough being the main port on the Rajang, rich from logging, coal mining and palm oil plantation. Houses were big, cars new and the infrastructure good. We had the sense we were in a very different environment from either Burma or Cambodia. The people were well-educated and enjoyed a European standard of living, or indeed higher.

Too often tourism offers low-grade unskilled jobs with few opportunities for self-betterment. It has to be admitted that, usually, non-local investors get rich whilst the majority of those employed in the industry stay poor. Throwing all their energies into the creation of a mass tourist industry is one of those mistake developing countries go through, like Spain in the 1960s or Thailand in the 1980s, and which they regret later.

Tourism can also be the last resort of basket cases desperate for a quick foreign exchange fix. In developed economies such as the UK, those employed are often immigrants or guest workers, employable local people being on a higher wage level and unwilling to take the jobs.

Yet the government minister known as Datu, which is an honorific Malaysian title like 'Sir', was desperate to put Sibu on the tourist map.

Seemingly the impulse came from some convoluted notion of civic pride not unconnected to his political ambitions. They were all inordinately proud of their city with its fiddly Chinese gardens and banal concrete urban sculptures and believed this would be of interest to the world at large.

We were directed to the market, one of the city's main attractions but it had little to recommend it, being just another typical Asian market. The waterfront with its many boat stations was again not very inspiring, cigar-tube boats, essentially airplane fuselages with the wings chopped off, sped off into the interior at great speed but were hardly picturesque or romantic.

We were invited to a grand lunch in Chinese restaurant called The Sheraton where all of Sibu's dignitaries were assembled, including the mayor, the harbourmaster and the great Datu himself.

This was very different from dealing with the Burmese generals, or Cambodian mafiosi, or indeed the Vietnamese communist cadres. These officials were educated mainly in England and a number had higher degrees including doctorates. This was high civilisation. Conversation was intelligent, sophisticated even. It was agreed that we would the next day make a recce up river to the Pelagus Falls where rooms had been booked for us in a jungle lodge.

I explained from our side what we needed to make the project work: help with importing the ship, registering it, securing the necessary permits and licences, and entry visas for crew and staff needed to set it up. The minister waved these worries aside assuring that all would be taken care of personally by him, that we would have carte blanche, even a monopoly for the first few years. Toni, then eleven got on rather well with the minister who asked him what he wanted to do when he grows up and was told "How do I know, I am only eleven?" This went down surprisingly well.

When asked what the principal attractions of visit to Sibu and the Rajang were the minister waxed lyrical about how this was the garden of the world, the most fertile place on the planet. We would show the tourists pineapple farms where the pineapples were the size of footballs. We would go to the pepper plantations, coconut groves and herb farms. Clearly the attractions were to be more agricultural than cultural.

So the next day off we sped up the mighty Rajang. Our cigar tube was extremely uncomfortable. The air conditioning was chilled to a close to freezing point and in our shorts and T shirts we were shivering all over. The windows were all misted up so we could not see anything of the scenery. A video with a zombie film blared throughout the cabin. The other passengers, mainly Iban tribesman, sat in serene comfort, seemingly unaffected either by the alien cold or the antics of the zombies.

To venture outside was dangerous as you were liable to be blown off. The vessel moved at a terrific speed and there was not much to hang on to. We ended up rolling up old newspapers round arms, legs and torso in an attempt to keep out the cold. Some hours later, and in a state close to hypothermia, we arrived at Kapit the main upriver town and back into the steamy embrace of tropical Borneo.

Kapit was also supremely nondescript. Other than a colonial-period bungalow erected by the Brooke Rajas, and now conserved as a museum, there was little of interest. It should be remembered that Sarawak was never part of the British Empire but ruled by the English Brooke family who in the late 18th century had been created hereditary rajahs and remained so until just after the war when they ceded the state to the British crown.

We were met in Kapit by the manager of the Pegasus Falls Resort. In an open speed boat the journey became far more interesting and we actually saw a crocodile, not to mention any number of birds including a rare glimpse of the hornbill, the national symbol of Sarawak.

The primary rain forest really was impressive, you cannot help be awestruck by its luxuriance. By contrast, the 'resort', set up by the Forestry Department some decades earlier, had seen better days. The Iban staff had long given up the battle with nature at its most rampant, the once-blue tiled pool was now verdant and teaming with pond life.

Attempts at landscaping, with roped walkways and stepped paths had long since reclaimed by Mother Nature.

Orders for dinner were taken at breakfast. There was a terrace with a good view of the falls and from here we could watch the cigar tube boats shooting the rapids with a sense of relief that we were not on board. We went for a walk along a 'jungle trek' established in more optimistic times however most of the rope bridges had rotted away and it became challenging as we scrambled up and down slippery ravines. I failed to follow Redmond O'Hanlon's advice to never, ever wear shorts in the jungle and was soon covered in leeches. We sought sanctuary in our hut to discover that the generator was switched off during the day and there was no air conditioning, and in the 100% humidity one ran rivers of sweat on a scale that not even monsoon Rangoon could induce.

The manager clearly had a good thing going with the hotel speed boat which apparently required astronomic quantities of very costly fuel. He took us off on day trips to explore the river and make a journey up the Baleh, the main tributary that joined the Rajang between Pelagus and Kapit. This was great fun and we would stop at Iban long houses to be invited in for rice wine and long jolly chats.

Most of the long houses had been rebuilt by the Malaysian government and resembled a cross between a bungalow and a railway train, an interminable stretch of a building with the main street enclosed to the fore to provide a communal area with private family accommodation off to the back.

They were not unlike a row of terraced cottages only with the street closed in. Given the high levels of precipitation this seemed a good idea, for it rains all year round here and in the actual rainy season, it rains all day every day for months on end.

Very few original wooden long houses survived but the ones we were lucky enough to see likewise had the same format of the closed street, raised high off the ground on stilts. Baskets of human heads were suspended from the roof. Some were just bare-boned skulls, others, perhaps more recent, with leathery dried skin and hair. These were family heirlooms and until relatively recently Iban young bloods would raid neighbouring villages in search of fresh heads which would be produced as proof of manhood to prospective brides.

Long houses and their surrounding farm areas could only support a fixed population. Thus nature worked out a very efficient system for keeping the number of surplus young males down without undertaking the carnage and chaos of war.

In the early days of the Brooke Rajadom a blind eye was turned to head hunting and the taking of Chinese heads was positively encouraged as a means of keeping their numbers down.

In one long house, I was told by a man with a glint in his eye how the practice was encouraged once again by the British during the Japanese occupation of the island. The Iban were staunchly loyal to the British who declared an open season on the taking of Japanese heads which clearly endeared Britannia to them.

Nowadays the young Iban warrior goes off overseas to earn laurels not by the taking of heads but by working on merchant ships or the oil industry. Instead of heads he returns to do his wooing with ghetto blasters, flat screen TVs and game consoles. These days the long house is 'wired' with wifi, satellite TV and of course everyone has a mobile phone. But if you bring out the rice wine it does not take long before they glaze over and relive head-hunting days of yore.

We felt fortunate that we avoided the 'drunken season' a period of months when the longhouses erupt into a bacchanal of inebriation – men, women and children drunk for weeks on end as part of some animistic propitiation, making the Scottish hogmanay rather pathetic by comparison. If a male visitor were to stay overnight in a long house convention dictates that, once properly drunk, he is the rightful property of any number of young maidens. This behaviour seemed shockingly promiscuous to early explorers, but anthropologists explain it as a way in which nature introduces new blood into isolated gene pools.

So what was the verdict on the Rajang? Navigable, easy to fly and in out of via Sibu and Kuching, amazing jungle, stunning scenery, and Iban cultural interest were the positives. The question was whether there was enough sightseeing and interest along the way? Could we find enough to keep our passengers busy and interested every day for several days?

I thought we could. When we had started on the Mekong there were few known attractions outside the main cities but we soon discovered much to see and do. We could do it again on the Rajang.

It was decided to send the Orient Pandaw the next year, from Saigon to Sibu, just a hop across the South China Sea.

In July 2009 I was back in Sibu to join the Orient after a safe passage over. A Sibu captain and crew had brought her over, having been instructed by nervous Vietnamese port authorities to hug a coastal route down Thailand and Malaysia and cross over the open sea at the narrowest point.

The master ignored this and just headed for the open sea, crossing as the crow flies and arriving in Sibu unexpectedly several days early to collect his 'one off' delivery payment. This was lucky, as no one had been found to insure the delivery.

A German manager who had been with us for a couple of years in Cambodia, and a core crew had flown over to take command and she was soon repainted, varnished and made ready for the coming maiden voyage. Other than the cigar tube boats and barges bearing coal and logs downstream there were few big boats on the river though I had read that during the Indonesian Communist incursion of the 1960s, British sea-going troop ships had been despatched up river as far as Kapit. We would be going further, to Pelagus and up the Baleh river and given the difficulties of navigation that lay ahead an experienced British captain had been hired.

Captain Steve had been master of a fishery protection vessel in the Falklands and seemed a rugged adventurous type, well suited to the challenges of uncharted rivers.

There had never been a river cruise ship in Malaysia before and their national ship registry did not have a class for river ships. They thus tried to make us register as a sea-going vessel, imposing standards which, by design and build, she could never comply with.

In the midst of such conundrums our benefactor the great Datu fell silent. Calls were not returned, emails left unanswered. We were on our own. We talked with shipping lawyers in the Malaysian capital Kuala Lumpur who proved even more mercenary than the bureaucrats. All sorts of complex legal structures were suggested to get round this maze of regulation.

In Burma you learn never ever to ask, you just go in and do it and sort out the paperwork later. That way it is easier for them to understand what you are talking about as they can see it. In Vietnam you get a 200-page memorandum detailing who does what and for exactly how much and when, and you pay not a cent more nor is it a day later than indicated. In Cambodia there is no point in asking anything as not much will happen anyway. But here in westernised Malaysia, with its British university-educated ministers and bureaucrats, the techniques of official obfuscation had been refined to new levels of obstructiveness. Despite many assurances and an (admittedly unsigned) memorandum of understanding crystallising these promises, the Datu had effectively disappeared.

Bribes far greater than anything ever encountered in the cantonments of Burma or the renal ministries of Cambodia were demanded. Eventually, thanks to our very efficient local agent and the dispensing of considerable sums we managed to get some form of temporary registration enabling us to sail.

All was ready, the ship and crew smartly turned out under the German's supervision. There was to be a grand opening ceremony before the maiden voyage in the full glare of Sarawak's media. TV crews had set up and the sun deck was lined with rows of chairs for the press corps. This was Malaysia with its free press and democratic political system, so unlike Burma where we would almost clandestinely put a new ship into operation, to avoid interference or provoke demands for some new levy from ministers and generals. And again so unlike Vietnam where they are all so busy getting on with things that no one would bother with the expense and loss of time over such ceremonial fripperies.

Here in Malaysia the press conference-cum-opening ceremony took on the proportions of a Roman imperial triumph. The object of honour was most certainly not Pandaw but the now-reappeared Datu himself.

After the Chinese drums and the Iban dancing girls and the Malay music representing all the ethnic communities present, the Datu launched into a peroration that went on for exactly ninety minutes without interruption in a highly-polished Queen's English without recourse to a single note. I have never seen such an impressive rhetorical performance and all this under the glare of the tropical midday sun on deck.

It was all thanks to him that Mr Paul and his family had visited Sibu, all thanks to him that this ship had arrived safely and been imported. It was all thanks to him that Sibu and the Rajang would now enjoy an unprecedented tourist boom and be famous the world over rivalling the great tourist sites of the world. The tourists would see for themselves the giant pineapples, the bananas the size of boomerangs, the coconuts from which flowed abundant milk, the record-breaking papayas and mangos unsurpassed elsewhere in the world. The tourists would marvel at the blessed abundance of Sibu and go home humbled.

There followed more Iban dancing and Chinese drumming followed by the sacrifice of a chicken on deck, and then as 'owner' my drinking of its blood, washed down with copious quantities of rice wine which the minister, who was a strict Methodist, abstained from. Thus the Orient Pandaw, launched in Vietnam according to Confucian rights with barbequed pig and burnt offerings of fake money, was now re-

211

dedicated according to the rights of the formerly head-hunting Iban. The Orient Pandaw is now in Burma where she has been rededicated according to Theravada Buddhist rites.

As it turned out, all this publicity was not to our benefit. Our raised profile resulted in raised prices as the traders and suppliers of Sibu quickly closed ranks to form a 'lets rip off Pandaw cartel' which we later broke by trucking everything in from Kuching at enormous additional cost. The main beneficiary was clearly the good Datu, son of Sibu, and now its saviour who had brought the blessings of tourism to his hometown.

Just what the intrinsic benefits of tourism to Sibu were was hard to say. As said, there were few visitor attractions, a distinct lack of cafes or bars or handicraft shops in which to spend our money, and no one was going to come back to the ship with a bag of giant pineapples. For reasons just explained, we had stopped buying stuff there. Clearly there were no intrinsic economic benefits to tourism. Rather the Datu and his fellow Sibuans sought the recognition of the world in the form of a flow of admiring tourists. These visitors would bestow prestige and the Datu would be politically re-elected as the man who brought the tourists.

Passengers embarked and we set off first down river to explore the Delta area. The sun set as drinks were served and we 'romantically' cruised past shipyards and factories on the outskirts of Sibu. Then dinner was served which proved inedible. The German manager, earning marks for effort at least, had attempted to construct complex menus based on local dishes and produce that proved totally unpalatable.

By the third day I along with a growing number of passengers were demanding burgers and fish and chips.

The passengers were mainly Australian with a smattering of Brits, all old Pandaw hands. This should have meant that they would be on our side but the fact was that they were spoiled by previous near-perfect Pandaw experiences and their expectations were high. An atmosphere of mistrust developed – everyone asking each other what would be the next disaster. The excursions were being taken care of by an old Australian hippy called Doug who had emerged from the tropical Sibu undergrowth and promised expertise in jungle trekking and local knowledge. However the logistics of arranging car transportation, not to mention tenders to take us ashore, were beyond him and passengers were growing restless with such frustrations, unable to get off the ship let alone set off on a shore expedition.

To compound this impression of our hopelessness Captain Steve had proved embarrassingly incapable of manoeuvering a vessel like ours alongside a jetty. An hour was spent hovering off the river bank at Kapit as he tried to make up his mind, and only when I snapped an order in Burmese to the Burmese first mate did the ship glide gracefully in up against a jungly bank in true Pandaw style. From then on Captain Steve was on a downward spiral, rarely emerging from his cabin, even for meals, other than an occasional strut to the bridge where the Burmese first mate ran things very efficiently.

Steve would appear at the office a couple of times a day moaning "Would someone tell me what is happening?" and I would suggest that if he spent more time on deck he might actually know what was going on. The situation was not helped by the fact that the star attraction of the first voyage, Redmond O' Hanlon himself had contracted some tropical disease shortly before being due to fly out. A rather butch Australian lady pursued me round the ship each day sarcastically calling out "Paul. Any news from Redmond?" or "How's Redmond, Paul?"

It was decided that I should give one of my talks to try and build up the expedition atmosphere a bit. Entitled 'The Pandaw Story' I elaborated on past Pandaw trials and tribulations – the fact that it took five years of trying before we made it to Bhamo, Pandaw II's maiden voyage and the sand bank, ships arrested by larcenous authorities, pirate attacks and that sort of thing.

There were murmurs and clearly I was not so much entertaining my guests as filling them with a sense of unease. There was the feeling that I was trying to play down the disaster of the Rajang by playing up past disasters. Perhaps I was, but I would call it creating an atmosphere. Clearly I failed.

The maiden voyage lurched from minor drama to minor drama, then from disaster to disaster. The food went from bad to worse and I confess when I went ashore at Kapit the first thing I did was look for a decent Chinese restaurant. Doug then disappeared from view, preferring to sit ashore in his truck that followed us up the river than face the music aboard. The captain became more and more elusive and the inflexible German manager absolutely refused to budge from his carefully constructed menu plan despite my pleading and the desperate cries of hunger from the passengers. There were highlights – booze ups and dancing in long houses being a blurry memory involving the imbibing of considerable quantities of rice wine and, on one afternoon's excursion, pleasantly inebriated dancing on the river bank in a funny headdress with a bunch of Iban braves, watched disdainfully by a very sober group of passengers.

I must say I was becoming disappointed in our Australian cousins who formed the majority of passengers on board and who — understandably I admit — felt they were not getting their money's worth. In the UK we are reared on an image of the Aussie as a sort of Crocodile Dundee character from the outback, swilling beer and not giving a monkey's about anything. The reality is that the modern Aussie is ever correct and well behaved. Roles seem to have been reversed and we British are now the drunken vulgarians whilst the Australian is a stickler for propriety. Clearly I was not popular as I spun yarns of sinkings and groundings, cruises that never went anywhere or even lost cruises. The bossy lady continued to hound me over the O'Hanlon disappointment while an ill-favoured retired Kiwi engineer with a Thai wife half his size and half his age could be found at all corners of the ship plotting with groups of fellow passengers. Vindictively, I later got my own back by banning him from the Indian maiden voyage and returning his deposit.

Mutiny was in the air, not just amongst the passengers but the crew who were jumping ship at each stop.

It was something of a relief to leave the ship and it all felt like a repeat of the Mekong maiden voyage. With the exception of that wonderful first voyage on the Irrawaddy Princess in 1995, when no one had any expectations, and India where we positively discouraged prospective passengers by painting a grim picture (resulting in everyone wanting to come), maiden voyages in general tend to be fiascos. Even when you remind people that it is a first try and to be prepared for the unexpected, for adventures and even disasters, people paying hard-earned money to come on holiday with us understandably have high expectations. The situation is not helped if passengers have travelled with us before and have experienced Pandaw at her best.

In Borneo over the following year we invested in setting up trails in the jungle and built a high speed tender to take passengers further upstream and into the tributaries and did much to try and enhance the destination. But the fact was that the only orangutan anyone was going to see was in the sanctuary in Kuching and no matter what we did the sightseeing remained dull.

I had calculated that, as with the Mekong, where when we started there was not a lot to do in between the cities yet had found and developed a good variety of shore excursions, we would find places of interest. Alas not. There is a limit to the number of long houses you can visit or boat trips up tributaries where the jungle, impressive at the first instance, quickly grows monotonous.

But the food did get better, becoming really quite good. We were able to offer a Pandaw service on the same level as in Burma or Mekong thanks to lots of hard work from the Burmese purser and all the team.

215

Another issue was crew. The Malaysian kids who readily signed up for this great adventure rarely lasted more than a few days before homesickness set in. Sibu was a prosperous middle class sort of city, the kids were well educated. They were less inclined to rough it in crew quarters like the Burmese or Cambodians. Keeping crew became a real problem. As had happened when we started on the Mekong, we started to fly crew in but that was beset with immigration problems and needless to say Datu, despite past promises, once again proved elusive.

When in port the Burmese crew would not go ashore for fear of the Chinese triads who would beat up foreign workers if they did not pay protection money. The boys were then approached by a Burmese mafia operating in the port who, for even more money, would protect them from the triads. If they did not pay this then would be beaten up by the Burmese mafia. Being thus caught by a double whammy, the Burmese crew decided to stay on board, never venturing ashore. We did manage to recruit some Burmese crew in the port who came from an arrested cargo ship, long forgotten and rusting on a mooring mid river. Unpaid and unable to get home, they had survived for months by hacking off bits of brass or other ship's fittings and rowing ashore with their trophies to sell to local scrap merchants in order to buy food.

Nor were the environmental aspects in Borneo conducive to the promised eco experience. How can you ruminate on the unspoiled glories of the rainforest when every half an hour a barge laden with hardwood comes chugging by? Similarly the coal barges, evidence of ferocious opencast mining deep in the jungle interior, chuntered by with a sinister frequency.

In 2010 a literal log-jam on the Rajang made international headlines. Hundreds of thousands of felled logs floated downstream and jammed up the entire Sibu port area. This was something incredible to behold. Then there were the palm oil plantations along the coastline – insipid, depressing rows of ugly stumpy palms stretching for miles where once the forest stood. No wonder the people of Sibu were rich, but at what cost?

Perhaps the most unpleasant aspect of our Borneo adventure was the amount of petty thieving that went on. On one occasion someone simply walked up the gangplank and walked off with the crew's TV. All the time people were slipping on board and pinching stuff, from both the crew and the passengers.

We had not encountered this before. In Burma for nearly twenty years now we have almost never had to deal with petty larceny on that level. Sibu was so much more prosperous than equivalent Burmese towns, yet the dishonesty we encountered there was shocking. Altogether there lacked an atmosphere conducive to trust and a sense of security. What with the cartel of suppliers to rip us off, the headaches of vessel licensing, the problems of crew and immigration obstacles for foreign crew, not to mention the many unfulfilled promises of the Datu, it was not working out.

We could probably have lived with all this but the fact that the sightseeing never developed made me realise that this was a potential loss maker.

We ran the Orient in Borneo for three years but it never caught on with the travel trade. Only our own old Pandaw hands had come through a mixture of curiosity and loyalty. Their reports had rarely been enthusiastic and with occupancy was falling so I took the decision to pull out.

The decision was made easier by the ongoing environmental disaster we could see all around us as forests were stripped for their hardwoods and the land claimed by palm oil planters. Interestingly, as soon as we announced we were pulling out, the remaining cruises filled up with people anxious to savour this last Pandaw experience before it closed forever. The Orient transferred to Burma in 2011 where she has been very busy every since. I do not think any of the crew regretted leaving. There were just too many things that were not right already, and too many that could go seriously wrong in future. We felt that we had had a lucky escape.

Losses in India

Everyone warned me: "Don't go to India. You will be ripped off." I ignored them, and for my pains did not simply get ripped off, but actually lost an entire ship.

That may seem like carelessness — how can you 'lose' a ship? The term usually refers to a sinking, or perhaps an act of piracy on the high seas. In our case the ship was removed from our ownership by less dramatic and more insidious means, but lose it we did.

It is a story that could only happen in India. Pandaw IV, which had done such distinguished service in the aftermath of Nargis was taken from us in 2009. Even now, several years later I still wake up each morning part filled with self-reproach and part grieving the loss of this once proud member of the Pandaw family.

As described, I had first visited northern India in 2002 for a recce on the Brahmaputra. However I had not pursued the project as we had become bogged down on the Mekong with its many difficulties and challenges. There was no time to be thinking of other destinations.

By 2004 things seemed to be calming on the Mekong and I began to dream of India once again. Seeking an Indian partner, I was introduced to one Mr Shiva, an Oxford-based organiser of trips to India.

Shiva came up to Edinburgh for a long lunch and discussions. He brought his fifteen-year-old son with him, which I thought was unusual for a business meeting, but I was later to learn that Shiva never went anywhere without some form of familial entourage.

Shiva was warm, friendly and very charming. The author of a number of works on Indian ornithology, living in a charming Oxfordshire village with his English rose wife Debbie, no one could have been further from my stereotypical conception of an Indian businessman. On account of his Indian public school education and

219

aristocratic Rajasthani origins, Shiva boasted brilliant connections amongst the higher echelons of the government elite.

We discussed various ideas but the one that really struck me was running a boat from the Yamuna River from Agra, location of the Taj Mahal in Uttar Pradesh, down into the Ganges and on to Varanasi (Benares).

What could be more romantic than a Pandaw moored off the Taj, then setting off for the temple-encrusted ghats (riverside steps) of the sacred city of Varanasi? Reading up on the Yamuna, the largest tributary of the Ganges, I learnt it had been used for transportation at the time of the building of the Taj Mahal and its broad expanse had often borne 18th century British visitors en route to the Mogul court.

Off I went to Agra, staying in a hotel owned by Shiva that had been an old family home which I was told was "just outside" Agra but turned out to be several hours travel away. As relations with Shiva developed I learned that "very close by" could be up to eight hours away on pitted roads. The hotel had been one of Shiva's less successful business ventures as he had spent a fortune renovating it to a high standard, hoping that Taj-bound tourists would stay there. The problem was that what was "close by" for Shiva was not nearly close enough for the wealthy tourists that he sought to attract.

At Agra a boat had been arranged by Shiva's brother Vishnu. Vishnu, proved to be a jolly character with great moustaches . Fond of whisky, Vishnu swaggered about with a Mauser hunting rifle "to keep the bloody dacoits off". Indeed the natives in this part of Uttar Pradesh were not that friendly, a number of local villages were homes to gangs of goondas or 'goons' as they are quaintly called in India. These gangsters are up for hire as muscle by local politicians intimidating villagers into voting for them in India's great democratic elections.

The boat was disappointing, a blue plastic rowing boat of the sort you might hire on the Serpentine. A massive parasol had been erected mid ships and we all squeezed in – a couple of boatman, Vishnu looking officious with his rifle and myself with a pole to measure water depths.

Off we puttered on an outboard engine. This was monsoon time and though the current quick, depth was little more than a meter, so in the dry season it would be just a few centimetres. The river meandered extravagantly through wonderful country, varied by hills, woodland and farmland. As always in India, thanks to Hindu vegetarianism, the birdlife was amazing. It was so unlike the Irrawaddy or Mekong where hungry carnivores have eradicated most birdlife.

After a day in the boat we had only covered an as-the-crow-flies distance of about ten miles so clearly river cruising on the Yamuna was not going to be practical.

Why had my reading suggested otherwise? Perhaps in the 18th century, prior to the great irrigation schemes of the British up river the river had flowed deeper? Anyway, my back was aching and bum numb after discovering reality the hard way. At that speed, and in such discomfort it was unlikely we were we going to reach the confluence with the Ganges in a hurry.

Fortunately our jeep was waiting at the next bridgehead and we could continue by road to stay in some sort of bird sanctuary run by one of Vishnu's friends. Vishnu and his chum sat together and demolished a bottle of Scotch between them as the night got hotter and hotter and the atmospheric pressure increased until I thought I was going to explode. Mercifully the clouds burst producing a profound relief and an unbelievably joyous sensation.

Next day we abandoned our blue tub and proceeded by car stopping at Bateshwar, famed for having the largest cattle fair in India with some very dreamy temples along the ghats. It was a mini Varanasi without the tourists and barbequed corpses. Then on to Kanpur where we did see corpses, people run over and left to decompose by the side of the highway as lorry upon lorry piled through in a black stream of exhaust fumes. Kanpur was an industrial centre and I was told, not without some pride, the most polluted place on the planet. That I could believe, there were factories everywhere billowing out black smoke. In the ongoing Indian industrial revolution this was the equivalent of the 'dark satanic mills' of Sheffield or Blackburn, only now its chemical pollution rather than good old-fashioned incinerated carbon.

So not a great stop for our Pandaw passengers.

I did get my first glimpse of the Ganges here, descending the riverbank under the bridge. The river was in its monsoon spate – violent and fast. No vessel large or small could possibly attempt to ride it. We pushed on into the night to Fatehpur and the promise of a hotel, a shower and a meal.

Fatehpur's promise proved illusory. We arrived in the dark, and in the dim street lights, characters lurked in doorways of seemingly derelict buildings. Dirty, bearded, with an air of looking for trouble the locals were not welcoming. For once Vishnu's Mauser was of some use, as a deterrent.

Fatehpur is known as the capital of the Uttar Pradesh badlands. No one, Indian or foreigner would go there voluntarily. The hotel ranks as the nastiest I have ever stayed in. The room's walls were smeared with a greasy filth. All surfaces had a stickiness as if coated with a gooey resin. The bathroom was so smelly that there was no way one would risk even using the shower.

The narrow hall outside, that served as a sort of reception area-cum-lobby was filled with more bearded desperados, sitting or squatting without occupation, observing our every movement in the same way a cat watches goldfish in a bowl.

After a meal in a sort of roadside transport café, the lights so dim we could (perhaps luckily) not see what we were eating we retired. Vishnu offered to share the room with me but I felt brave enough to go it alone, positioning a chair behind the door and sleeping fully clothed in a deep embrace with my rucksack.

And so the journey continued, motoring down the Ganges to Varanasi where I hopped on a plain to Delhi and then that night got a flight to London, so exhausted that I fell asleep before takeoff and woke up on landing at Heathrow, having slept right through the in-flight service.

Clearly the Yamuna was out in any season and the Ganges was too wild a beast to consider during the monsoon. It would be necessary to return in low water times and assess it then.

Reading Eric Newby's book *Slowly Down the Ganges* (1966), I noted that he seemed to spend a lot of time run aground. On the other hand until the 1940s the British had run streamer services up to Patna in Bihar and much earlier, before the advent of railways, to Varanasi and beyond.

It was decided with Shiva to form a joint venture company in India. Expensive advice was sought from top shipping lawyers. A ship would be built in Burma and leased to the Indian company, thereby protecting our investment. Meetings were had with the Ministry of Shipping and this scheme was officially blessed as legal and correct and we took further counsel from a top firm of shipping solicitors in Bombay.

We had built Pandaw IV in 2004. It turned out to be our unlucky ship that just seemed to invite disaster. Four is an unlucky number in Burma and U Soe Naing, our shipbuilder, advised me against using it.

Unusually, and stupidly, I ignored his advice. This was uncharacteristic as, deep down, I am as superstitious as your average Burman.

The story of what happened to Pandaw IV in 2004 when she was ready to sail is told in a previous chapter. After her arrest by the Burmese military in 2004 it was another five years before we could get her out of Burma. We ran her on the Irrawaddy in the intervening years but she was surplus to our requirements there: our Burma business had shrunk, the result of sanctions, the failed monk-led "Saffron Revolution" of 2007 and then Cyclone Nargis in 2008. So much bad news had put people off. However the ship had earned her laurels during Nargis saving so many lives and with so many babies born on board, we thought that the good luck that had brought would have had expunged any ill-omens.

By 2009 our problems in Burma seemed to have gone away, or rather been forgotten about. It was a bit like when I was banned in 1989, or after we did our runner with Toni in 2000. If you are patient and wait long enough, past transgressions are for all parties conveniently forgotten.

With my return to Burma in 2008 for Nargis I was able to renew a number of contacts and was assured by a well-connected Mr Fixit that I had long known that he could obtain the necessary export permits and licences, secured by six-figure payments to the minister and his minions.

I made a number of visits to Calcutta in order to ensure that we would have the correct licences and permits on arrival to enable us to operate. At the same time, travelling by car I followed the course of the Hooghly River from Calcutta up to where it joins the Ganges at the Farraka Barrage.

On another occasion I flew from Bangkok to Bodh Gaya and then travelled overland to Varanasi exploring the holy places of Buddhism, which I found very moving, before getting stuck in a day-long traffic jam in Patna where sometime before a flyover had collapsed and blocked all the roads.

Patna was akin to hell in my eyes. It took three hours to cross the town in search of the river where I had hoped to check the *ghats* or landing stages but we never found the river in the mayhem of the city's traffic.

Everyday Shiva would call me from Delhi, often for a couple of hours at a time, and wax eloquently on all his contacts, connections, school friends in high places, and so on and all that he was doing to make it happen. However, I noted that he seemed to avoid any of the real preparatory running around in Calcutta, leaving this to a very pompous young army captain.

He would take me round various government offices introducing himself as 'Captain' which often seemed to evince a smirk from the various officials who were clearly running circles around him.

Calcutta seemed to me to be an enlarged version of Rangoon. The same streetscapes, the same banks and commercial buildings all built around the turn of the 20th century. In fact many of the architectural practices, often Scottish, who had set up in Calcutta opened branch offices in Rangoon. They were parallel cities separated by the Bay of Bengal and built according the principals then prevailing in the commercial grid of central Glasgow, imposing steel frame architecture that enabled the play of grandiloquent external features. Only in Calcutta the scale was different, the buildings even larger and grander and the city so much more spread out as befits a former capital of the Indian Empire.

One felt a familiarity entering decrepit government buildings and up the red betel nut-stained stairways, the pong of ordure wafting around, tea boys delivering sticky tea, the endless transportation of lunches delivered in tiffin carriers, not to mention the crows, the rats and the rubbish everywhere.

It was just like home. These days, with the ascendency of China, it is easy to forget that Burma was for a hundred years administered as a province of India under the British Raj, something the Burmese were not very happy about. So much of Burmese culture, like that of elsewhere in Southeast Asia, comes from India, not just the Buddhism that arrived from the 8th century onwards, but the food, the dress and the general culture.

For one thousand years Indian influence permeated Burma and then the British arrived and formalised things by making Burma part of the Raj. Step off a plane at Calcutta and all this comes instantly home.

Back in Rangoon, Pandaw IV, soon to be renamed the 'Bengal Pandaw' was made ready. We re-engineered her and changed the propulsion to an inboard system, knowing that there would be no local expertise to maintain the outboard rudder propeller system in India. A set-up team was appointed under Neville Joseph, one of our most trusted and reliable managers, himself a Burmese of Tamil origin.

Export documents ready, a tug was hired from Calcutta. There were several false starts – bad weather, engine problems and the such like but eventually the tug set out and crossed the Bay to reach Rangoon a week or so later. She picked up her tow and returned to Calcutta bearing our beloved Pandaw IV like some great prize. Meanwhile Neville and his Burmese crew flew over to Calcutta to pick up the ship on arrival. Shiva had been unable to find a crew so we sent over not just a master and a chief engineer but an entire crew who could handle such a ship.

Despite heavy seas and weather warnings tug and tow made it to the mouth of the Hooghly and the pilot station at Sagar. Shiva and his English wife Debbie, had actually appeared in Calcutta in person and had arranged the hire of a mini bus to take the crew down to board the ship. At this point Neville later reported to me that Shiva and Di would not board the ship or even get out of the bus and show themselves before the local officials.

It would seem they were desperate to see the ship for themselves for the first time but for some reason dared not be seen to be in any way connected with it.

The crew then got the engines started and proceeded up the Hooghly with a local pilot and were instructed to moor up river close by to Outram Ghat and the city centre.

And then everything went dead.

The crew proceeded with unwrapping the ship after its ocean passage and cleaning it up. I checked with Shiva. What about formalities – customs, immigration, port clearance, etc? Normally when a foreign ship comes into port a swarm of officials descend. But over a week had gone by and nothing. Shiva assured me everything was taken care of, repeating that had the contacts right up to ministerial level.

I grew uneasy, for this was not normal. Then I got the call. The ship had been arrested and the crew all placed under house arrest on board. Shiva went completely silent on me and avoided all calls. I despaired for Neville and the team and after three weeks of inconclusive negotiation decided to fly to Calcutta and see if I could resolve matters myself.

Once there I was not allowed on board and the vessel was moored mid stream and under observation and it was impossible to get out to her as all boatman had been ordered not to go near the ship. Negotiations ensued with the head of customs.

Initially the vessel was arrested under anti-terrorism laws. This was in the wake of the November 2008 Taj Hotel attack in Bombay. Then it was claimed that we were trying to smuggle the ship into India. The tug also was arrested and apparently it had some history of smuggling teak in from Burma. A massive six-figure fine was levied, meanwhile our team was to be deported as they had the wrong type of visa.

The crew had been prisoners on the ship for over a month now and with no diesel for the generators I knew conditions on the ship would be bad. Then I got a call from the hotel reception asking me to go to the hotel entrance as some people were asking for me and they would not let them in.

I went down and there was Neville and Phoe Koe the cook both in mufti. Neville being Indian, dressed in an old *longyi* and grubby T shirt with a few days of stubble clearly could move around unnoticed and Phoe Koe who may have Indian blood in him, looked just the part too.

They looked a right pair of Calcutta street ruffians, it was no wonder hotel security would not let them in.

We went to a café round the corner. They were in good spirits, even enjoying the adventure, but they confirmed that conditions were bad on the boat. They were out of drinking water and had taken to drinking the water of the Hooghly. Not surprisingly some of the boys were getting sick. Food was short. It was not good.

And where was Shiva? Once again he had disappeared, leaving the pompous little captain to negotiate with Bengali officialdom, notorious as the most corrupt and unpleasant on the planet.

In the end I agreed to pay a $120,000 fine and once again met with the head of customs – an enormously fat man who sat behind a desk the size of a billiard table in an office the size of a village hall. I think he was actually quite shocked that I agreed to pay.

I had gone to see the tug owners who I had hoped might sympathise and assist but they just shrugged their shoulders as if this sort of thing happened every day and it was all part of an elaborate waiting game to see who would hold out longest. We did not have the luxury of time or patience. We had a crew to think of and then in a couple of months the passengers would arrive and the ship had to be made ready.

One thing I did insist on with the head of customs was that I could visit our ship. After the meeting I was taken out in a customs launch and boarded her. The crew were in good spirits despite what had happened. They had received some aid from a seaman's mission and were full of stories. Like Neville and Phoe Koe they had been sneaking ashore cadging rides in passing fishing boats. The ship was dark, almost hulk-like. With no electric power the lads had been unable to do much work and she was shabby after the sea passage needing repainting and a lot of hard polishing.

Then Shiva threw down his trump card. This was the moment he had been waiting for. The arrest of the ship and the customs case had been just a prelude to soften us up and psychologically prepare us for the real shock. Shiva produced a letter from the ministry of transport stating that a foreign-owned vessel could not operate on Indian Inland Waters. This was entirely contrary to the top legal advice we had received and the outcome of all the meetings I had with transport ministry officials.

The plan had been to charter the ship from our offshore company which owned it, to the local joint venture company in which Shiva was the majority shareholder and we the minority shareholder. This company, 'Pandaw India', had been set up to manage and operate the ship not to own it. It was too late to turn back, the ship was on the Hooghly, having paid heavily to get her in we would be hammered again to get her out. Some said we would never get her out.

Shiva offered the only solution: register the ship in the name of Pandaw India. Though I was a minority shareholder a shareholder agreement would be drafted giving me effective control of the business. I had no choice but to agree. The ship was re-registered in the name of Pandaw India and then Shiva through down his next card – the foreign investment law stipulated that for transportation a foreign investor could only own 20% of a joint venture company and thus my shareholding was further diluted.

However, as said there would be a shareholder agreement to ensure we at Pandaw retained control. Shiva's lawyer was summonsed and produced a hundred page draft of this agreement. We then went through the ritual of discussing it in a hotel conference room over a couple of days. All was agreed but when it came to the crux Shiva was not ready to sign. He had to get some tax advice from his accountants, we would sign it next time.

The crew were subsequently deported back to Burma. Again I was powerless to prevent or even influence events. That sense of impotence was deeply frustrating. It was ironic that in the 19th and early 20th centuries the Irrawaddy Flotilla ships were almost entirely crewed by Bengali lascars (sailors and militiamen) under the command of Scottish officers. And indeed the original flotilla came from Bengal to Burma in 1854. Here we were 150 years doing things in reverse, a

Burma-built ship with a Burma crew now showing the lascars how to do things. Only the Scottish management remained – that was me.

Neville was allowed to remain and our German manager flew over to set up the hotel side whilst I returned to the UK. Reports from Neville and the German became more and more worrying. Shiva had put his brother Vishnu in charge, together with the officious captain. In order to register the ship the local Bengali surveyor insisted on hundreds of thousand dollars-worth of structural changes on the ship in the name of 'safety'.

The one ship yard that could do the work did not open till noon each day and at least two days each week were lost in religious festivals of one sort or another. Things moved slowly in West Bengal. With a communist-led government, the state was effectively run by an alliance of militant trade unions and political mafia. It is the one part of India that the economic boom has passed by, due to the incredible levels of bureaucratic obfuscation, union militancy and attendant corruption.

Tata, now the largest car manufacturer in the world, built a state-of-the-art car assembly plant just outside Calcutta but it never opened as they refused to bow to such corruption. West Bengal is that sort of place – an economic basket case where it is impossible to get anything done. The one upside of such rampant inertia is the preservation of so many splendid buildings. No property developers here!

Shiva's people went on a spending spree buying mountains of equipment for the ship. We were bankrolling the whole set up and as the bills started coming in we grew more and more alarmed. The German could do nothing to control them. Shiva had put in his own people, all Shivaasthanis like himself, as the Bengalis were supposedly so unreliable. The German became more and more despondent, they would not consult him, an experienced Pandaw manager, on anything.

Shiva just charged in and arranged everything according to his own ideas, having never actually run a ship before. There was no cost control, no system of accounting, cash just flew away. Meanwhile crates piled high on the quayside containing tons of supplies and equipment most of which was never to be used.

Roser and I flew out a few days before the inaugural cruise. From the moment we arrived we sensed something was wrong. For one thing I had booked rooms at the Oberoi, a favourite hotel. However the driver Shiva sent absolutely refused to take us there and instead took us to the Taj where we learnt Shiva and Debbie were staying.

We found Shiva in the lobby. He had set up a sort of court for himself there and all day various people flowed in and out to see him, politicians, journalists, contractors, old friends and of course his famed 'contacts'.

There he was in all his splendour, the man of the moment. He somehow thought I would join him on the sofa and spend the next few days likewise holding court. Whenever I suggested going to see the ship he would change the subject, waving the notion away like some tolerant adult before an insistent child. After a day cooped up in the hotel I decided to hire a car and go to the ship myself. The German and Neville were on board and I was receiving distress calls. Things were pretty bad and the first group were supposed to be arriving the next day. However I had no idea where the ship was and Calcutta is vast and the Hooghly long.

Shiva got wind of this plan and soon squashed it dragging me into another interminable meeting with his lawyers to discuss the still unsigned shareholder agreement that once again did not result in his putting signature to paper. This time the trouble was over concerns about foreign exchange controls and the policy of the State Bank of India or something.

That night Debbie discovered that it was our wedding anniversary and expensive gifts were bought from one of the Taj boutiques. Later we found they reclaimed the cost from expenses charged to us.

Eventually I lost my temper and insisted that we be taken to the ship. Shiva relented and a car was arranged taking a couple of hours through the suburbs to find the ship miles upstream. The plan had been to cruise from the city centre but Shiva had decreed that it was too dangerous to pass under the various city bridges, which was rubbish as there was plenty of air draft. And thus we found everything revolved around Shiva's decrees which were based on neither experience nor intuition but rather bloody-mindedness and sheer stupidity. You could not argue, you could not discuss. He could outtalk an army and one wilted exhausted just at the thought of listening to one of his discursive explanations that could last anything from an hour to half a day.

The ship looked terrible. There were welders, with sparks flying, busy making the structural changes insisted on by the surveyor. These were totally unnecessary and merely intended as an exhibition of the surveyor's power. The ship was half painted and nearly all the varnish polish on once-pristine woodwork had been weathered away during the sea passage and was now looking mouldy and mucky. There were at least a hundred crew and workers on board, it was impossible to tell them apart, and most were lying on the decks, or in the passenger cabins, asleep. Unopened boxes lay stacked everywhere containing hotel equipment. There was enough stuff to fit out five hundred-room hotel. And the passengers were checking in the next morning.

I have known new ships where the passengers boarded an hour after the last shipyard worker has left. At Pandaw we are not strangers to last minute panics, but this was incredible.

Amazingly, overnight, the German managed to get the mess cleared up and the rooms ready, all with untrained crew. The passengers arrived having been bused two hours across the city after their long haul flights and I think were too bleary eyed to notice just how bad the ship looked. It was so unlike Borneo where everything on first impression was so spic and span and Pandaw-style. But there we had a dozen of our own people to show the locals how to do it. Shiva in his infuriating arrogance, having arranged the deportation of our expert crew as part of his take over strategy, believed that a bunch of village boys from Shivaasthan could just walk in and run the whole thing.

As always with the incompetent or inexperienced the solution to any problem is to throw more people at it. There must have been a crew of over fifty and crew quarters only had twenty five berths. As a result the movie theatre on the lower deck had been closed off and when you went down there were several rows of bodies curled up asleep. These people were not enthusiastic bathers, nor were they in the habit of de-odorising, so the atmosphere can be imagined.

The passengers were an intrepid bunch and I had been sure to warn everyone in a personal email of what to expect. Consequently there was little disgruntlement and people were very supportive. From the start this was clearly a Shiva and Debbie show.

Of course this hurt my ego, I was used to being the kingpin of any cruise. Suddenly it was Shiva on the Tannoy night and day with an endless barrage of mundane information, actually so banal it insulted the educational levels of our average passenger. The ship had not got the correct liquor licences for the states it was to cruise through so only beer was provided though Shiva seemed to have a private supply of wine that was only produced at 'top table', much to the annoyance of the excluded.

We proceeded rather gingerly up the Hooghly. Fortunately there were some lascars who knew something of handling a vessel but as Shiva dominated every detail they were too nervous to do much. Shiva had hired a sort of flat-bottomed ferry that followed us and insisted in shuttling passengers ashore for sightseeing even though I spent whole mornings in long discussions with Shiva who refused to let the lascars bring the ship alongside to let the passengers off. "India is not Burma, Paul, you do not know our rivers". Our flat bottomed, shallow draft Pandaws are designed to go alongside almost anything and jetties are totally unnecessary. Eventually I lost my rag and forced the captain to go alongside but then I discovered the lascars had no idea how to tie the ship up. In best Pandaw fasion I had great fun jumping off the bow with rope in hand and making he fast round a tree. The lads soon got the hang of it and I quickly gained their confidence and taught them how to handle the ship. They were actually keen to learn and I soon revised my opinion of the Bengali lascar and realised that with leadership and training they were good seamen.

The Hooghly really is a marvellous river. Not only is the West Bengal countryside lovely, with colourfully-dressed peasants, but there is a wealth of things to stop and see. Breathtaking terracotta temples, the splendid neo-classical Hazarduari Palace at Murshidabad, built by a Scottish engineer for the Nawab there, plus numerous very picturesque villages.

At every stop a media circus of TV cameras and press photographers awaited and Shiva, suddenly a commodore astride his flagship, would launch into a great performance: charismatic, ebullient, glowing with pride and sense of purpose. We would catch snatches of interviews, "I have brought this ship from Burma", "We have invested in buying this ship" and suchlike. Roser and I became increasingly worried: a horrid, sinking feeling hit us. Up to now, beguiled by Shiva's charm I had believed that all would be well, he would sign the shareholder agreement, our investment would be safe. Now we realised just what had happened – a massive confidence trick somehow combined with an ego trip.

Then one evening after a few glasses of wine Debbie let it out of the bag, she cast her eye around our magnificent ship and said, "To think we now own all this". We had been had.

So sick did we feel as all this dawned on us that we decided to get off halfway. We just could not sit there any longer, the duped victims of a most spectacular coup. We returned home in a state of depression. Messages from the German only reinforced the realisation that all was lost. To make matters worse the hygiene, food quality, safety were appalling yet we carried all the risk.

We wrote to booked passengers warning them that they would not receive the usual Pandaw service and offering to refund people if they preferred not to go. No one took up the offer. In fact there were no serious complaints and I think because the river cruise through India was so good, with so much to see and do, and so incredibly beautiful, that people did not mind the bad food and rubbish service.

Over five hundred people had booked through us and though we controlled the cash flow it gave us no voice at all for cut off the cash flow and the booked passengers would not be carried. Rather Shiva used these blank cheques as an excuse to rack up the most incredible expenses. Low hanging high voltage cables over the river involved bribing the power company $10,000 every time we passed to switch off power. Apparently half of north India would black out as crew used bamboo poles to lift the thick cables over the top of the wheel house. Crossing Bihar armed Maoist insurgents on horseback would take pot shots in the air as the ship passed. We were forced by the state government to hire at an absurd cost a detachment of special forces for 'protection'. As we passed through three states we were hit with triple taxes on everything.

Indeed, the ship's daily operating cost was over double what it was in Vietnam and Cambodia. There was little of the shore support we take for granted on the Irrawaddy or Mekong with good mechanics and engineers who can move fast to fix things. Navigation on the Ganges was tough – after the monsoon the flow rates are very high and then in the low water season there is not a lot of water. We lost a propeller and none of the shipyards in Calcutta could help so had to have one cast in Saigon and flown in from there. Distances were huge and the logistics of sightseeing and excursions ashore complex. On one occasion passengers were all put in a bus to go to Varanasi and the bus driver set off in the opposite direction for Bodh Gaya, only after about five hours did anyone realise the mistake resulting in a ten hour bus trip. As the water levels dropped each trip the ship would cover less distance until it could only get as far as Patna. Despite this it was a considerable achievement, another first for Pandaw. The British had abandoned steamer navigation on the Ganges soon after the introduction of the railways to India in the 1850s, and until Pandaw, no one had dared to try it since.

So Shiva had our ship. We had spent half a million dollars delivering her and refitting her, then we bankrolled a loss-making operation for that first season rather than let down the passengers booked by cancelling their holidays. Bookings for the next year looked good — clearly as a river experience the Hooghly and Ganges were winners — but nevertheless we took the decision to pull the plug. There was no point in continuing to bankroll an operation that we did not control, which had all sorts of health and safety challenges, and which was losing money.

As I write the ship is still there. Not surprisingly Shiva very quickly set up his own marketing operation. We tried to sue him through the courts in India and he counter-sued but after several years this has still got nowhere. I am told that, the Indian legal system being what it is, it could take several more years before anything happens, if it ever does.

Meanwhile he has the ship. Every so often Shiva makes contact to try and solve the problem, nearly always there is a catch, another attempt to con more money out of us, or to try and get us to drop the lawsuits with what I take to be false promises. At the last meeting he once again came with his son, now a university student in the UK, and after listening to all the usual waffle I said: "But Shiva, you stole a ship" he merely smiled and looked rather pleased with himself, the proud parent showing off to his son.

Debbie, who was suffering from cancer, sadly passed away recently. Extraordinarily, he had even brought her along to a meeting at the Travellers Club in London, using her as part of an elaborate scheme to persuade us to abandon the lawsuits.

"Debbie is dying" he said patting her knee, "she has not much longer to live, let's resolve this matter and be friends".

In this case "being friends" apparently amounted to me signing over my remaining shares in Pandaw India for nothing, calling off the lawyers, and chartering the ship back from him at an exorbitant rate.

What are the lessons to be learnt from this episode? Obviously you should never invest in India, never trust any business person from that country no matter how creditable and respectable they seem, cut your losses early, and so on.

But of course, I have learned no such lessons. No entrepreneur worth their salt ever would. The truth is I would go back to India tomorrow and try it all over again, probably making variations of the same mistakes all over again. After all, you have to keep trying.

During the so-called Great Recession that began in 2008 with the collapse of Lehman Brothers and which still continues at time of writing six years later, Pandaw managed to triple in size in numbers of ships, in passengers carried and in revenue. We did this without borrowing. Indeed we have never leveraged ourselves, mortgaged ships or sought loans, apart from a small loan from a friend to get Pandaw I refitted back in 1998. Prior to 2008 investment managers would look at us and shake their heads and say 'something wrong here, no debt'.

We were able to build ship after ship through something called 'self-financing', apparently an alien concept to most bankers, accountants and MBA types. It is nice to pretend we acted on some moral principal — 'neither a lender nor a borrower be' and all that. In fact we probably would have borrowed to finance this rapid expansion if we could, but no sane bank would lend to a venture running ships in hazardous navigational environments in countries with dubious regimes.

Actually in East and Southeast Asia expansion funded by cash flow is not an alien concept at all. It is called the 'Asian family business model'. It would not work in the West because taxes and cost of regulation are so high, and, because everyone is so in thrall to the banks to pay for their housing, they need to be paid huge amounts to live. In the West most of what people earn is split between the banks, for housing, and the government, for usually unwanted and unnecessary 'services'.

In emerging economies with low or no personal tax, people are not caught in this tax-and-mortgage trap and end up with more spending power. They are thus happier and of course all that spending further enriches the economies. In Asia they sit on cash and in the West we sit on debt.

At Pandaw we fell into the former category and thus have happily weathered revolutions, various pandemics and global downturns.

With twelve ships, over three hundred employees and over 10,000 high end passengers carried a year up till 2014, for nineteen years, I ran the whole show from a laptop at home in Scotland. I have never had an assistant or a secretary. I have never had an office. We had evolved to a point where we have various key people doing key things, mainly home working like myself. Our bookkeeper, Ms Bee, sat in Saigon and our reservations support ladies in Singapore. All are young mums and work flexible hours around their child care duties. It was only in 2013 I was persuaded to take on a marketing bod, who sat in the Cambodian capital Phnom Penh and helped field enquiries.

For nearly twenty years Pandaw had no sales and marketing department and PR was a totally alien concept. When you buy a ticket on a 'normal' cruise ship 50% of what you are paying will go to the bank to cover the finance cost of building the ship and 25% will be direct marketing costs. So your 'actual' cruise cost is just 25% of what you pay and out of that the operator must make a profit. At Pandaw with no finance and virtually no marketing costs we got to keep all the ticket money and spend this on two things – building more ships and funding the Pandaw clinics.

From time to time, at moments of self-doubt, I had 'consultants' come in and they would shake their heads and say this is not how it is done. Not according to some MBA manual on how companies are supposed to be administered. Yet somehow it worked for all those years. The proof is that we made money and kept on building more ships. Something seems to have gone badly right.

Nor did I, as business owners often do, feel compelled to micromanage every little detail. In fact I have been light on the tiller. My working day was short and I had lots of time to potter in my garden, play golf, go sailing and spending time with my son Toni. I can afford the time because I do not have endless meetings with a management team, nor a board to schmooze and discuss everything with.

Light on baggage, I have been able to move fast, seize opportunities and fix problems rapidly. I would not be able to do this without the loyalty and dedication of our purser team and the crews under them and I would not have been able to do this with a top-heavy management team.

This might sound ideal, but it is not. The loneliness at times has been unbearable. Tapping away on a laptop doing one's hundred emails a day answering one hundred questions can become depressing. Attempts to appoint a CEO in 2009 to take all this away and free me up nearly resulted in the company's collapse. It may look easy but it is not.

On three occasions in the past five years, when worn out and in low spirits, I have succumbed to the temptation to sell the business and have accepted the advances of various suitors. Apparently the business is worth a lot of money now and Roser and I could retire in some comfort. On each occasion we have gone quite far down the aisle before taking fright. We only have to go out and stand on one of our boats, surrounded by crew, many of whom we started with two decades ago, and the tears well up and we find we just cannot do it.

It is not as easy as it used to be out there. There is a lot more competition and our one-time monopoly of river cruising in Burma and the Mekong has long been shattered. Those happy days of living off referrals alone sadly are over. I am the first to recognise that we need to spend money in marketing and get our message across: the message being that there is an alternative to big white modern boats where everything is covered in Formica and you cannot open the windows. Pandaw is teak and brass, colonial heritage and being outside all day not cooped up in an air-conditioned cabin, or sitting huddled in your anti social private balcony. Pandaw is just so much more civilised. And that is why 45% of passengers who travel with us have been with us before. Surely the highest repeat rate in the industry and the reason why we do not have to do a lot of marketing.

It may sound a dream business model but by early 2014 I reached a cathartic moment following the sinking of one of our ships at sea. The Saigon Pandaw was on a delivery voyage being towed by a tug from Saigon to Rangoon and was reported lost at sea by the tug master. Fortunately there was no one on board.

The story remains shrouded in mystery and could fill another chapter, suffice it to say that we soon learned that it was not sunk as reported but rather sold by the Indonesian tug master to some pirates who towed her to an island and stripped her bare. Some weeks later they took her out to sea and sank her and filmed it too. They even posted the clip on YouTube (http://youtu.be/lrS_Oy8wEMI), which shows the vessel being sunk while the tug crew film the spectacle in what sounds to me like guilty silence. After this drama involving a long sea search working with Vietnamese Naval Intelligence I returned home to Scotland at a low ebb.

A friend put me in touch with an experienced business person who was prepared to look at how we run the business and make a survey of how it all worked. I think he had quite a shock, a mixture of admiration and horror, but he managed to persuade me to invest time and energy in putting in a proper management structure. Whereas I was convinced I had the most efficient business model in the world I came to realise that it was inefficient and that the main element of inefficiency was me. Why? Because if anything happened to me the whole show would collapse. Anyone valuing the business would see me as the biggest problem. Further, after the loss of the Saigon, not to mention past disasters in India and the imprisonment of Nwesu, there was a limit to the amount of psychological hammering that the human mind can take. Already by your early fifties you start to feel confidence and potency ebbing. You no longer feel up to long days at your desk and endless trips. It is time to slow down. A decade of chronic insomnia, living on an average of four hours sleep a night often led to physical collapse through sheer exhaustion. Whereas in my forties I could live with this by my fifties I could not. Something had to change.

We set out a strategy and plan to bring in top level people to take over the various functions that I had up till then taken care of myself: a marketing office was established in London that centralised efforts and included IT development. A chief operating officer was appointed for Asia who has been steadily building a new team of expatriate managers that rotate round the ships from a base in Thailand. New finance and accounting systems were developed and a new reservations system is currently being built.

I found I had been living in a cloud of negativity for years, having seen it all before a hundred times, I had given in to the old tropical malaise. Now full of positive energy once again I really enjoy working with bright top level people, trying to pass on experience and knowledge. Probably they find me a bit of a bore as I waffle on about the good old days but I like to think all this coaching is passing on something of the company's lore. So positive has all this made me, and with so much more time on my hands, I am back exploring rivers again. Great plans are afoot!

Roser and I get out to Asia once a year for a long stint, usually over December when our son Toni comes out for the school holidays and joins us. Much of our time is spent on issues of style and presentation. Roser rushes around nagging the pursers over dirty curtains and half-dead plants. I push for spanking white paintwork and gleaming decks. Only we seem to be able to do this, the pursers get too tired to see anything and the expats we employ to oversee them either do not fuss over such matters or are too Orientalised to notice much anymore. Whilst we are quite conservative, and encouraged to be so by the pleading of old and regular clients not to change anything, when we do try to introduce some new way of doing things, we find our crews are even more conservative than we are. It took me years to eliminate horrible smelly buffets and when I introduced outdoor dining on the Katha Pandaw the crew threatened to resign and old 'pax' (industry-speak for passengers) boycotted the new ship. Now the Katha gets the highest rating in the fleet.

In 2013 we launched the five-cabin, ninety foot, Kalay Pandaw known by all on the river as 'Baby Pandaw'. This is our home when in Burma. Hotels there remain challenging and attempts to rent houses and flats a nightmare of administration with endless problems with water, power, bugs, etc. It is so much easier to live on our own houseboat and just drift around according to where we want to be stopping and visiting ships when we pass, supporting crews and pursers, bearing supplies, but most importantly meeting as many passengers as we can in order to get a feel for their experience.

At last, after nearly twenty years of running around chasing ships and sleeping anywhere, on the office floor, on the bar floor and, often enough, on deck, we can do this in comfort and style. The Kalay we built ourselves, using our own engineers to design and supervise the construction on a bit of riverbank just opposite our office on Strand Road in Mandalay. It was slow, but they did it on budget and on a per-room basis cheaper than any of the commercial yards we had been using. It was like being back where we started with the first Pandaws in the late nineties. She is a fast boat, we overtake all the other cruise ships and with a draft of a couple of feet can sail a straight course when larger, deeper draft ships are compelled to zigzag round the sand banks. Cruising on the Kalay this winter was an eye-opener for me and I realised that our future at Pandaw was to build smaller and get further, away from the big white ships.

The greatest difficulty over these twenty years has not been the untameable nature of the rivers, the corruption and bureaucracy, Burmese generals, Chinese triads, Viet cadres. The challenge has been a human resource issue. I do not refer to the crews, who are keen and loyal and see a Pandaw job as a job for life. Not the pursers, the backbone of the fleet without whom we would be rudderless. I refer to the supervisory level, staffed by expatriate managers.

I am afraid we long ago stopped counting the number of expats who have passed through our ranks. The two industries with the highest turnover of staff are probably marine and hospitality. In river cruising and thus Pandaw the two meet — often disastrously. It is the nature of shipping that crew sign on and off, so it has been for centuries, but it means we take on a manager from a cruising background, train him up only to find after a few months he is off on another ship or to another job on the slenderest of whims. Hoteliers are little better. A glance at an hotelier's CV can make you dizzy, every six months taking up a new appointment. There seems to be a great nomadic tribe of them out there, particularly in Asia and the developing world, all the time moving from job to job. The moment they are in a new job they are looking out for the next, and of course the internet, with so many recruitment websites, does not help.

We tried senior sea captains or chief engineers in the role of Marine Superintendent. There was 'Wee Donny' from Glasgow, who interviewed so well. He told us he was a 'hands-on sort of guy', who liked to get stuck in there and fix things himself. Based in Yangon after a mere two weeks in the job he rarely made it past the bar on his way, mid morning, to the office. So I tried him on the ship and again the only energy dissipated was the long walk from the cabin to the bar for a morning beer that would extend through the lunch hour, the afternoon and evening and then on into the small hours, socialising in a very jolly way with the passengers. Then there was Jari the Finn, an enormous sea captain we sent to Phnom Penh who made the Green Vespa bar at the end of the dock his office. He was known to down thirty beers a day as he transacted company business. For these old sea dogs, coming off the sea and the discipline of a big ship and into places like Rangoon and Phnom Penh, with cheap beer, easy-going girls and pubs and clubs that never close it was like landing in paradise.

245

Successive managers that we let go in Rangoon stayed on, there was one bar which was more like an ex-Pandaw employees club and all of course sitting there all day cursing the company. We found it almost impossible to find people with the discipline to stay on course. With ships dotted around, far apart and often far from port in various strange countries it would be impossible to even begin to consider imposing any such control over such a motley bunch of characters. If you are going to work in wild, frontier places you are going to attract wild, frontier types

I can only count two or three really great hoteliers out of the fifty or so we employed over these years. There was Ghilberto of course whose name and style, often infuriatingly, lives on amongst the Burmese he trained. There is Madame Chantal, ten years with us and still haranguing the poor crew into cleaning behind the fridge. She often ends up donning her rubber gloves and doing it herself whilst the Burmese look on in wonderment. Such people are dying breeds, hands on and leading from the front.

Then there were all these extraordinary characters that one remembers with amusement. Gustav the mad German chef who was always getting into trouble – on his first voyage to Bhamo the crew had a whip round to have him contract-killed — life is cheap in Bhamo. When I heard the rumour by long distance phone call I managed to persuade the purser to give him another chance. By the end of the second voyage Gustav and the purser had become inseparable friends. He was the best chef we ever had and would rise at four in the morning to do the breakfast bake. He also made amazing jams from strange tropical fruits. He did have a tendency to lose his temper, not in Ghilberto's *Commedia all' italiana* style but more Wagnerian – laden with menace. And he did have the tendency to lose his temper with government officials, on one occasion with the Vietnamese border guards who were delaying the passage of the ship so as to extract an additional bounty (as they do).

After that episode we had to pay 'compensation', and write a letter to assure the government that he had been sacked and left the country. We transfered him to Burma where he was so nearly "hit" in Bhamo.

Then there was the case of Jacques, a Frenchman, we hired in Phnom Penh. He took a room at a riverside hotel and from there would send me weekly reports without ever setting foot on the boats. He had not been seen by any of the pursers or crew for months and when he was finally located offered no explanation or apology. When we dismissed him he took us to court in Cambodian suing us for three years salary, holiday pay, lost bonuses, and psychological damage – an amount running into hundreds of thousands of dollars. Actually on the last count he may well have been shocked into some genuine sort of psychological damage as in socialist France no one is ever sacked and if it happens it is considered a life-altering trauma. The case dragged on for years and went from the divisional to the high courts. In the end it all came down to who could make the high court judge the highest offer and a sort of silent auction ensued over several months with various brokers posing as advocates acting as go betweens. In Cambodia an advocate is essentially a broker between one of the contending parties and the judge and justice all comes down to how deep your pocket is.

So we learnt not to hire French people in Cambodia. We tried David, a rather nice but shy American hotel manager. He did not hide in a hotel ashore and lived aboard the ships, indeed this had been written into his contract. After a couple of months, it emerged that he rarely if ever left his cabin. I am not sure whether he was more terrified of the passengers than the crew. Communications with the purser were restricted to text messages from his mobile phone. Meals would be delivered and left on a tray outside his door. Like Jacques he was assiduous in his weekly reports to head office conveying an impression of great industry and diligence. However unlike Jacques he did not put up a fight when asked to go. Rather he was incredibly polite and thanked me for the experience and told me I had the most wonderful business he had ever encountered.

Deciding to try someone from within the river cruise industry for a change, in the hope that they might fair better we hired Johann from Switzerland. Johann had worked for Viking River Cruises, one of the top river cruise operators in the world and came with amazingly good references. He arrived in Phnom Penh and within two weeks I received a long and detailed report detailing all the areas of the ships that required improvement, renewals and reequipping. Essentially he wanted to convert every single ship in the fleet into a copycat of a Viking ship. He supplied a quote from a local supplier he just happened to know, that ran into fifty pages and came out at over a million dollars. Basically anything 'Pandaw' would be eliminated, nearly everything from teaspoons to chillier rooms would be changed. When I counselled that he wait a few months and learn about what we do and how we do it he immediately resigned and was never heard of again.

There were good guys too of course. An Austrian called Franz was a fantastic manager and never have I seen our ships look so good. He was in Burma and did such a good job that I transferred him to the Mekong. This was in the first start up year there and after the occasion of the ship's captain's arrest he suffered some sort of nervous breakdown with the stress of it all. One can hardly blame him. A ship stuck in port with fifty baying Americans is enough to drive the sanest man crazy. He just walked off the ship and disappeared. Some weeks later his father contacted me trying to track him down. I believe he turned up on a Thai beach.

Chantal, our hotel director from France who loyally worked with the company for ten long and dedicated years, could be too tough. In 2012 there were attempts on her life from an unknown crew member in Vietnam, presumably for some slight or perceived hurt. She was staying on the Mekong Pandaw off season and one night the ship caught fire near her cabin. The crew reacted well and brought it under control. We did not think it had anything to do with Chantal. Then a week later there was another fire in the night, again right outside her door where some pots of inflammable paint and varnish had been stacked. Luckily Chantal escaped just in time but the fire raged up the aft stairwell and the sundeck awning caught fire and was destroyed. Again the crew reacted well but this time we knew there was an arsonist on board. This is how things are in Vietnam, make someone lose face and it is a knife in your guts or worse. We never identified who the culprit was but the prompt installation of CCTV cameras put paid to further attacks.

Crews can be volatile and easily upset. A few years ago in Burma I had my first ever mutiny. In this case purser and crew refused to sail a ship unless a fairly large amount of money was delivered to them. It looked like a straightforward case of blackmail, as the next morning fifty passengers were due to embark and they all knew that if the ship did not sail we would suffer disruption on a scale that could put us out of business, I spoke with the purser by phone and agreed to his demands pending a full investigation.

On investigation it transpired that the crew really did have a real grievance. In fact the purser had been pocketing their gratuities and then blaming the company for holding them back.

And thus the human resource challenge or rather nightmare continues to this day and in moments of despair I have feared that there is no real solution. I think one of the sad things is that because of the huge educational gap that occurred through the 1990s and 2000s in Burma under the SLORC regime, there is a lost generation and it is difficult to find amongst our middle management level people with the education and breadth of vision to rise to an executive level. We have tried, but it does not work. Sadly the only management model the Burmese know after fifty years of totalitarian rule is, well, totalitarian rule. For this reason Burmese crew beg me never to put a Burmese boss in charge. Put the nicest of Burmese in a position of power and overnight he or she becomes a monster.

We found the Khmers (Cambodians) lacked the ambition and did not want to assume responsibility, seeming to prefer being nannied by decision-making expats. The Vietnamese were all too ready to assume executive responsibilities, but then they would discriminate against the Khmers and other nationalities, promoting their own relatives and party comrades. We tried Singaporeans, but they are so boxed into the toy town world of Singapore, where everything is cushioned, controlled and sanitised, they cannot cope in the wild frontier world of the places where we work. Put a Thai in and the Khmers will kill him. Put an Indian into Burma and there will be a mutiny. And so on. I wish there was an answer.

Having proudly pioneered river travel in six countries – Burma, Thailand, Cambodia, Vietnam, Malaysia and Indian — and on six great rivers — the Irrawaddy, Chindwin, Mekong, Rajang, Ganges and the Kwai — it came as something of a shock when competitors started emerging. I found it quite difficult to take, and handled it badly. This is where we set in motion something that we believed at the time was fairly altruistic (a win-win all round for the traveller and the local communities, with low environmental impact) to something that has become a monster. For a time we received almost daily press releases for the launch of yet another big white horror on either the Mekong or Irrawaddy. Fortunately on the Irrawaddy their range is limited by their deep drafts and they cannot reach the 'real Burma' and are confined to the tourist traps. Sadly on the Mekong navigational limitations restrict even our range and already the congestion is appalling.

There was of course no way we could have stopped all this and it could be argued that it would have happened anyway, without our pioneering work. We did though enjoy a near monopoly on these rivers for over ten years. To date none of the other river cruise operators have engaged in community projects like school building or healthcare. They are rather cynical profit making exercises that put little back. At times it has felt that we have run a training school for all our competitors with a haemorrhage of highly trained people lured away by offers of higher pay.

Many regret it. As one hotel manager on another ship said to me the other day "better to be a barman on a Pandaw than a manager with someone else". Many of our old team are not tempted by such offers, realising that the long term benefits of working for Pandaw outweigh the short term temptation of higher pay with other companies. Usually there are catches, like they do not get paid off season, or get no healthcare or provision for eventual retirement as we provide, things they do not understand at the time.

The first jolt we experienced was what happened to our dear old Pandaw I in 2004. As mentioned, we had chartered this ship from Inland Water Transport, the government department that operates a huge fleet on the Irrawaddy. A new regime at Inland Water Transport had emerged, under greedy and ignorant army officers, hungry for bounty and quite unlike the old gentlemanly school of retired naval officers. When they tried to raise the already exorbitant charter fees, and with all the operational headaches of getting them to supply fuel, spare parts and engine maintenance, as described in an earlier chapter, I had decided to let the ship go.

This was a huge mistake. Pandaw I may have been expensive to run and a pain to operate but she had a talismanic quality and symbolised all that we stood for. I had expected IWT to come back with fewer demands but this was where I miscalculated.

Adriano was a young Italian who we had employed in our Rangoon office. A slippery character he had been fired for dishonesty. In his year at Pandaw had learnt much about our ships, operations and market. Adriano had managed to persuade a group of rich Chinese to acquire the ship from IWT. By 2002 Burma was fast becoming an effective Chinese colony as sanctions barred Western firms from investing there. This made it open season for the Chinese, the majority of whom had migrated across the border from the badlands of South-West China. Rough and tough, these borderers instinctively knew how to work the Burmese military and government in a way that no Westerner would have the gall to do. They dressed Burmese, spoke Burmese, ate Burmese, married Burmese, worshipped in Burmese temples and thus could break cultural barriers impervious to most Westerners.

If I requested a meeting with a minister it would inevitably be a stiff, formal occasion, bound by protocol and spectated upon by a great entourage of followers. A Chinese could go round to the minster's house at night, go in the back door and have a kitchen table meeting with the minister's wife at which, decisions would be made, and largesse would be doled out.

In the end Adriano and his Chinese friends hired the old Pandaw I for 500% less than what we were paying, while also managing to have her re-engined at government expense. By then Burma had changed. Where once an annual bottle of Johnnie Walker Black Label would ensure full ministerial cooperation it was now necessary to go in and leave the keys of a brand new land cruiser on the minister's desk.

And these Chinese were cash rich. They came from Kokkang and the other borderlands where there is only one way of making lots of money, and it isn't by manufacturing sherbert dip.

Now relocated to Rangoon and Mandalay they could launder their poppy-derived profits in property and in buying up legitimate businesses, in particular travel-related businesses through which it is easy to turn large amounts of money. River cruise ships were of particular interest to them. These could be built in Rangoon for cash and then the proceeds from ticket sales or charter revenue would be remitted to banks in Singapore.

At first I was dismissive of this takeover of Pandaw I, doubting that it would impact much on our sales. But Adriano was clever and quite shameless. He used the Pandaw name, and copied exactly our schedules and itineraries and thoroughly confused the market. Travel agents had no idea whether they were booking them or us. We were losing business.

Then in 2004 in the wake of Chit Su's imprisonment and following the arrest of the new Pandaw IV we were down a ship and took a decision to maintain our long cruises, while letting go of the short cruises. This gave Adriano an opening to move in and take over all our short cruise bookings, and we, while disgraced and discredited, lost an entire market segment.

It is even possible to speculate that Adriano and his Chinese gangster friends had masterminded Chit Su's arrest and the (thankfully temporary) downfall of Pandaw. They were poised to take over our other ships too, expecting them to be confiscated in lieu of unpaid taxes and then auctioned off cheap by the government.

As previously related, we saved the Burma business because we had the cash resources to settle such demands on the spot.

Later Adriano started building ships himself. I remember sitting him down over a drink and explaining to him that a creative genius like he could do better than just carbon copying. That they could develop their own name and brand, and design new ships differently for a different market. This seemed to strike a chord as Adriano, like not a few Italians, is vain. He had some form of an architectural diploma that was a source of great pride to him, and thankfully he went off and designed ships very different to the classic Pandaws, more like floating hotels than expedition ships. We wish them well.

On the Mekong we were likewise being challenged by the end of the 2000s. Here the story is quite different to that of Pandaw I but just shows how things work in Asia.

I have mentioned the ubiquitous Mr Dong, who had gone from being an office runner to our key man in Vietnam. Mr Dong was very ambitious and there was no way we could have held him back even if we had wanted to.

In 2008 we built our first ship in Vietnam, the Orient Pandaw, which Mr Dong had project managed with great efficiency. Mr Dong had ambitions: he wanted to be an owner not an employee. He also had long antennae, and if any one of any importance was to visit us in Vietnam Mr Dong made sure he met them, even if meant hanging around in a hotel lobby all morning waiting to pounce. On one occasion the owner of one of the top American river cruise companies was visiting, with a view to chartering one of our ships. Somehow Mr Dong manoeuvred one of his coincidental meetings in the lobby of his hotel. The American, had not really liked the Pandaw teak-and-brass experience, preferring a big white boat along the lines of his other ships. Business cards were exchanged.

Then some months later Captain Rob was in Saigon to do some consulting work for us on a new ship and was whisked off by Mr Dong to a meeting of his Vietnamese 'friends'. He was shown plans of a new ship and asked if he would project manage the construction. Rob was appalled and called me that night – I had no idea. Mr Dong had put together a consortium of Vietnamese investors to build the American his ship. Mr Dong at that time was a full time employee of Pandaw. Only in Vietnam could this happen.

The next thing we heard was that a second ship was under construction in Saigon and that Mr Dong was involved in its construction as well. It seems that the first consortium had fallen apart and one of the investors, to spite the others, had decided to build a ship of his own. In the end both groups fell out with Mr Dong and he ended up with nothing and came back to us, tail between legs.

We solved the problem by taking him off the payroll and saying that he was now a 'consultant'. He still gets lots of work from us on the old 'better the devil you know' principal. There would be no point in having a row and firing him as the next man would be just the same. Now, thanks to Mr Dong's encounter in that lobby, there are dozens of ships on the river, most of them big and white. For as soon as the American came in so did all his competitors. These craft are more like floating hotels than real ships and are constructed with hotel materials which easily fall apart with the vibration and movement of a ship. They have a maximum lifespan of five years before they become too down-at-heel and then the charterers move on to the latest big white ship on offer.

Perhaps the most calculated act of plagiarism was that of a certain Swiss travel agent. We had worked with Klaus for years and I regarded him as a close personal friend. Klaus had a daughter called Ludmilla and in 2003 had suggested that we give her and two of her Swiss friends a job on the Mekong as guest relations officers or GROs. Just out of college, this seemed a good idea at the time as being Swiss they would speak lots of languages and hopefully relieve both the pursers and guides of much of the day to day information giving to guests. However things soon went wrong when the three girls took boyfriends from amongst the crew, all Burmese with wives and families at home. When in port wild nights were had in the nightclubs. Our key players were appearing for breakfast service with shaky hands and bloodshot eyes.

The other twenty-three crew who had not got lucky with the Swiss girls went around in a torpor of frustrated jealousy, though many got their chance later as the Swiss girls were great believers in sharing their charms. There was a bad vibe on board. Our German manager became convinced there was a drugs problem and it was decided to search the purser's cabin as he had become the seediest and most run down of them all. The German manager informed me that he had done a drugs course and knew what he was looking for. We peeled back the bedclothes and mattress to find nothing as the bleary eyed purser miserably looked on. Then the manger went through the drawers and exclaimed 'got it' producing a number of round white balls each about

255

the size of a small marble. He held one out before the purser and with a Clouseau-esque air of triumph cried out "what is zis?" the purser replied "a moth ball". I took one and sniffed it. Yes definitely a mothball.

Later the manager performed an audit of the accounts and here proved more successful – money was missing and the purser, more hungover and miserable than ever, could offer no explanation. The purser was let go and he did go and took all the other Burmese with him. He was the *saya* and the others were beholden to him. That's how it is in Burma.

Suddenly we were without several key people and fortunately as Roser and I were on board, along with the manager and his wife, we were able to keep services running in good old all-hands-to-the-pumps style whilst we rather hastily borrowed a number of Khmers from a friendly local hotel. Soon after the Swiss sirens departed, to a general sigh of relief.

Some years later Klaus took to chartering one of one of our ships in Burma and his daughter Ludmilla was dispatched to Burma as his manager on board. This was a very different Ludmilla to the one we had known several years before and she clearly had grown up a bit and applied herself efficiently and diligently for a couple of seasons on the Irrawaddy without incident. We formed a good opinion of her.

Then Klaus informed me over one of his friendly phone calls that he was building a boat in Burma that he intended to send to Bangladesh to operate in the delta there. He had always had an interest in this area and I thought nothing of it. He was using our old ship builder U Soe Naing and we wished them well. Then we discovered that they were using one of our designs, a new concept I had worked on with U Soe Naing but had yet to build. This was a river vessel not the coastal vessel that Klaus assured me he was building. The cat was out of the bag and it was indeed a ship for the Irrawaddy. Ludmilla was to manage it and carried off several key Pandaw staff including one of our best pursers. She had spent her two years on the Irrawaddy with us learning every detail of the business right down to the shipyard where we built our boats and cherry picked the best crew. The bosun, Ludmilla's current boyfriend, was promoted to general manager and U Soe Naing the proxy owner. Then they took our largest UK client, with whom we had had worked with for a decade and a half, who preferred knock down rates to comfort and service. Business is war, but it is less straightforward than most wars. You often never know whom the enemy is until it is too late.

All these stories of Adriano and Pandaw I, Mr Dong in Vietnam, of Klaus and Ludmilla in Burma, are but a sample of the challenges faced in business. If you are an originator it is inevitable that people are going to try and copy you. I doubt if we could have avoided any of these scenarios. Looking back there was inevitability about all of them. Yes if we had kept Pandaw I it may have held Adriano and his Chinese triad friends back in Burma, but not for long.

Of course someone was going to start building ships on the Mekong and Vietnam is full of energetic Mr Dongs. If Klaus and Ludmilla had not built their boat in Burma, someone else would have. But I think what hurts is that nearly all of these ventures were inaugurated and then run by people we had trained and invested time in.

A nd thus it was that we unleashed a monster – river cruising in Asia. It is not very edifying now to turn up at the Phnom Penh city jetty and see ships of all shapes and sizes jostling to get in, moored several abreast, their generators pumping out black smoke. I shudder to think that I was the one behind it all. There are similar problems of congestion at Pagan and Mandalay too. Soon there will be more and more river cruise ships in both Burma and the Mekong. They all religiously copy our itineraries and the communities we once took pride in supporting have become spoilt. I discovered that the many touts and vendors who harass our passengers at the Cambodian weaving village are actually bussed in from Phnom Penh – they even know our schedules. To think ten years ago the locals would shyly show us their handiwork and had no commercial notions at all. Burma will not be far behind with the scams, touts and so-called trickle down benefits from tourism.

I had once argued that river cruise ships had a limited environment and social impact. They are self-contained and unlike a hotel or resort do not need roads in and out, power transmission, water supplies and sewage works. Indeed on a ship all this is self-contained. We can get in and out of communities without disturbing them. Alas now when several ships turn up simultaneously and all these tourists tramp through some pristine village I am appalled. Am I the guilty party, the one responsible for it all? Yes, probably, and I do feel guilty and part of me is ashamed at what I unleashed.

Yet I go on building ships, albeit these days they seem to be getting smaller and smaller, and I am constantly aiming for smaller rivers and new frontiers. Shipbuilding is a rather expensive addiction for me and I love to play with new ideas and designs. I think now our business model has evolved to point that the big American companies will no longer copy us as to them such projects will make little financial sense. It was hard enough convincing them that a thirty-cabin ship could be economic, nothing less than a hundred cabins is their standard model. In Burma economies of scale do not work. The bigger you get the higher your costs. Buy one egg in the market and it is 10 cents. Buy a dozen and it goes up to 20 cents each. In Burma there is a converse economy of scale, which is why small remains beautiful.

Despite my guilt complex I am at the same time very proud of what we have had the opportunity to do. We took a bunch of kids out of villages and trained them into highly polished professionals who take justified pride in what they too have achieved. Many of them have been able to send their sons and daughters to college and university, nearly all support extended families of up to a dozen dependents, taking care of the healthcare of elderly aunts and uncles or the schooling of nephews and nieces.

We currently employ about three hundred people but through them feed more like 3,000. Then there are all the suppliers and contractors; people associated with the company – drivers, guides, porters on the docks, farmers and marketers. Suddenly 3,000 dependents becomes a far larger figure.

The crowning achievement of our years in Burma is the Pandaw Charity. Though we had been involved in a couple of projects prior to Nargis in 2008, in particular funding the construction of a new wing of the U Hla Tun Hospice at Mandalay and the Yandabo Village School, it was only with Nargis in 2008 that we realised our true role and mission in Burma. Perhaps Nargis for me was a moment of atonement, a chance to redress omissions that had resulted in Chit Su's imprisonment in 2003. Certainly Nargis was a life-changing moment for me and also I think for many of our people. It was then that we realised that all those years of plying up and down the Irrawaddy carrying well-heeled tourists had a meaning. We had acquired a skillset second to none and possessed the logistical and practical skills to go and do what no one else could achieve with speed and efficiency. All that we had worked and trained for, so many years, pointed to Nargis. After Nargis we established a proper charity registered in Scotland and were able to maintain this momentum.

The Pandaw Hospital Ship has continued its operation in the Delta area to this day and we have been able to continue to support a Nargis orphanage in Maubin, west of Rangoon and facilitate the construction of another Nargis home in Mandalay, paid for by two very generous Pandaw passengers from Australia. Over ten schools have been built in river villages up and downstream from Pagan, in areas that receive no benefit at all from tourism. With close contacts with these villages we moved from school building to healthcare, establishing our first

259

clinic at Gantgar in 2009. Today there are over seven of these with a medical and support team of twenty rotating between them.

In 2003 we established a central diagnostic clinic at New Pagan to which patients may be referred from the outlying villages. We handle about 5,000 treatments a month and all medications are free. We cover an area of about 250 square miles supplying the only medical care available to over twenty villages in this area with a total population of over 100,000. As people do not have cars and public transportation is not-existent some of these village are to the people who live in them remote and they are so poor they would never have been able to reach or afford treatment at the one government hospital at Nyaung Oo. We fund most of this from our profits so when people book a ticket to travel on one of our ships a fair chunk of the ticket price goes to support the clinics. It works out about the same as what we would pay in corporation tax if we were incorporated in a developed country. Thanks to the low tax regime in Asia, we get to decide where to spend this money and not governments, who tend to spend it on maintaining themselves rather than on the people.

This year is our twentieth anniversary and when things are weighed up there is much we all at Pandaw can be proud of: the enduring design of our ships, the fact that we have always been first up any river, even the fact that we are imitated by so many.

The year 2015 also happens to be the 150th anniversary of the founding of the original Irrawaddy Flotilla and there is some satisfaction in reviving its traditions. There have been many mistakes – nearly all mine, and as told some of these have led to disasters.

In the way such things are normally understood I am a hopeless leader and an even worse manager, yet somehow the ship sails on, if only through the common bonds and strong loyalties shared with our crews. We now have the children of our original crews working on the Pandaws, as perhaps my son may in the not too distant future. Likewise we actually have the sons and daughters of many of the people who first sailed with us twenty years ago signing up for river cruises.

Problems do not go away: there are no magic solutions, but with age one does perhaps cope with these problems better and one learns to manage the stress and worry.

In the early years, when Burma was sanctioned and a politically correct press told people not to go, we felt guilty but knew that the benefits to the Burmese people outweighed the cloud of opprobrium under which we lived.

Despite a real regret at having been the inspiration for what is essentially a fairly unpleasant industry, I still believe that the benefits to the ordinary Burmese outweigh the negatives. It is also comforting to think of the many thousands of very satisfied former passengers we have been privileged to carry over the years, with an enjoyable mailbox each morning filled with appreciative reports, and a tendency for many of our passengers to return again and again.

All said, I just have to stand on the deck of a Pandaw as she chugs serenely up the greatest of rivers, as dawn comes up like thunder, and the temple-bells are ringing, just as Kipling described in his barrack room ballard 'Mandalay', to be overwhelmed by a sense of romance and adventure.